THE IRRESISTIBLE MR WRONG

THE
IRRESISTIBLE MR WRONG

The Robson Press

First published in Great Britain in 2012 by
The Robson Press, an imprint of Biteback Publishing Ltd
Westminster Tower
3 Albert Embankment
London SE1 7SP

ISBN 978-1-84954-199-2

10 9 8 7 6 5 4 3 2 1

A CIP catalogue record for this book is available from the British Library.

Set in Bodoni and Adobe Garamond Pro by Namkwan Cho
Cover design by Namkwan Cho

Printed and bound in Great Britain by
CPI Group (UK) Ltd, Croydon CR0 4YY

It is presumptuous of me, an aged male, to attempt to write about these six women with empathy. I would not have dared to do so without the help of three women editors who have guided me in those pathways of the heart denied me by my gender. This book is gratefully dedicated to them: Marcelle D'Argy Smith, Nina Risoli and Jaime Brahms.

CONTENTS

What's wrong with marrying rich women? Those little bastards who criticise me don't understand. I took them simply as women.

And what's wrong with taking presents from a woman? I give them too, even though I give a ring and she gives a bomber. An aeroplane is not the moon, it's a toy. If you can have a bomber you have it. So what?

Porfirio Rubirosa

INTRODUCTION

Why do women fall for scoundrels? Not all women certainly, but an identifiable number of them – including almost all heiresses – find themselves drawn to, even marrying, a thoroughgoing bastard who cheats on them, steals their money, abuses them physically and mentally, then dumps them. Why, to these otherwise balanced young women, is Mr Wrong irresistible? What is it about him, what is it in them, that causes it? In short, what is the nexus between wealth, celebrity, sex and self-destruction?

This is the serial biography of five women who were all serially married to the same man: Porfirio Rubirosa. All, plus Zsa Zsa Gabor, the Hungarian adventuress who did *not* wed him, were advantaged and privileged individuals. They shared one characteristic: power. The father of the first, Flor Trujillo, owned a whole *country*; Danielle Darrieux was a movie star by the age of sixteen; Barbara Hutton, the 'poor little rich girl', was extravagantly wealthy; Doris Duke the richest woman in the world; Zsa Zsa was endowed with beauty, wit and glamour; Odile Rodin with looks, talent and youth. All were 'born in a happy hour' and gifted by good fortune. They had

– on the face of it – *choice* in how they ran their lives, together with control.

Rubirosa was vulnerable only in one way: he had no money. There, except for Odile, the women held the material advantage. Yet without hesitation they abjectly yielded that power to a dominating male with no conscience in exploiting them.

Flor at seventeen was an innocent and Rubirosa an unknown quantity (perhaps even to himself then), but the women who followed her as his successive wives were fully aware of his nature and his past before they married him. They knew he was a boozer and hell-raiser, compulsively promiscuous, a jewel-thief and unscrupulous crook, that he exploited and beat up women, and had been involved in two murders. He'd concealed nothing from them and enjoyed his reputation as a cad. Yet *nothing* could deflect them from their focused determination to capture him as a husband. Why should they elect to make such a choice, for which they paid so extortionate a price both emotionally and financially?

He was known to everyone as 'Rubi' and, displayed in the shop window, his image was alluring. To look at, he was an attractive item. Although not tall (5ft 8in), he had dark wavy hair and a permanent tan; he was either one quarter or one eighth black, resulting in an enviable skin tone. His nose was broad (he would have it fixed) and his lips thick in a high-cheek-boned handsome face. His body was slim, fit and well-muscled; he moved with an athlete's grace, fully at ease within his own skin.

For a woman meeting him while in his thirties – by which time his early macho brashness has long been replaced by the confidence he can have any woman in the world – he represents a desirable sexual proposition, if one to be approached with caution. He is a 'playboy' and predator, a creature of his time and place and social circumstances, a man who has been *created* by women and defined by the lovers who made him famous: Christina Onassis, Ava Gardner, Eva Perón, Gene Tierney, Countess Maritza of Spain and Queen Alexandra of Yugoslavia, plus countless others.

He possesses looks and sex appeal, a quick smile, good teeth and bedroom eyes. An adolescence passed on the fringe of the in-crowd in Paris has gifted him with social ease, wit, and opportunistic guile. He can converse engagingly in several languages. He is romantic, bold in his wooing, generous and impulsive; he never bores. His technique has proved irresistible, for he *listens* with his whole attention on the woman confiding in him. He remains mindful, sensitive, sympathetic; she believes he understands her.

These characteristics form the basis to his persona, but it is enhanced by a number of worldly skills. He is an able horseman, a boxer and a fencer; he dances, skis and plays tennis well. He is a rated polo player, knows how to pilot a plane and handle a racing car nimbly as he can a pony. All these pastimes which so well suit him cost money, and here lies the fundamental flaw in Rubi's world. His image is without solidity. He possesses the tastes, energy and appetite for the life of a celebrity playboy – but he lacks money. He's blithely indifferent to it except as a necessary resource; he has no desire to amass capital, only to have fun and spend freely.

Rubi also lacks something less tangible than cash. He is an entirely social animal and, as a fish in a bright-lit aquarium, entirely dependent on his artificial environment to give him life. He is alive only among others in the setting of bars, restaurants, resorts, in a glossy milieu composed of glamour, gossip columns, photographers, seductions and escapades. With Rubi, what you see is what is, he has no inner resources. If he's alone in a room there is no one there.

Perhaps to compensate for this existential lack of substance, providence has gifted him with a singular and outstanding attribute.

In the 1960s the giant pepper grinders brandished by waiters in fashionable trattorias were named 'Rubirosas'. His third wife Doris Duke states that 'he had the most magnificent penis I had ever seen'. Her godson, Pony Duke, quotes her saying, 'There has never been anything like it … six inches in circumference … much like the last foot of a Louisville Slugger baseball bat.' The society photographer Jerome Zerb, who followed him into the men's room in Deauville casino, reports, 'It looked like Yul Brynner in a black turtleneck.' And Truman Capote wistfully eulogises about 'that quadroon cock, a purported eleven-inch café-au-lait sinker, thick as a man's wrist'. In the fashionable world it had the nickname and reputation *toujours prêt* – always ready.

Yes, Rubi was phenomenally well-endowed, and certainly this formed part of his attraction but, as many hundreds of women could testify, you did not have to wed him to sample it. It was on offer to any female bidder and for the right price it was available for rent. Rubi possessed more. He had an air of natural entitlement, a charismatic presence and with it charm, which worked not just on women but also (most) men. He behaved as he felt like behaving and saw no reason not to do so. Yet he was no braggart and happily told stories against himself. He was worldly, suave, he had an air of mystery and reeked of danger. Twenty-five years before the invention of James Bond, he set the prototype – except that Rubi served no country but himself.

No woman in her right mind wants to marry James Bond. That's not what he's *for*. To marry Rubi was an equally misjudged self-destructive act. To understand why these particular women took that mortal step it is perhaps necessary not so much to scrutinise him as examine *them*.

CHAPTER 1

FLOR TRUJILLO, DOMINICAN REPUBLIC, 1932

Homesick is how you get when you have to return there.

That, anyway, is how it is for Flor as she stands in her First Class cabin watching the steward gather together her many items of luggage, twenty minutes before the liner's arrival at the dreaded shore of home.

Rather than the single dollar bill the boy would have got from other passengers, she tips him a five (worth around $100 today, but even a trainee celebrity is obliged to exceed), instructing him to bypass Customs on arrival – 'Tell them who I am' – and to load the bags directly onto one of the presidential limos he will find drawn up behind the quay. She checks her appearance for the last time in the mirror, which reflects the image of a slender seventeen-year-old girl with bobbed black hair in a small cloche hat and short-skirted linen suit, then quits her cabin to come on deck when the liner is still a mile from shore.

Even with the trade wind ruffling the surface of the sea, the heat and blaze of light strikes her like a blow. She pulls down her dark glasses to shade an all-too-familiar view that evokes nothing but abhorrence. In the distance the close-packed buildings of the capital swarm up the flank of the mountain in rambling disarray. From the monumental sixteenth-century cathedral at its base rises a terraced maze of streets whose first tier is made up of the once-grand but now crumbling public buildings of the Zona Colonial; above these spread ascending levels of church towers, forts, roofs of rose-coloured tiles then, higher yet, a warren of clapboard houses and ramshackle old wooden mansions, painted in pastel shades of blue, pink and red, faded by the sun which washes out all colour from the scene.

Flor Trujillo © Press Association

The dilapidated city expanding up the mountain rests upon a shoreline rimmed by the Maleçon, a tree-lined boardwalk stretching as far as the eye can see toward the outer barrios and the shanty town, obscured by distance and the fume of charcoal cooking fires.

A dark green band of mangrove swamp grows beneath the paseo, varied by the alluring glimpse of white sand beach.

Flor Trujillo stands glaring at the idyllic view with fierce resentment. Many would have seen that sunlit prospect of palm trees, beach and lushly forested mountains as a tropical paradise; she knows it to be a prison. The picture-postcard scene fills her with revulsion. This was the stifling cage she grew up in, more restrictive than any convent … and she, little fool, believed she'd escaped it. What delusion, what naiveté to imagine so when *no one* escaped Him, least of all his first-born daughter.

But for the past two years the fact is she *had* eluded him. She'd petitioned her father to allow her to go to school in France. Of course he'd been reluctant, but he wanted her smart and savvy and cosmopolitan as he would have liked to be himself. It had taken persistence and timing, but eventually he had yielded. So, with paternal acceptance if not approval, she had escaped into another existence she'd only read and dreamed of, thrilling in its liberty and promise. She had come to know the City of Light with its galaxy of worldly pleasures – not *all* of these though, for she was chaste and, even in Paris, closely chaperoned. Though not invariably, for vacations were spent with school friends and their parents in Biarritz, or skiing in Megève and St Moritz. At the exclusive girls' academy, initially she'd felt a misfit. 'Naïve, thin, with legs long like a stork's, unable to speak French, I was the shy tropical bumpkin, the classmate of girls who included a princess. Now I, who had only ridden a burro, had a thoroughbred horse of my own…' But she is quick-witted and adapts fast. Gawky and unsure at first among such sophisticates – the black girl from wherever – then with growing confidence in her looks, Flor learned how to play the game as it's played in this world and run with its bratpack, gaining casual acceptance as a cadet member of the international set with her own mestizo style.

Meanwhile in the course of that two-year span – during which she received no word from her father – she had *changed*, altered beyond recognition by experience, by association and self-assurance, but also physically. She had developed from a gauche Creole adolescent into a young woman in the flower of her youth, with the blood's sap running in her veins, bold and aware of herself and what she wants from life. *And this is not it.* The liner she is aboard has slowed to quarter-speed to enter port and she is about to step ashore onto the island where she least wants to be in all the world. *But what choice has she?* Conscious that in France his daughter was slipping away from him, he had yanked on her string and she had obeyed him, as all obeyed him – or else. The Great Benefactor had sent for her and she was coming home.

Now close to land, the surface of the sea is smooth, sheltered from the breeze by the mountain, and the smell of the island steals across the water to embrace her: the fragrance of spices, flowers, fruit, with ever-present beneath it the whiff of rotting garbage and human effluent. Her gorge heaves at the familiar stench, she almost gags. She will never be free of this stinking hole till someone shoots him.

As if on cue, as the liner clears the harbour beacon, altering course to come into port, his is the first image she sees before she even registers the crowd upon the quay. A giant poster of the Benefactor occupies the full height of the customs warehouse. Wise guardian of the people, unsleeping in his devotion, his watchful gaze scrutinises them unblinking – and seems to look directly at her. The portrait is an immense version of that same icon that hangs in the place of honour in every home throughout the island. By it, and spanning the full width of five houses on the waterfront, stretches a banner with scarlet lettering six feet tall: GOD AND TRUJILLO. The President recently has considered reversing the order of the two priorities.

Great Dictators, whether building a memorial to their rule or exterminating their enemies, do nothing by half-measures. A homecoming must *be* a homecoming, a first-born's welcome a state occasion. The harbour quay is usually a marketplace where turbaned women in the shade of brilliantly coloured awnings lord over stalls heaped with pyramids of tropical fruit; it is always busy. Now the place is a roiling mob of people jigging in the harsh glare of the sun. A military band is playing, its members' shiny black faces throttled by the collars of their gold-frogged uniforms. To the flash of brass and crash of noise, the crowd in their brightly varied rags are shifting to the sound, calling out and rocking to the blare in a rising fog of dust kicked up by their stomping feet.

Behind the crowd, in the shade of the Customs House, stands a platform elevated to shoulder-height above the tumult. The stage is occupied by some twenty men grouped around their principal figure. All are in uniform. Two or three are older, their chests spattered with medals and coloured ribbon, the rest in their early twenties, some even younger. Their white tunics, worn above breeches and highly polished riding boots, are broad shouldered, tight fitting, nipped in at the waist. They express swagger and machismo – which might be expected, for they have been designed by the President himself for his bodyguard with the same close attention as he has selected the youths who wear it. All are slim and fit, handsome, white or pale of skin, and all are aware they are on parade.

At the centre of this cadre of young officers rises a dais, upon it a piece of furniture Flor recognises. The President seldom travels anywhere – even the short distance from Palace to harbour front – without the throne chair in his baggage train. It raises him head and shoulders above those attending him and its tall backrest conveys imposing dignity, while the elevated step where his pygmy feet rest remains unnoticed – along with the fact that the Benefactor, though the ideal of Beauty, Wisdom and Truth to all his people, wears built-up shoes and has unusually stunted legs. But this is a subject which, among many others, is never discussed aloud on all the island.

The ship has disengaged its engines, drifting to a stop. A tugboat butts it through a narrowing gap of oily water choked with splintered crates, rotting fruit, garbage and small dead fish. From the deck, Flor's glance passes over the Guard surrounding their Leader and is drawn ineluctably to the personage at their centre. Unwillingly, in a stew of emotions that includes aversion, fear, pride, awe and ambivalent love, her gaze focuses in upon the occupant of the throne chair. Clothed in a starched white linen suit, with eyes hidden behind dark glasses, her father stares back at her, his mouth pursed in a customary moue of murderous discontent.

A shiver passes through her, despite the heat. She flinches, her look slides away… abruptly coming to rest, startled, on one of the young officers who stands by him. 'I noticed him instantly,' she says later. 'Handsome in a uniform that had a special flair, even his gold buttons looked real.' Electricity pricks across her nerves as she becomes aware he is looking directly back at her. The crowd and everyone on the quay are gazing at her, but his look alone has caught and held her. For a long moment, which while it lasts feels endless, their glance extends and a signal flashes between them, what the French call a *touche*. 'It was love at first sight,' she explains afterward.

❧

Flor's welcome home is warmer than she had feared. Her father, absolute despot of his country, is unpredictable in his moods. The President could be a monster, terrifying in his rage. At other times his face would light up on seeing her, he'd draw her close, embrace her, stroke her hair; press a wad of $100 bills into her hand, urging her to buy toys, clothes, another pony, anything her heart desired.

Today, following the harbour-front reception and back home in the presidential mansion above the town, the President is in unusually benign paternal mode. Pride shows in his face as in his shrill high-pitched voice he examines the daughter who has returned to him no longer a schoolgirl but a young woman, slim, chic, spirited and sexually attractive. He is proud of his possession. Flor is questioned closely on her studies, on the classmates with whom she has passed her vacations, who she has met and connections she has made, on the wealthy and international milieu of which she has become a part.

His interest is more than fatherly. For Trujillo his daughter is an ambassador for the country – a country so obscure that most in the wider world are wholly unaware of it and, if they are, only as a backward slum rotting somewhere among the islands of the Caribbean. Trujillo has a passionate ambition to *rebrand* that image: to put his country on the map and entice here the beautiful, rich and famous – that glitzy côterie known as Café Society who follow the seasons with their yachts and retinues; to attract capital, investment, development and publicity to the tropical island which he rules as his private fiefdom.

The President is pleased and gratified by all Flor tells him of how she has spent the last two years. He instructs her to throw a lavish party, inviting all her friends.

Her true friends are in France. She canvasses those she knew in the Dominican Republic when she lived here. Some have moved to America – those permitted to do so. Others receive the invitation with unconcealed alarm, explaining that in the interval their families have fallen out of favour and they would not be welcome at the Palace. Some have fathers who have disappeared; their offspring became non-persons, dangerous to know. They, too, cannot come to the occasion. When the evening arrives the guests mainly are children of the generals and colonels composing Trujillo's staff. Most Flor knows only slightly, many not at all. Only one girl, Lina Lovaton, who had attended the same military school as herself, can really be called a 'friend'. This is not *her* party but her father's. Everything in sight belongs to Him – and even her friendship with Lina will one day be appropriated by the dictator when she becomes his mistress.

The soirée creaks awkwardly into being, stiff, formal and frowsty. In France she has grown used to more sophisticated and vibrant occasions than this; she'd forgotten how dreary such events here were. The tin-pot republic exists in a time warp, governed by antiquated Spanish protocol. Fashion and modern manners have not penetrated this provincial backwater. Her father's circle of cronies is made up of sycophantic functionaries, with wives who are either frumps or vulgar show-offs, every one of them obese as their husbands. Their children, her peer group, are hicks, the girls graceless and subdued beneath the watchful gaze of their duennas. Only when dancing do their straitjackets loosen to the merengue, native rhythm of the favelas. While it plays their bodies shuck and bump within their starched outmoded dresses, supple in the negro beat… only to freeze when the number ends and, in silence, they return meekly to the custody of their chaperones perched on small gilded chairs around the walls.

As always the President maintains his own space in the large high-ceilinged ballroom, encircled by his cabal and attended by a handful of the personal Guard posed stiffly behind him. Soon after his late arrival when the party is already under way – his appearance signalled by the opening bars of the national anthem while all rise respectfully to their feet – Flor's glance seeks out the faces of these crisply uniformed youths. And there among them she sees him again, the young officer she'd noticed on the quayside at her arrival. As then, he is staring directly at her. She drops her glance at once… then looks back. For the second time a *touche* passes between them.

From her few friends at the party Flor ascertains what she can of him, though none of them knows Lieutenant Rubirosa personally. What she learns – from Lina – amplified by what she gleans later, is that he'd been born into a respected and cultured family. His father served as ambassador of the Republic in Paris during the First World War. As an adolescent Rubirosa had been schooled in that city, like her, and he'd remained there after his father had been recalled to the island. However he failed his baccalaureate and was in turn summoned home in some disgrace. Enrolled at the capital's best law school, he had played polo, boxed and led an active social life during which, at a party at the Country Club, he'd been noticed by Trujillo and summoned to present himself. Rubirosa had been invited to join the great man's table where, it seemed, he passed the unspoken test, for the following morning he was called to the Palace and given – not offered – a commission as lieutenant in the Presidential Guard… and directed to the President's own tailor to make his uniform, and to his personal shoemaker for riding boots with spurs – a look Trujillo favoured in the young men he elevated to attend him.

This evening at Flor's party Lieutenant Rubirosa remains dutifully in his place, close to the person of the Leader. Neither he nor she finds an opportunity to speak to the other.

The heat and humidity in the capital grow intolerable in full summer, when the trade winds cease and not a drop of rain falls for weeks. No breeze stirs in the narrow streets of tottering gingerbread houses where the air lies choked below awnings and overhanging balconies festooned with heavy creeper. Mules' hooves clop against the cobbles, shouts and cries bounce off bare walls and tiled floors. The uproar never ceases: carts, motors and horns, children and stray dogs. Doors and windows stand open to the street, Mexican music crackling from the radio in every house along with the smell of sweat and old clothes, cooking goat's meat and the fume of charcoal.

Ninety-eight per cent of the population remains trapped by poverty in their steaming barrios, but those who can escape the city. The President removes his family and entourage (including Rubirosa) to his country estate. There Flor rides out on her thoroughbred Arab stallion, accompanied by a groom, and passes the rest of the time in decorous idleness, watched over either by family or a duenna.

But 'as in a good script, we found ways', Rubirosa will explain later. More was communicated by glance than word, though once the two were caught speaking together in French by Dona Bienvenida, Flor's spiteful stepmother, who had replaced her own mother as the dictator's wife. She reported the incident to her husband. Trujillo was livid, his reaction immediate. Rubirosa was banished to duty at the military fortress of San Francisco de Macoris, where he was restricted to barracks.

So the two undeclared lovers find themselves separated in the traditional predicament of medieval romance – which they solve as young lovers have always solved, by ingenuity, subterfuge and smuggled notes.

A ball is due to be staged by the municipality in the town of Santiago. It is usual for local governors to seize on any opportunity to curry favour with the President, and it is clear to all that his daughter is destined for a starring role in the country's affairs. The prospect of a suburban repetition of her earlier lacklustre dance fills Flor with gloom, but it provides an opportunity. Though it is hard to find privacy to make the call, she telephones Lieutenant Rubirosa at the fortress to invite him.

A few days later, after improvising an appointment with a medical specialist, he comes to the ball. There he approaches Flor, bows, and asks her to dance. They dance… and continue to do so for five numbers in a row, observed by countless eyes while tongues wag. And it is noted that this is not the limit to the young man's audacity. Taking time out, the two stroll together *in public* beneath the lit-up trees of the town's dusty plaza, animatedly talking together in French. 'From that moment,' Rubirosa says, 'I was in love, and Flor as well.'

⚜

Informers are everywhere, part of the system; denunciation forms a recognised method of self-advancement. Even before the ball ends, the President is apprised of what had taken place. *What impudence!*

Vengeance is swift. Next day Rubirosa's sword and revolver are taken from him, he is stripped of his uniforms and expelled from the army. On the instant he becomes a non-person, and he knows this is not the end of it. The President is notorious in his wrath towards those who displease him. A gang of psychos and thugs lurk close to hand, prepared to torture, maim or kill to fulfil his whim, adept in the refined barbarities of their calling.

Rubirosa knows that his life is under threat. He considers escaping from the island, 'but to leave would be to lose Flor. And to lose Flor would be to die. But to stay would also be to die.' Dispatching a note to her, he borrows a pistol and hides out in the stables on one of his uncle's plantations.

His note to Flor is intercepted and carried to the President, its bearer tied to a palm tree in the garden and whipped before Flor's eyes. Appalled, she locks herself in her room, rejects meals, and refuses to see or speak to her father. An aide is sent to reason with her, but she is implacable. 'Tell my father that I want to marry the man I love, and I *will* marry him. Otherwise I would not be worthy of being his daughter.'

Meanwhile Rubirosa's mother, fearful for her son's life, seeks an audience with Trujillo and goes to plead for him. Cautiously, in a tone designed not to rile him, she points out that the family are respectable and loyal. Her husband had served his country honourably and with distinction throughout his career. Where was the shame if Lieutenant Rubirosa has asked the great man's daughter to dance, accompanied her on a passade around the town square? Where was the affront to Him if the young couple had fallen in love?

Perhaps it is Dona Ana's sincerity, perhaps Trujillo's intuition this personable youth could prove of use to him, perhaps a flicker of concern for his daughter's happiness, just possibly the remembrance that he too had once been young and ardent; more likely though on that particular morning his Furies are not with him. Whatever the explanation, the President does not hear out the mother's plea. 'Enough!' he shouts, and his fist slams the surface of the desk. 'That's enough! They will marry right away.'

The origins of Presidente Rafael Trujillo were veiled by the spin of myth to have become legend, for to the inhabitants of the island he stood on a par with God; his banner bore witness to their twin omnipotence. But to an impoverished, illiterate, provincial population gossip is the stuff of life, and the facts – though seldom and only furtively discussed – were available to all. His grandfather was a Spanish policeman stationed on the island, whose illegitimate son spawned a litter of eleven children, one of them Rafael.

How far the boy's nature was shaped by deprivation and abuse, by lack of education or redemptive role model is impossible to say. After reviewing his career it is natural to conclude he was *born* a brutal thug. The dark was present in him at his nativity and later would expand until it possessed him. He showed street savvy from the start, joining a gang of hoods named 'The 44' on reaching his teens. Short, wide and hard, he became an enforcer, using blackmail, violence and terror to collect. Not that he often had to employ such tactics. He had a *presence*, a menace that induced others to yield. He was working as a telegraph operator for $25 a month when he married the peasant woman who would become Flor's mother. Poor, their worldly wealth amounted to one burro stabled in the garden of their palm-thatched house, but Trujillo had a keen sense of appearance. He owned only two white suits, but his wife spent much of her time washing and pressing them. Soon he became a security guard on a sugar plantation and in the role acquired a taste both for uniform and tyranny.

At this time, just after the Great War, America was an imperial world power who had colonised – a word never uttered – several islands in the Caribbean. Santa Domingo was occupied by a military force of US Marines. The exemplary manner in which Rafael Trujillo imposed discipline on a disaffected rabble labouring on a plantation in near-slave conditions under the heat of the sun became known to the military authorities. He was effective, 'without scruples', it was noted with approval. He sounded like a useful man, the sort they were looking for. In 1918 he was awarded a commission in the National Guard, which was officered by marines. Readily allying himself with the occupying power, his ascent up the ranks was swift. When US forces finally quit the island in 1924 Trujillo had risen to command of the National Army. Six years later he led a coup against President Vasquez, installing himself in the become-vacant office. Soon after, the island's capital, Santa Domingo, was renamed Ciudad Trujillo and that crucial year of 1930 inaugurating his regime was designated Year One of the new republic.

Eleanor Roosevelt, Rafael Trujillo and his wife

With his meaty hand slamming down explosively upon the desk the President had issued his decree: *Enough! They will marry right away!*

Never could he reverse his decisions, for to do so would be to show weakness, but afterwards and not for the first time he wishes back the consequences of his impetuous edict. Behind the implacable façade lurks a man of passion whose violence is barely held in check. He feels toward his first-born daughter a fierce possessive love. She is his own flesh, the child that he has *made*, not just biologically but by taking charge of her upbringing after divorcing her mother, sending Flor to board at military school at the age of nine. There she learned discipline and obedience while remaining wholly dependent upon Him.

> Call it masochism, my slave-blood psychology coming out, but I *had* to submit to Trujillo's will. For in my tangled emotions he was not only papá, cajoling, demanding, ordering, for whose love I thirsted insatiably – perhaps above my husband's – but the demigod Generalissimo Trujillo, bizarre, fateful, omnipotent. Like the humblest Dominicano I prospered and suffered under his rule and came to think of him as immortal. I had succumbed to the Dominican neurosis, a willingness to swallow anything because it came from Trujillo.

Papa was God, didn't the two receive equal billing? He had fashioned her from the start and at fifteen dispatched her to finishing school in France to polish his creation. Yet the creature was not made in his own likeness, but rather its opposite. Crassly ignorant himself, coarse, unravelled, unsophisticated, deficient in all the graces, he has a clear picture of how he wants her to be.

What Trujillo desires for his daughter and his ambitions for his country are the same. The island that forms his fiefdom is a feculent midden, the population subsisting on one of the lowest per capita incomes in the world. He intends to transform the place into an international destination rivalling Venice or Monte Carlo, a luxurious world-class resort for the rich and famous. Through personal determination alone he will impose the appearance if not the structure of modernity upon the capital and adjacent coast. Santa Domingo will become a favoured luxury watering hole and playground for the cosmopolitan smart set. And his daughter will become the symbol to the world of this brave new republic, elegant, smart, high-toned, above all modern; the epitome of chic and style.

That was Trujillo's intention, which he'd never doubted he could achieve. He could impose his will on others, why not upon Flor, his creation? It had not entered his mind that in the process of European grooming the creature would gain a will of its own or a taste for freedom and independence, a teenager's urge to rebel.

The President is used to dealing with those who oppose him: he has them taken care of. To have Flor dealt with in the same way is inappropriate and counter to his feeling for her. And to have Rubi banished or disposed of would alienate her beyond recall; it would make her his enemy so she too would have to be dealt with in her turn.

Thus it was that upon this occasion on the murky battlefield of the dictator's mind Love won over Death – but this is still relatively early in his career during which, later, Death will prove always to be the safer option.

But the President is displeased, and when He is vexed those around him tiptoe in mortal terror, frantic to avoid his path. From the day he announces they will be married, he severs contact with the young couple. He is icy in his detachment, refusing to address one word to either.

Meanwhile he takes charge of every aspect of their forthcoming wedding: orchestration of the splendid ceremony, briefing the Archbishop, the wording of the invitations, the guest list and the lavish reception afterward. The President will give away the bride, still attached to him by an invisible chain. Rubi's best man will be the American ambassador, Arthur Shoenfeld, whom he's never met but who represents the new republic's patron, the US. A strategic relationship which well suits the State Department; Trujillo may be a monster but he is *their* monster.

The nuptials are set, the details are decided and the country's leading newspaper, *Listin Diario*, records that 'the genteel couple have united their pulsing hearts in emotion' and announces 'the most aristocratic wedding ever recorded in the social annals of the Republic'.

For the genteel couple themselves all this comes as something of a shock. As Flor puts it, 'Five dances in a row, two circles around a park, an innocent flirtation, and I was to marry a man I scarcely knew.'

The pair's chaste incipient romance has jumped fast forward into a situation neither had planned or contemplated, far less discussed. There has been no opportunity to *talk*, or gain knowledge of the other's past or flesh. Supervision over them has been constant. The two are strangers, designated partners in an arranged marriage.

For Flor this dalliance with Rubi had originated as a gesture of defiance to her father, a statement of independence. Rubi had happened to be standing in the right place at the right time, wearing a uniform in which most males look their swaggering best. It was very easy for women – now and later – to fall for the *image* of Rubi. Dark, handsome, slender and erect, he looked the part. On sighting him Flor had developed an instant crush – many women would later do the same.

Of course, to her it feels like love. Crushes do, and seventeen-year-olds are seldom analytical or self-aware. But her reason for marrying him is traditional, even primal, for it has applied since pre-history – to escape from home. 'I was infatuated by now, and also wild to leave my prison, to run like hell from father, an instinct that was to propel me all my life.'

And Rubi? He is twenty-three, fit and bold. For a macho Latin stud to roll over and acquiesce to an arranged marriage is the response of a man lacking balls. And Rubi *has* these, and the apparatus that comes with them will receive further attention in this book, indeed will form a leitmotif to the narrative. But neither Rubi's tackle nor male pride rears up in protest at this takeover of his life. Complaisantly, he goes along with the plan. He is confident of his own worth and what he is bringing to the wedding feast.

For him, marriage to Flor poses no dilemma. His nature is that of a gambler, a chancer. He will become known as a unscrupulous gigolo but in one sense he remains a romantic until the end. He believes instinctively that if he seizes the present the future will provide room-service and a fairy godmother pick up the tab – and this will remain so all his life. For him this marriage is no sort of choice.

Rubi, who will spend his entire life among the privileged and well-heeled, will remark later that Trujillo is the only really rich person he has ever known, 'He owns a whole country.' In the republic the Great Benefactor is the source of all wealth, all power, all patronage, and blithely Rubi steps forward with his bride to drink at the toxic font. The dowry he receives for saying 'I will' includes the distinction of a public identity: he is appointed Secretary to the Dominican Legation in London, their passport to liberty. The couple is given $50,000, a house in the grounds of the presidential mansion and a Buick convertible with chauffeur and their entwined initials embellished in gold leaf on the door.

On 2 December 1932 Flor marries the first of her nine husbands and Rubi secures his starter heiress, the first of five wives. So, together and in love, they climb into the Buick and set off for the world stage and the roles they believe life owes them…

CHAPTER 2

FLOR TRUJILLO, DOMINICAN REPUBLIC, 1932–37

The crowd of gaudily over-dressed wedding guests applauds as Flor and Rubi drive off from the mansion, high on hope and delusive liberty. They have defied the Benefactor and survived, the world lies open before them … but first there is the matter of sex to resolve. Flor has to be deflowered.

Her bridal night is spent in their new house in the grounds of the presidential mansion that Trujillo has given them. There her mother is waiting to greet the couple with a bottle of chilled champagne, for she has not been allowed to attend the ceremony, 'A ritual she was to follow after so many of my marriages,' Flor will recall thirty years and seven husbands later. But that is a remark made by a woman a great deal more worldly and cynical than the teenager she is today.

Sexually she is wholly inexperienced, innocent even of heavy petting. The sophisticated brat pack she'd known in France had been experimentally wanton in their ways but she'd been constrained by her Catholic upbringing and the value her provincial culture set upon virginity. 'You must realise that Latin girls are as jealously guarded from young men as the women of any Moorish harem,' she explains. Whereas Rubi has extensive acquaintance with sex; he claims to have enjoyed his first encounter aged thirteen. He is skilled in the arts of love, and he's not about to take her by force.

Flor has been told about the mechanics of the deed, school friends breathlessly have confided its details. And shortly before the wedding in a scene of tortuous embarrassment she'd been formally instructed in the act by Dona Bienvenida, her stepmother. Only the knowledge that she'd soon be clear of this insufferable parental custody enabled her to endure it.

So Flor is theoretically prepared for what is in store, but later that evening when, dressed in a pink negligee, she is waiting for Rubi beneath a tent of mosquito netting and he returns from the shower and drops his towel, for the first time she *sees* it…

Much has been said and written of Rubi's organ, and by many. In the 1960s the giant pepper grinders flourished by Italian waiters were known as 'Rubirosas'. A broad female clientele have testified to the awesome reality. Its reputation will firm up into legend and later wives will comment on that particular consistency, neither soft nor hard, along with other aspects … but now it is the *sight* alone that causes Flor to shriek, leap out the bed and race in terror for the door. She makes it into the passage with Rubi in pursuit. 'I ran all around the house while he chased me,' she recalls.

He grabs her, attempts to calm her without success. There is no rape, nor penetration that night. He is neither a cruel nor brutal man in lovemaking unless the moment calls for either. But eventually the ritual act of consummation has to take place, though it is a messy, painful business. 'I didn't like it because I bled so much, and my clothes were ruined. In time, he began to make love to me in different ways, but when it was over my insides hurt a lot. He was such a handsome boy and so charming that I let him do whatever he wanted. But he took so long to ejaculate that by the end I was a little bored.'

⁂

The morning after, Trujillo strolls across the green carpet of the Bahama grass of the mansion's well-watered grounds to inspect his protégés and wish the young couple well. He glances around their new home, pleased by what he sees. Expansively he informs them that today they may settle in and organise the staff but in future they will have lunch with him and Dona Bienvenida at the mansion. 'And Flor,' he adds as he leaves them, 'my son Ramfis is going to visit you.'

She is aware that her father has a mistress and that a young half-brother, Rafael Jnr, exists, but it was never discussed openly. 'I had learned well that, in Trujillo's Republic, when you knew something you knew nothing, absolutely.' Next day a car drives up with three maids, a chauffeur and a soldier minder. A nurse emerges, carrying a little boy of three in ringlets, wearing red velvet shorts and a French-lace collar. With him comes a gift from his mother, a box jammed with silver, marquise-cut diamond jewellery and lingerie with Paris labels. Flor takes her little brother in her arms, he screams and kicks with fury. 'For years he was to resent my very being,' she explains.

This wilful, precocious infant, who is treated with such deference by his attendants, is a monster in embryo – the tyrant's first-born son who stands to inherit the sceptre and the isle. From the start Rubi is more successful with the boy than Flor, laying down the foundation to a bond that will become vital to him in the years to come, ultimately his very lifeline. Though Rubi has little love for infant children he possesses a sure instinct for expedience.

The couple had received numerous wedding gifts. 'They jammed a whole room,' Flor says. Very many people sought to ingratiate themselves with her father, an even greater number to remain in his fickle favour. Presents included watches, silver, 'rings without count' and a $10,000 pair of earrings for the bride. And from Trujillo the house, the Buick, the $50,000 dowry. Of them all, the gift the two prize most is the promise of Rubi's posting to the embassy in London, their passport to an international milieu both long to re-enter, now with improved credentials and their own status within it.

In the days stretching into weeks following the wedding no further mention of that appointment is made by Trujillo. In sharp disappointment they come to realise that prize has been withdrawn. Marriage he has permitted; their liberty and independence he cannot condone.

But meanwhile the living is easy. Theirs is a comfortable wooden house with trellised verandah and slatted jalousies shading its windows from the harsh blaze of the sun. It has its own swimming pool and comes equipped with the latest American devices including gramophone and radio. There is a housekeeper and cook; Flor has two personal maids who see to everything and pick up after her; Rubi a valet, masseur and boxing coach. One room is fitted out as a gymnasium and ring for himself and Kid Gogo, the Dominican champion, now his sparring partner and resident pugilist. The mulatto prize fighter doubles as their minder, accompanying them if they go out at night. Not that there is anywhere to go. Trujillo's plans to transform the place into a fashionable resort are still but a dream and, despite work on the drains, air quality in the capital remains execrable – though when the trade winds are blowing the odour is only intermittently detectable further up the mountain, where the young couple live.

The occasional whiff is a small price to pay, as life for the pair of them has become the greatest fun. They've suddenly acquired a visible independence together with the toys of modern luxury. Both relish the experience for its novelty. They're like kids dressing up and playing at being adults, and with it they're in love.

'Rubi took to the easy life and so did I,' says Flor. His nominal occupation as Undersecretary in the Foreign Office carries no responsibilities and requires no skills except a pleasing manner with foreign dignitaries and potential investors in the island. He and Flor are capable in the role, it comes easily to them. There is a steady stream of entrepreneurs looking for opportunity, but most visitors are from the republic's patron, creditor and master, the United States. These men – they are always men – have to be looked after, seated by someone articulate at dinner, cultivated, schmoozed. Trujillo's own social skills are rudimentary, he's wholly lacking in charm, and at times resentfully aware of his deficiency. His court, the cabal of cronies surrounding him, are little more than thugs with dolled-up wives incapable of anything but Spanish. Style, elegance, sophistication, conversation are at a premium on the island.

This period, the Great Depression of the 1930s following the Wall Street Crash, is the worst of times for Trujillo to attempt to realise his grandiose fantasy of creating a luxury resort. Not only is he facing political opposition at home, which he quells by infiltration and brute force, but acute financial crisis. The country is massively in debt to the US and the treasury is empty. Franklin Roosevelt, the President, sends his lawyer fixer Joseph E. Davies to sort out its chaotic finances.

Trujillo's meetings of this nature invariably are conducted one-to-one; he trusts nobody with key secrets. But unusually Flor and Rubi are present on this occasion when the matter is discussed over dinner at the mansion. And rather than pleading as a supplicant against further financial sanctions, Trujillo's message to Davies is unambiguous: *Get the US Government off my back.*

Flor watches as in the course of that evening Davies is converted from critic to supporter, won over so effectually that he returns to Washington not only extolling Trujillo's leadership but recommending that the US grant a moratorium on the republic's debt. 'Father had a genius for imposing his will on others,' Flor says. Davies was not the first, though to date the most influential, of those friends in high places the dictator acquired to his cause. He assembled one of the most powerful lobbies in Washington which at the climax of his rule in the 1960s was costing $6 million annually (around $50 million today). This sum devoted to sanitising the public image of his tyranny was exceeded only by the price of what would become the most extensive spy system in the Western hemisphere. By 1961 the network required $8 million to run, and it was estimated that one in five of the population (of three million people) was a paid informer.

⚜

For Flor and Rubi, playing house is a frolic. For exercise they go riding or swim. They sunbathe by the pool while served with long cool drinks. Neither of them is a great reader but they scan American magazines and *Vogue*. The latest fashions haven't reached here yet – not that the tiny minority of women who might afford them could begin to carry them off.

There's not much in the way of company. Only occasionally are there international guests to dinner at the presidential mansion, when drinks and wine are available, proper food is served and there's some attempt at civilisation. Every day the couple are obliged to eat there and usually it is just with Trujillo and Bienvenida. Only plain fare is on offer: rice and beans, no drink, no cigarettes, no small talk. 'A bit like two slaves dining with the master,' Flor describes it.

Rubi's job involves no actual work. He rides, plays polo, gambles, cruises bars, and is casually unfaithful with other women. Flor is upset and furious but this is standard Latin behaviour and he is unrepentant. Her sophistication is only a veneer, she's still a teenager with ideals, boiling passions and jealousies, hormonally erupting and every bit as Latin as he. There are rows and stand-up fights. She goes at him and once he whacks her back. Hysterical, in tears, she flings herself into the Buick and drives to the Palace, bursting into a meeting to tell her father of the outrage.

Next day Rubi is summoned into his presence. Ensconced behind his enormous desk, eyes shrouded by dark glasses, the dictator presents a figure of considerable menace. He is terrifying in his rages, capable of having a man maimed or killed for some perceived affront, but Rubi knows that to show fear is fatal. Unapologetic, he readily admits to striking Flor – she had abused him like a fishwife, behaved in an unladylike manner and failed to respect him in his own home. So yes, he'd smacked her one.

There is much Trujillo detests about Rubi, those same elements in him that he envies: looks, cool, education, charm. He's chafed by the rivalry of the old bull for the new stud in the field. But there is also much they share: Catholicism, pride, machismo, attitude to women. For both, dominance in the home is an unquestioned stance. Trujillo has no respect for Rubi, he has no respect for anyone

27

who works for him, he belittles and humiliates all around him. He's aware his son-in-law is a drinker, a gambler, a lightweight. He knows he cheats on Flor – all his movements are reported to him – but Rubi's whoring is as standard and mundane as his own; he'd have been more jealous had the couple been faithful and happy together. He knows, both know, that to slap an unruly wife is necessary at times. It's the natural order of things, he's slapped his own. There is no penalty.

None of the landowning class or self-styled aristocracy cares for Trujillo, though like everyone else they are afraid of him. They consider him a jumped-up peasant. He has dealt with their conde-scension by recruiting their first-born sons into his Presidential Guard, effectively bringing their parents into line. After Flor's marriage many of Rubi's relatives receive government appoint-ments. Like a traditional godfather the dictator looks after family and his aged mother is sacred to him. Every evening after a promenade along the waterfront accompanied by twenty or so of his generals, he calls on her between 6.30 and 7, then visits his mistress and son before going home for dinner with Bienvenida at 10 p.m.

Bienvenida's family have been favoured by Trujillo, her brother has been awarded the coveted post of ambassador, heading up the Dominican embassy in London. Now, at one of those stilted lunches at the mansion in the torpid heat of afternoon, Trujillo breaks silence to announce that she is shortly leaving on vacation to visit him, then make a grand tour of Europe. Later Bienvenida, who is childless, confides to Flor that Trujillo 'is dying to have chil-dren and wants me to see a top Harley Street specialist about it'.

When the date of Bienvenida's departure dawns – and it dawns quite soon – Trujillo escorts her to the boat. He embraces her fondly in farewell, pressing the usual package of $100 bills into her hand. For three days following, Flor and Rubi are not required for lunch at the mansion. A team of workmen has been brought in to redecorate the private quarters. The whole place is in disarray for at the same time all the servants have been let go and a new staff installed in their place.

When the work is done and the mansion sparkling with fresh paint and smelling of polish and beeswax, Maria Martinez moves in with her son Ramfis, plus baggage and a ton of personal effects. She'd been a stenographer at the National Palace when Trujillo's eye first lit upon her and he picked her as a mistress. When she became pregnant he suggested an abortion, but she refused. So instead he married her off to a Cuban in the Dominican army and shipped them both to Havana. Against his wishes, she returned to the republic to give birth to Rafael Jnr. Flor considers that she's been smart in the way she played her hand. 'Little Ramfis was the trump she used to ensnare Trujillo.'

A new mistress-in-residence makes no difference to the country but domestic regime change is immediately apparent at the mansion. Maria is no plain submissive Dominicana like Bienvenida or Flor's mother, but a beautiful imperious woman of Spanish temperament who dares to talk back to Trujillo. She makes her presence felt, and for Flor the inevitable problems with a new stepmother are exacerbated by the fact that Maria is almost the same age as herself.

Flor and Rubi's residence has no privacy; not even a fence divides it from the mansion's grounds. Trujillo is an early riser and has the habit of strolling in on them when the whim takes him. One morning he drops by casually to say that he's going to marry Maria.

Overcoming her dismay, Flor attempts to appear delighted by the news. 'What was there to say? I was upset by the things father did but I accepted him as a natural law unto himself, a man who could do what he willed with his life, mine or anybody else's… And so I went to father's civil marriage to Maria.' *Everyone* who's invited attends the ceremony. Not to would be an unforgivable affront. All are keen to express their joy in the Benefactor's union; the provincial aristocracy and the brash new order in their vulgar finery are as one. Costumed as for comic opera they make up a motley throng, but the strangest member of that wedding party is Ramfis, now six and a full colonel in the army, wearing dress uniform, sword and medals, drinking champagne and chatting with his ADC.

⁂

Flor believed that her and Rubi's fall from grace was prompted by an item in a Haitian newspaper reporting on a state mission to the republic where all were impressed by their 'elegance'. The piece applauded them as the best dressed, best educated, most popular couple in town. There was no mention of Trujillo, who resented the omission.

Soon after this Rubi, who is bored by his non-job, becomes involved in a speculative venture. 'There was the matter of my dowry,' Flor explains. 'Both Rubi and I longed for some independence of our own, though neither of us had much business sense…' There were always a number of dodgy entrepreneurs hanging around the Palace, seeking Trujillo's approval to their various schemes. One of these was Felix Rexach, a Puerto Rican engineer who had done a deal with Trujillo on a project dear to the dictator's heart.

At the bottom of El Condo in the heart of the Zona Colonial, the fortress of Santa Domingo looks down on the estuary of the Ozama River where it bends into the sea by a pocket beach choked with garbage. This is where the original harbour had been set up under the protection of the fortress's guns. Then it was perfectly suitable for the shallow draught vessels of the period, but now Trujillo has a vision of turning it into a deepwater harbour capable of receiving cruise liners, and constructing a marina for the yachts of the super-rich he wishes to attract here.

Rexach had built a harbour in Puerto Rico and possessed the credentials for the job. He'd carved out an apparently successful life that included homes in Paris and the Côte d'Azur and a semi-famous wife known as La Môme Moineau (the Raggedy Sparrow), a Parisian nightclub chanteuse. In the restricted social life of the capital where everyone knows everyone else it was inevitable the Rexachs and Rubirosas became acquainted. French-speaking, travelled and sophisticated, the four are distinctive in this social wilderness. A bond forms between them in which Flor and Rubi spot an opportunity for themselves. Somehow they've learned of a second-hand dredge for sale in New Orleans. Rexach is schmoozed into agreeing to charter it for use in the harbour project if the Rubirosas buy it.

'For once I gathered courage,' Flor says. Choosing the moment, she asks her father's permission to use her dowry for the purchase. He consents, but with the comment, 'I don't have much faith in either second-hand machinery or this investment.'

The dredge is acquired and towed to the island. It is old, rusty and not an imposing piece of equipment. Flor and Rubi are dismayed when they see it, nor is Rexach overly impressed. It is put on trial in the most difficult part of the harbour.

❧

A private off-the-record life is impossible on the island. Where you go, who you speak to, what you say invariably is noted. Having no life worth the name of their own, the populace lives vicariously by gossip. It is soon whispered that Rubi and the Môme Moineau are having an affair. Rexach is early to pick up on it and he is sore. He has anyway by now acquired his own dredge, a larger and more modern rig. He informs Trujillo that Rubi's dredge is inadequate; moreover a hazard, for its gas-powered engine risks blowing up and destroying the port.

Neither Flor nor Rubi can obtain a meeting with Trujillo to get a hearing. They are frozen out of the deal. Rubi demands from Rexach that he refund them the price of the dredge – and he refuses. The couple are stricken. The President is furious and their capital, the money they'd hoped would fund their escape, is gone. Beside himself in anger, Rubi acts on impulse.

❧

The cobbled waterfront is an open market with stalls selling fruit, vegetables, flyblown meat. Carts with coloured awnings vend orange juice and peeled sugar cane; hawkers peddle cookies and small balls of salt. The over-ripe air is thick with the smell of sweat, shrill in the uproar of the ragged mob; all poor, malnourished, many defective, diseased, deformed. A blind woman begs, rattling a tin, eyes that are white scabs; a legless man goes by walking on his hands like a swinging egg.

The crowd parts to let through a splendid figure: Captain Rubirosa in the dress uniform of the Presidential Guard, wearing a revolver on his belt. He's accompanied by the solid bulk of Kid Gogo, shoving a way to the quay where a launch is waiting, engine running. They step on board, the boat puts off with the two upright in the stern and chugs through the river's sluggish flow, afloat with broken branches and debris, toward Rexach's dredger at the construction site. The shallow water is discoloured by soot, sargasso weed, effluent and hundreds of dead fish in a wide stain spreading out to sea.

Their approach has been noted from the dredger. When Rubi comes aboard closely followed by his minder, Rexach is already on deck. The two march right up to him. 'I leapt at him, grabbed him by the collar and shook him like a carpet,' Rubi writes. '"Thief! If you continue waging war against me and don't pay me right now what you owe me, I will destroy you!" He was terrified. He collapsed. He promised everything I wanted.'

It is an impetuous action on Rubi's part. Later he will learn greater subtlety in the exercise of bluff. Very understandably, Rexach runs to Trujillo in high alarm. He's been assaulted, threatened. Rubi will kill him, he can't continue with the work.

Trujillo is not just a patron but a partner in this project and loyalty a commodity he receives not gives. There is no reason to worry, he assures Rexach, 'Four officers of my Guard will accompany you and let Captain Rubirosa know what it will cost him if he touches one hair on your head.'

❧

Trujillo never communicates his disfavour in person. The individual who transgresses is no longer acknowledged to exist, but the sentence is delivered by messenger. Always the same man, Flor says, a terrifying creature known as General 'Magic Eye' Alvarez, so named because the giant negro has one crude glass eye set in its own fixed stare. Magic Eye brings the news that their home and Rubi's job are no more, that they are a shameless ungrateful pair no longer acceptable on the island.

Although her father lives less than a hundred yards distant across the lawn, no way can Flor reach him to appeal; 'We had become non-persons.' Their money is gone in the dredge, but Flor has jewellery. Rubi borrows where he can though with little success, his record with debts is not good.

They pack. Nothing in the house belongs to *them*, they take only what they can carry and board a plane to New York. 'So we "deserted" Trujillo. To father, anyone who made a move independent of HIS wishes was a betrayer,' Flor explains.

⁂

The couple arrive in Manhattan just before Christmas 1934. They don't even own winter clothes and can scarcely speak the language. They are entirely unequipped for real life; they don't possess a single marketable skill between them. They rent a room in a sleazy Broadway hotel. 'It was a nightmare, as Rubi disappeared to play poker with Cuban gangster types while I waited in that dingy hotel room, watching the Broadway signs blink on and off. When he won we ate, when he lost we starved.' And Rubi is less than supportive in these hard times. 'He would come home at 6 a.m., his pockets stuffed with matchbooks scribbled with phone numbers of women. Angry, brutal, he shoved and hit me when we argued.'

A colony of expat Dominicans exists in the city. Headed by a Dr Angel Morales, it is made up of opponents to Trujillo who have fled the island, together with those family members who've managed to escape. Several have suffered imprisonment and torture under the regime; Trujillo's daughter and son-in-law are emphatically not welcome in their community. There is also a well-staffed Dominican consulate (and spy centre) run by Flor's uncle, but disgraced and expelled from the President's favour, the Rubirosas are untouchables who cannot be invited. The couple are broke, cold, at odds with each other and friendless.

Their only contacts are Rubi's three young cousins who have grown up in the city. 'They were tough teenagers (when I saw *West Side Story*, it reminded me of them), good-for-nothings who had never worked.' One of them is Luis Rubirosa, nicknamed 'Chichi', who gains his living from petty crime and boasts a police record for robbery and assault.

Flor is appalled by Rubi's relatives, but he – who needs company and action to exist – continues to see Chichi. And his connection to criminal low life does not go unnoticed. Trujillo may have cast out the couple but his nature compels him to keep tabs on them.

Then, when they are at their lowest point, redemption comes out of the blue: a cable from the Palace. They are pardoned and recalled from banishment. Even more astonishing, the summons includes the news that Rubi has been elected to the Dominican Congress.

They move back into their house above the capital, untenanted since they left it. And they are received again in the presidential mansion, though Flor's welcome lacks warmth. Trujillo will never be able to forgive his daughter who defected from the destiny he'd planned for her. Anyway, he doesn't *do* forgiveness.

She is demoralised by her father's coldness. Shaken and humiliated by their months in New York, she yearns for affection, for the father who used to take her on his knee and call her '*mi princesi*'.

But 'that was the peculiar genius by which he ruled – by belittling people, making you feel insignificant, sapping your self-esteem.'

But once again they have a home and the appurtenances of wealth, even if they do not *own* these, and there is staff to look after them. Though they possess no capital of their own and no independence, Rubi now has a salary. His job is a sham, the Congress itself a charade where Trujillo makes his entrance to open proceedings wearing lifts, full uniform with plumed fore-and-aft hat, and presides over an assembly whose business is solely to approve his edicts. Its members are appointed and dismissed on whim, its function purely ceremonial.

Why, Flor wonders, has Trujillo recalled them? The answer comes quite soon, when Rubi announces that he's off to New York on a 'special mission' for her father. He's away for two weeks and when he returns he's bearing a raft of presents for her. His spare suitcase is filled with new dresses and other gifts. She welcomes him back with delight.

On the day following Rubi's departure from New York, Dr Morales (who had served as Interior Minister in the republic and later as Vice President of the League of Nations) presided at a meeting of Dominican exiles in Manhattan. Also present was fellow insurgent Sergio Boscome (son of a Dominican general killed in a 1930 shoot-out attempting to kill the new President Trujillo), with whom he shared an apartment on Hamilton Place. After the meeting, Morales went on to dinner, Boscome returned to their apartment. He was shaving in the bathroom when he heard the cries of their landlady. A man brandishing a pistol demanded to know where Morales was. When Boscome rushed into the living room, his face covered with lather, the assassin shot and killed him. The police investigation named Morales the intended target, and ten months later presented sufficient proof to a grand jury to indict Chichi for murder. But he had vanished from the city.

Back on the island, the successful mission has effected a rapport between Trujillo and Rubi that excludes Flor. The two men have become close and are off on a trip together when one night there is an insistent hammering on Flor's front door. The servants are roused and she comes down to find Chichi in the hall explaining, 'I had to leave the States because they are after me.'

He moves in with them – an inconvenient guest, for he has no money and behaves as though Rubi owes him. He bosses around the staff, shows no inclination to seek work and passes the time lounging by the pool ordering drinks. Flor is exasperated but Rubi is curiously reluctant to throw him out. One evening the couple comes home to find the problem has been solved. The servants explain that 'strangers' surrounded the house and took him away. 'We never saw him again and my husband would not comment on the affair. When the New York police tried to extradite Chichi, the Dominican Government's answer was '*No such person exists.*'

⚜

The junta of generals around Trujillo is chosen for its loyalty and ruthless capability to implement his will. He does not trust the old 'aristocracy' with positions of authority, the members of his cabal are effective but uncouth. Yet the various embassies that his vanity has led him to set up in foreign capitals require more than barbarians to represent the republic in the image he desires, and he is woefully short of personable candidates who know which fork to use at dinner. Rubi is named Secretary to the Dominican legation in Berlin.

This is 1936. Hitler has been Chancellor for three years and in that time has reordered the chaos of a humiliated bankrupt country execrated by the world and saddled with crippling reparations, transforming it into a thriving economy while purging all opposition to Nazi rule. He has reduced unemployment from six million to less than one and halved the crime rate; sales of clothing, furniture and household goods are up 50 per cent and the standard of living higher than it has ever been. The Führer has rekindled the national spirit and enjoys popularity close to worship.

Trujillo is an ardent admirer of both Hitler and Mussolini, and envious of what they have achieved. Once he'd complained to Flor about the smallness of the stage providence has granted him on which to display his talents, while Hitler has a seat at the high table and is an international player. The Führer's army has just reoccupied the demilitarised Rhineland (formerly German territory) in defiance of the Peace Treaty, which imposed such ignominy upon the country, and Berlin is hosting the Olympic Games.

The feel-good factor in the population is close to hysteria. Their mood has been fanned into such heat by Joseph Goebbels, Minister for Propaganda. A weedy insignificant man with a club foot and accompanying grievance, he is a charismatic public speaker but, above all, a brilliant propagandist.[†] He also possesses a flair for the spectacular that matches Hitler's own histrionic style. By means of choreographed displays, parades and the rituals of Nazi Party celebrations, he has been instrumental in creating the Führer myth. It is of course a help that the Propaganda Ministry enjoys absolute control of the media and the arts.

---

†   The emergent dictatorships were quick to seize on the advertising and promotional techniques resulting from mass media. Almost all of the methods currently employed in political advertising in Britain and the US were first defined by Hitler in *Mein Kampf*.

For a young couple on the make this is an expeditious moment to relocate to Berlin. Hitler is actively wooing the countries of Latin America with the aim of recruiting them into a natural alliance of dictators against both Bolshevism and Democracy. The couple are seated in Hitler's box at the Olympic Stadium, invited to attend the Nuremburg Rally, and fêted by both Goebbels and Hermann Göring. It is the life both have long thirsted for, a milieu they'd met with in youth – though not on this level. Rubi, who has greater experience, learns fast but Flor, who sees it differently, is daunted. 'Rubi and I were alike in so many ways, neither of us really good-looking, both mixed-up Dominicans in love with the high life, hungry for what money could buy, but unable to earn an honest living on our own. "The day I don't have money," Rubi vowed, "I'll kill myself. I need it to live the way I want to live."'

His work, as ever, is negligible. He fences, he rides, he parties. Of course they attend parades and receptions as a couple. But Flor has no German and not everyone speaks French; she is conscious that the 'chic' she was so admired for in the Caribbean is not seen in quite the same way here. 'Rubi was cutting a swathe on his own, but what was I? How could I, still a provincial Dominican girl in her early twenties, unworldly, badly dressed, mousey, compete with Rubi's women? My particular *bête noire* was a certain Martha, who had enchanted Rubi at an Italian winter-sports resort. Soignée, blazing with diamonds, she was everything I was not...'

One day a box is delivered, containing twenty-one magnificent red roses. 'I assumed they were for me, until I saw the note addressed to Rubi, "For the twenty-one days we have loved each other."'

She cries to Daddy: *I hate this! Solve it, get me out of here!* But she knows he's a pitiless god with no heart left; her letter is strained and formal.

I have learned a little German and seen a lot of the country, and have admired the great work of Hitler. But nevertheless I'm not happy ... They don't invite us to their dances, and I don't have the chance to meet anybody. If it isn't too much to ask, I'd like you to transfer us to Paris ... There, I'd have occasion to attend many conferences and get to know better the French literature that I like so well. Please let me know if you can comply with this request.

Daddy comes through, but Paris provides no answer to Flor's unhappiness. The cosmopolitan set she'd known at school here has long dispersed to their own countries. Rubi though is instantly at home: 'As soon as I arrived in Paris invitations began pouring in. I was out every night, often alone. My wife objected ... she could not keep up with me.'

It was hideously demoralising for Flor, not at all what she'd dreamed of, hoped for. She hadn't even *chosen* to be Rubi's wife, the part had been forced on her. For a while it had been the greatest fun while they played at being adults in their tropical villa, mixing the latest cocktails and practising routines to the latest records from America. They were both great dancers. In the capital's one decent nightclub – where they were instantly recognised, of course – other couples often had stopped to watch them and applauded.

Now romance has gone there's little that unites the couple. Though understandably depressed, Flor is realistic about the relationship (and surprisingly unembittered – they will continue to sleep together whenever their paths cross over the next twenty years, whatever their marital situation, and between them they racked up fourteen marriages). She says, 'Our marriage hadn't been a matter of love, or even sex. Like most Latin males, Rubi expected me to be the docile wife, waiting at home for him, no matter how much he dallied.' She realises that a different relationship with him is not possible. Set in the Latin mould, he is what he is and no woman can change him. Their marriage is over and there is nowhere to go but home.

⚜

Meanwhile, back on the island Trujillo has continued to prosper. He has taken over much of the fertile land, redistributed some, but retained the best for himself. He personally controls both sugar cane and tobacco, the principal exports. He has put in roads, provided electricity and running water to the capital and instituted further work on the drains, though to little effect. Any word of personal criticism is 'speaking against the republic' and a criminal offence subject to arrest and torture. The country belongs to him body and mind, but a soaring ego knows no bounds; he has need of a cause for his people to march to, and a suitable group on which to focus any latent discontent.

Hitler has racial purity, Fatherland and 'living space' as patriotic cause; for victim caste he has the Jews. Conveniently available to Trujillo as a readily identifiable hate group are 'the Blacks'. He has negro blood himself, almost everyone on the island is of mixed blood and like many he uses make-up to lighten his complexion. Yet he is a negrophobe. In the west of the island numerous Haitians have crossed the ill-defined mountain frontier in recent years, to find work on the several large Dominican sugar-cane plantations, and remained squatting in the territory. Three months before Flor quits Paris to return home, Trujillo arbitrarily declared his country officially White, and put into effect an active policy of '*blanquismo*'. On his orders a ragtag army of goons armed with guns and machetes descended on the area to cleanse it of Haitian squatters. These were the same colour as everyone else but grew up speaking French rather than Spanish patois. The local population was subjected to certain tests, one of them to pronounce the Spanish word *perejil* (parsley), awkward for French speakers. Get it wrong and they were hacked to death. The butchery was relentless, close on twenty thousand people massacred. However, so remote is the area and so complete the control Trujillo exercises over the Dominican press that no word of the killings leaked for weeks – and then the international media was more engaged with Hitler's plans for war than some past atrocity on the other side of the world, of which no photographic evidence existed.

GOD AND TRUJILLO! Hoardings displaying the slogan are everywhere on the island. As is another: TRUJILLO WE LOVE YOU, and the message is no less than truth. Astonishingly, this corrupt, brutal overweight tyrant is *loved*, even worshipped, by his people; he's the great Father of all. And the Daddy to whom Flor comes home.

⁂

She still thinks of him as omnipotent, as do his people. That's the image she's had of him since infancy. Yet, despite the evidence of his coldness, harshness, cruelty, she believed he'd take her in his arms, hug her, restore her and set the world to rights. 'Did I love him, or any of my husbands for that matter? I don't know to this day. Perhaps … all my life I wanted only to be pampered by father.' She confides that on this occasion she longed for him to embrace her, give moral support, soothe and restore her shattered ego … but also to come up with money to return to Paris on her own terms and make something of herself.

Secretly, I wanted no divorce, for Rubi was the husband I'd married in the church … For the first time in my life, I poured out my heart to father, telling him about my wild quarrels with my husband, adding up my complaints like a child. Then I grew afraid as I watched the terrible satisfaction on his face…

Then, in his shrill voice, Trujillo starts to shriek. A torrent of filth pours from his mouth as he denigrates Rubi 'in gutter language', disparaging, vilifying, ridiculing him as so often he's done to others in public, reducing them to rubbish. Trujillo's rages are a terrifying performance. Most are cowed to abject silence. Flor is shaken, deeply hurt, 'If he felt this contempt, why had he married me off to him?'

The rant ends as suddenly as it began. Abruptly he hands her an automobile catalogue, telling her she can choose any model she desires. His behaviour is familiar to her, 'Cash was the only language of love that father knew.'

But at least she understood that language and takes it in her stride. From the brochure Flor chooses a top-of-the-range Buick, asking that it be delivered in Paris. 'But then comes Papa's fiat: "I'll never let you go back to that man."' Next day his lawyer calls on her to arrange a divorce.

'I meekly complied. This was to be the pattern of my marathon marrying. I would think, naively, if I divorce and start afresh, *this* time Papa will approve.' He never would – expressing his disapproval in one case by going so far as to have her husband murdered – nor will she ever break free from Daddy until his assassination twenty-four years later, and perhaps not even then.

But now she has cut free from Rubi, and done so before her spirit is broken. She's an optimist – as nine marriages surely indicate. Back in the Dominican Republic, she sets to remaking a would-be independent life.

And Rubi? He is fired by a furious Trujillo from his employment and remains alone in Paris. No, not alone, Rubi is congenitally unable ever to be alone, but once again he's single, a man lacking income and on the make in a big city at a critical moment in history, for the Second World War is about to break out.

CHAPTER 3

DANIELLE DARRIEUX, PARIS, 1940–41

I t was the sound that told people life had changed – probably forever. When the citizens of Paris woke up on that spring morning in 1940 the noise reaching them from the street outside was unfamiliar. The usual din of traffic and autohorns had gained a deeper resonance, a heavy rumble identifiable solely by the old – and that only after a second of shocked astonishment.

It was the creak and grind of heavy wooden wheels, the clop of farmhorses dragging wagons over the cobbles. The great peasant carts each contained a whole family, plus most of their belongings piled high around them. The slow-moving stream of horse-drawn vehicles was broken up by cars trapped in its flow with overheating engines, mattresses and suitcases roped to the roof, open boots jammed with prams, bicycles, carpets and anything that could be crammed in the gaps between.

The journalist Fleur Cowles, staying at the Ritz while covering the early months of the war for *Life* magazine, became aware of the unfamiliar sound as soon as she awoke. She dressed and went downstairs to discover its cause. As she was crossing the lobby the

Concierge stopped her to say, 'You must leave Paris, madame, the Germans are coming.'

'How do you know they're coming?' she asked.

'Because they have reservations,' he said.

❧

For a week the sky over Paris was black with smoke from bonfires of burning files by every government building. People stood still in the street, craning their necks to stare up into the empty air, looking for paratroops. The roads were jammed with refugees streaming into the capital from the occupied countries of Denmark, Holland and Belgium, while a counter-flow struggled in the opposite direction as Parisians abandoned their homes to escape south. No trains were running. The railway stations were closed and guarded by soldiers. People gathered outside, rattling the locked gates in desperation.

On 11 June the French army cut the telephone lines and abandoned the city. An advance squadron of German tanks reached Porte St Denis next day and a truce party went forward on foot with a white flag to negotiate peaceful entry into the city, but came under fire from the rooftops. They retired, and General Küchler ordered an all-out assault for 8 a.m. next morning. That the city was saved from bombardment was due to the American ambassador, William Bullit, who received a surprise call appointing him Mayor of Paris, just before the government fled the capital to relocate elsewhere. Though the post was well outside the usual career path of a US diplomat, gamely he accepted, contacted Küchler and assured him German forces would meet no opposition. Paris was declared an 'open city'; the right to resist was surrendered in exchange for peaceful occupation.

That same day a column of helmeted Wehrmacht troops marched twelve abreast behind a band down the Champs-Élysées, and a huge swastika was raised above the Arc de Triomphe. General Studnitz became military governor of Paris, requisitioning the Hôtel de Crillon as his headquarters. The Ritz, the Raphael and George V were taken over by the High Command with similar lack of fuss, continuing to provide the service for which they were renowned. Hermann Göring, in search of something rather more grand, annexed the Senate building, the Palais du Luxembourg, for his personal HQ.

Wehrmacht loudspeaker vans toured the streets, warning everyone to stay indoors. Panzer columns of tanks clanked down the main avenues, followed by military trucks filled with helmeted soldiers seated to attention with rifles upright between their knees. Paris became a dead city; all its buildings were closed, every shop locked and shuttered. Once again the sound of the capital changed: no traffic except military vehicles, but the added ring of countless black metal-tipped boots striking on the cobbles.

On 17 June the new Prime Minister, 84-year-old Marshal Pétain, appealed for an armistice from Vichy, where the government had fled. The formal capitulation was signed at Compiegne, in the same railway carriage in which Germany had surrendered to France in 1918.

By now 100,000 French soldiers lay dead and two million were prisoners of war. To the south of Paris a dense mass of refugees dragged their way down dusty roads in columns stretching as far as the eye could see. The verge was littered with belongings they'd thrown away and cars abandoned when they ran out of petrol or their motors seized. Some had a pram, a makeshift cart or wheelbarrow heaped with baskets, bundles, sacks. Their clothes were torn, crumpled, filthy; they'd worn them for days, slept in them by the road. They were thirsty, hungry and exhausted, many were in tears, pulling along whining children by the hand. In among the endless procession were horses, cattle, dogs. The sun beat down from a cloudless sky, unbearably hot.

In Paris, when people emerged onto the streets after the curfew, great red flags with swastikas flew everywhere; huge Nazi banners draped the frontage of government buildings and hotels, obscuring several floors. German road signs stood at all major intersections. Every clock was set forward one hour to German time. A black-out was in force, but except for buildings with generators there was no electricity. The telephones didn't work. The unwatered flowers drooped in the public gardens and the leaves of the plane trees withered in the heat. On the Left Bank sheep belonging to refugees from northern France grazed on the uncut lawns of the Palais des Invalides. Yet the familiar architecture of the city remained intact, unscarred by bomb damage. The occupation had brought with it no *Sturm und Drang*, instead – unique in history – it provided a model of good manners.

Wehrmacht trucks patrolled the streets distributing food to the population. It was handed out by smiling ruddy-cheeked soldiers with bared blond heads. At first their reception was wary, but quickly these healthy young animals were seen not to be dangerous. They winked at young women, who tossed their heads in disdain then glanced back flirtatiously. Restaurants and cafés reopened to receive these new uniformed customers who were liberal in their spending; they were polite, paid for everything and tipped well.

Paris became an enormous garrison. Flush with unspent wages, soldiers clattered into luxury shops to buy clothes for wives and girlfriends, and expensive gifts to send home. At the Café de la Paix on Place de l'Opéra and the fashionable open-air cafés and brasseries along the Champs-Élysées more than half the customers were German. On entering a café they took off their belts and flung them with a crash on the marble-topped table before sitting down. Backs of chairs and empty seats were hung with steel helmets and revolvers. They called for champagne, laughed, smiled at everyone, patted the children at near-by tables, gave them sweets and cigarette cards, let them examine their weapons. At first these kids were snatched back by their parents, less often as time went by. People were hugely relieved at the behaviour of the 'Boches', impressed, even enthusiastic.

At night the streets rang with song and cheers from the victorious celebrating soldiery. These happy high-spirited young men soon acquired girlfriends. The law of nature ensured fraternisation. Parisian women dyed their bare legs the colour of nylon stockings, and inked a line around the thigh to show where they stopped. Paris had been the capital of love and earthly pleasures for so long the inconvenience of war could not be allowed to extinguish its civilities. The tone was set early: on the third day following occupation when the curfew was lifted, one of the better brothels displayed a sign, BUSINESS AS USUAL AFTER 3 P.M.

❧

There was another face to this coin of German courtesy, a face marked with brutality and persecution, and the inhabitants of Paris will catch glimpses of it quite soon, though they prefer to avert their gaze. But for the moment the business of daily life, though restricted, was not particularly oppressive. *On doit continuer de vivre* – as a city tribe Parisians are the most pragmatic species on earth.

The arts also continued, particularly the theatre. The occupation prompted a theatrical revival in the city; the German officer class was avid for culture and entertainment. There were 400 new productions in Paris during the occupation, including new plays by Camus, Sartre, Cocteau and Jean Anouilh. The cinema also continued to do well as it had throughout the latter half of the 1930s.

One of its stars was 23-year-old actress Danielle Darrieux, who by now had made twenty-nine films, including the international success *Mayerling*, directed by Anatole Litvak, in which she starred opposite Charles Boyer. Several of these pictures were Franco-German co-productions filmed in two-language versions. She was as popular with German audiences as with those in her native country. In the autumn of 1940 she completed filming the romantic comedy *Premier Rendezvous*, directed by the highly rated and much older Henri Decoin, to whom she'd been married for five years. This was produced and distributed by Continental, a German company set up by Joseph Goebbels, whose Paris office was run by his nominee, Alfred Greven.

⁓⁂⁓

At the end of September, three months after the occupation of Paris, Danielle is invited to a party thrown by Count André de Limur, a French diplomat with a taste for show business and fashionable company.

Her last film *Battement de Coeur*, also directed by her husband, has just been released to considerable acclaim. *Premier Rendezvous* is in the can and currently being edited for distribution. She is an established star with an international reputation at the height of her career and this party is in her honour.

She makes her entrance and is welcomed by the Count with due *éclat*. The others there are far too sophisticated to be hushed or show awe, but every eye circumspectly is on her as she is led on a circuit of the most important guests. One of the men presented to

her is a deeply tanned Latin American of about thirty. He is introduced and she reaches out her hand. He takes it, bows and raises it
to his lips to kiss the back of her fingers, '*Enchanté, madame.*' His
velvet voice has a faint but exotic accent. And what a delightfully
melodious name: Porfirio Rubirosa.

Danielle's host, the Count, leans to her to stage-whisper in her
ear, 'Be careful, this man is dangerous.'

She smiles, and those within earshot chuckle at the words.

⚜

Danielle had been born in Bordeaux into a middle-class family.
Her beloved father, an eye-specialist, died when she was eleven,
leaving little inheritance. His widow and three young daughters
relocated in Paris, where Danielle went to school, showing herself
to be imaginative and bright, with notable musical talent and a
good voice.

Mother was ambitious for her daughters and prospects looked
brighter in Paris than the provinces. But money was tight and she
had to give singing lessons to help out. Danielle explains, 'One
of her pupils was married to a husband who had some sort of job
in films. He sometimes came with her to class and mentioned to
maman that he had two film producer friends who were urgently
looking for a thirteen- or fourteen-year-old girl to play the lead in
their next picture. The several they had already tested all came over
as too old for the part. He suggested to maman that the daughter
of the house should go see them.'

Her mother, who was well aware of the reputation of gentlemen
in the film business, baulked at the notion, but Danielle insisted. 'I
was inquisitive and stubborn by nature; I was determined to try for
it.' Maman relented and Danielle, wearing her best sky-blue frock,

set off alone for the production offices. There she ran into one of the producers about to leave for the studio at Epernay, where the film unit was shooting tests. So struck was he by the slim animated tomboy with her impish grin, he proposed that she accompany him there.

Clambering into his big car, the underage schoolgirl who wanted to get into movies and the middle-aged producer who was casting one drove off for the studio. A key scene, since ever.

Arriving there without incident, Danielle found a number of girls, older than herself, waiting to be tested. Unlike them, she'd never attended stage school and was without any experience. But she took the pages of script given her and sat down to learn her part. When it came her turn before the lens she showed no nervousness. She spoke her lines spontaneously. What struck everyone was her vivacity, an irresistible gaiety; she had a natural gift for comedy.

Next day she was recalled for a further test. 'I had to play a dialogue scene with a very good-looking young assistant director (out of shot) who I had to call "Maman" while in floods of tears.' For a fourteen-year-old without any dramatic training to be able to summon desolating emotion and tears on command was a remarkable feat. 'After a week of waiting without any particular agitation or impatience I learned that I'd got the part.'

She was that rarity – a natural. A teenager with a sunny nature and face spilling over with merriment and infectious high spirits, the camera loved her, and so did the public. She was immediately signed for another picture, *Coquecigrole*, which went into production that same year.

Other French film actresses of the period were all in their thirties, playing much younger roles on screen. By chance, accidental timing and God-given talent, Danielle created a brand that was hers alone. In 1932–3 Danielle completed three films, the following year no fewer than six. Her audiences watched her grow up on screen, saw her blossom and come into flower as a young woman. She had thousands of fans by now in both France and Germany, who copied the way she cut her hair, did her make-up, her look, clothes, style. She was a recognised star – and at the same time a most dutiful daughter. Her salary went into a bank account controlled by her mother. Success did not turn her head and there was no teenage rebellion; between filming she studied design at L'École Commercial and played cello and piano at the Conservatoire.

In 1935 she was cast in *J'Aime Tous les Femmes* by its director, Henri Decoin, whom she'd met on her previous picture when he was hired to rewrite the dialogue, adding lines specifically designed for her. An experienced cineaste more than twenty years older than she, he was captivated as much by her personality as her talent – indeed the two were inseparable, her screen persona was an aspect of herself. She married Decoin in the winter of that year, aged eighteen.

The reception to *J'Aime Tous les Femmes* was enthusiastic, the director-wife partnership were rehired for *Le Domino Vert*. Then in 1936 director Anatole Litvak offered her the starring role in *Mayerling*. The picture had a prestigious cast that included Charles Boyer and Jean-Luis Barrault. Danielle's part – that of the young mistress of the Empress's son involved in a tragic love affair ending in a joint suicide pact – called for a wider emotional range than she'd previously attempted. She was doubtful of her capability, but Decoin encouraged her to accept the role. 'I always believed in him and obeyed him in everything. Without his advice I would always have remained a pretty young thing singing and playing in minor films and would probably have left the profession quite early. He knew how to make me into a proper actress, to realise my worth. It is due to him and him alone that I became what I did become.'

In *Mayerling* – which proved a huge success, not only in France and Germany but internationally – she gained a new dimension in her work. As a comedienne she could get an audience to laugh and shriek with delight, as a tragic actress she could make them weep. 'Until now I hadn't really taken my job very seriously. I enjoyed it and it amused me to do it, but that's as far as it went.'

With this new commitment to her art came the offer of more and very varied parts, but also a punishing schedule. Between 1936 and 39 she completed ten films, four of them directed by her husband. Most were Franco-German co-productions, some shot in Berlin studios.

In 1939 she started shooting *Premier Rendezvous* with Decoin as director. In it she played an orphan who runs away from her boarding school. At twenty-three she was still a slim gamine with a cheeky face, she could get away with teenage roles. The picture was produced by Continental. 'As I'd very often filmed in Germany (along with many other French actors) I didn't have a very clear idea of the significance of that particular company or what it represented,' she explains.

It was then, after the filming of *Premier Rendezvous* and while the footage was still being assembled in the cutting room, that she was invited by Count André de Limur to a party where she meets Rubi…

⁂

Rubi takes her extended hand in his, folds it in his own and bows to kiss the knuckles, '*Enchanté, Madame.*' Straightening up, he looks her back boldly in the face. Her host murmurs something about him being dangerous and she smiles at the remark. Then the Count's touch on her elbow urges her on to meet the next important guest.

The mix of people at the party reflects the occupation; there are a number of smartly uniformed German officers present. The barrier between victor and defeated has broken down quite quickly, assisted by the continuing presence of an international community in Paris. Cosmopolitan smart society has no frontiers, for the rich are their own nationality and nothing can disrupt the interconnections on which their life depends. The film business has long been a Franco-German collaboration, its actors and actresses possess a following in both countries. Every major country maintains an embassy here, for America is not yet in the war. Many of their staff are at the soirée as the host is himself a diplomat. The French author Claude Mauriac writes that at a similar party of Mrs Jay Gould's he was 'stupefied to be shaking hands with one of those German officers whose contact I find so repugnant on the Metro … the champagne and atmosphere of sympathy and youth made everything too easy. I should not have been there.'

Danielle does not speak with Rubi again until she's about to leave the party, when he offers to drive her home. She hesitates, but Count de Limur points out that they live almost next door to each other in Neuilly…

All private cars had been requisitioned on the second day of the occupation; petrol is sold exclusively to those with ration coupons. The only vehicles allowed to drive the streets are required to display SP plates (Service Publique), granted solely to doctors and those in the international community in favour with the High Command. It is characteristic of Rubi that he possesses a car with chauffeur, plus the correct plates and gas to run it.

Nothing happens on the drive to Neuilly, he does not hit on her, doesn't even suggest a further meeting. She is still married to Henri Decoin. It's been a successful partnership, he's been instrumental in advancing her career – and she his. They are living together and still on good terms but, after five years, there is no longer the same sexual chemistry between them; aged forty-four, he's become more of a father figure. The girl child he married has grown up to become a woman and star in her own right, with her own bank account and a desire to run her own life … yet the terms of an established relationship are very hard to change.

A few days after Limur's party Danielle runs into Rubi at a nightclub, then again at Maxim's, the smartest restaurant in Paris, frequented by both French and Germans, where the cuisine remains excellent. This time he asks her for a date. It is followed by others.

Rubi has come on in the three years since his last wife left him. Where there was once a cocksure swagger is now a laid-back urbanity. No rough edges remain visible. Of course he is perfectly dressed by the leading Paris tailor, preferring dark suits woven in a mix of silk and wool to the heavier cloth standard at the time. His shirts, ties and specially made underpants come from Jermyn Street. His shoes are custom built; no one could call them lifts but the heel does add a crucial half-inch to his height. Yet these elements do not entirely account for the change. The puppy fat has gone from his face. The mouth is still full and sensual, but the rather podgy nose has acquired a fineness and definition that wasn't there before. His hair, expertly cut by the best barber in town, is no longer crinkly though it tends to curl. No trace remains of his racial or provincial origins and he's grown in *presence*: he has a reputable job, a house in a fashionable neighbourhood, a car with chauffeur, salary, expenses, and the façade of a man of substance. Yet he does not appear to take his respectability too seriously, he's great fun to be with. A shade taller than Danielle, he is faultless in his role and manner. The New England philosopher Emerson re-states a truth communicated to him by a Boston grande dame of that period 'who declared that the sense of being well-dressed imparts a feeling of tranquillity religion is powerless to bestow'.

Rubi and Danielle make a glamorous couple and no one fails to be struck by them. For her this is flirtation, an assertion of independence. Their affair is not covert or conducted in out of the way places, but played out in public at a handful of smart restaurants and nightclubs. She is still living with her husband and conceals nothing from him. Their marriage has been lacking the vital spark for some time and he takes the development with good grace.

So this is a dalliance of an acclaimed movie star at the height of her career, with full confidence in her worth, who is invited everywhere and requires a handsome escort and suitor who looks the part. Rubi plays it exquisitely. He writes, 'This might have been an agreeable flirtation, a light episode of the sweet life in the eyes of others. But one day she said to me, "I'll tell you, I think this is very serious for me."'

'For me too, Danielle,' he answers.

CHAPTER 4

DANIELLE DARRIEUX, PARIS, 1941–45

Why do some women fall for shits? Perhaps this trawl through the lives of six who did so may flag up aspects of their character and provide notes toward an answer, though one which illuminates *them* rather than the love object. Any hypothesis is partial and incomplete without reference to the particular shit. You had to meet Rubi in the flesh to get an idea of it.

There were the looks – we obtain an idea of those from photographs – and there was the bearing, his poise and laid-back assurance, plus the obvious fitness and vigour. There was the silky voice and accent, the teasing lightness of delivery and alert attentiveness to how you replied. Presentation and performance he'd finessed to an art. Yes, he was personable but there was more to it than that. The word charisma is now devalued to become a cliché, in Rubi's case let's call it 'mystique'.

What added to Rubi's allure was the hint of mystery; he enjoyed a louche reputation. This did not stop anyone from inviting him as a guest – he was amusing and entertaining. Though some were jealous, most men liked him. He was an exhilarating presence and dependable set dressing at any gathering. People were only titillated by the rumour that he was a crook.

When Flor walked out and Trujillo fired him in a rage at the casual way he'd treated his daughter, Rubi was in poor straits for he never had any inclination to save and possessed no money of his own. When he met Danielle Darrieux three years later he was a man of substance with a house, a job, bespoke wardrobe and chauffeur-driven car. It will be of no surprise to learn that he came to this privileged estate by a curiously winding stair.

Danielle Darrieux

Life had not been easy after he'd lost his job. However the Dominican ambassador in Paris (Trujillo's elder brother) had rescued Rubi's face if not his salary by finding him a place in a legation serving both Holland and Belgium. That had collapsed with the German occupation of those countries but he'd hung on to his diplomatic passport and residence. Unsurprisingly in these straitened circumstances he found the answer in a woman, one he had kept on the hook since their affair in the republic. La Môme Moineau was back in Paris, living at Rexach's luxurious townhouse while her husband remained involved in further construction projects in Ciudad Trujillo. She didn't have a career as a chanteuse any longer and was well past her prime, but she owned a fleet of cars, had plenty of money and an established place on the circuit. Rubi was expensive and unreliable, but he represented a stylish feather in her cap.

Of great advantage to Rubi in his career (which was social climbing and seduction rather than work, he despised work) was that he was completely without conscience. It opened the range of possibilities wider than to most. The Spanish civil war – particularly the communist forces' siege of Madrid – had caused a number of the city's wealthier residents hurriedly to move elsewhere, some of them in such urgency they were unable to take their assets with them. One such individual was Majuel Aldao, owner of the leading jewellers in Madrid, who had been obliged to leave a substantial portion of his stock in a safe, guarded by a trusted employee. Anxious to recover this while the man remained so, he made Rubi a proposition: that he use a Dominican embassy car with diplomatic plates to drive to Madrid, collect the jewellery, and bring it back to Paris in the diplomatic pouch.

The Raffles-type adventure appealed to Rubi's romantic nature. It fazed him not at all that he no longer was on the embassy staff and did not have the use of its cars, still less custody of the diplomatic bag. He'd performed several small favours for the Dominican ambassador, who permitted him still to use the term 'consul' in describing himself; he was confident the matter could be arranged.

The smuggling trip held further promise in that he knew another refugee keen to move his assets out of Madrid. Johnny Kohane, a Polish Jew previously resident there, had left behind some $150,000 in gold bullion. A plan was hatched. Rubi obtained use of the embassy's Mercedes and, for a fee, borrowed the uniform and passport of its Dominican chauffeur, who bore a passable resemblance to Kohane. With Rubi seated in style in the back, Kohane drove the car across France and into Spain – still torn by civil war – by way of the frontier post at Port Bou.

For almost two weeks Aldao, expectantly waiting in Paris, received no word from Rubi. Then he reappeared, without Kohane but bearing two thirds of Aldao's jewellery together with a harrowing tale. It seemed that leaving Madrid the two had been halted at a road-block by a party of armed men. Kohane had slammed his foot down and crashed the barrier, but they'd been pursued and fired on. Kohane had been killed in the fracas and he, Rubi, was extraordinarily lucky to have escaped alive.

Rubi knew how to spin a tale. Years later, back in Trujillo's employ, the dictator would praise his diplomatic skills: 'He's a great liar and the women like him.'

But where was the inventory that had been with the jewels, Aldao wanted to know. Rubi said there had been no inventory when he collected them. But Aldao was not convinced and made his own enquiries, discovering that the embassy's Mercedes had sustained no damage in the fray; it was unmarked by a single bullet hole.

There was little he could do and he'd at least retrieved two thirds of his gems, but he remained sore. Many men were sore at Rubi just then, with good reason, and the list would grow – pretty soon someone would shoot him.

It required money to be Rubi, the running costs entailed in keeping up the façade and maintaining his reputation were high. He'd never possessed capital wealth, though he'd rubbed up against it often. La Môme Moineau had been happy to pay for his company, but she'd come up the hard way herself and saw life too clear to fund him in an independent lifestyle. However, now he had collected. He was in the chips and back in the game.

Aldao wasn't about to publicise the smuggling caper: it made him look a sucker. Nor was Rubi tempted to brag about it, but inevitably there were rumours. It detracted from his social desirability not a whit: *This man is dangerous.*

A few months after his successful theft, Rubi was once more living his life to the full when one day he received a telephone call from the Palace in Ciudad Trujillo. On the line was an aide who said, 'The President, who is beside me, would like to know if you could see after his wife and son, who will arrive in Paris in a few weeks. You will have to find them a house of appropriate size, accompany them, show them around…'

'I was so stupefied that I couldn't answer straightaway,' Rubi recalled. 'At first I wondered what sort of a trap it was. I couldn't see one.'

He rose to the occasion, as always. He met Dona Maria and Ramfis off the boat at Le Havre, concealing his astonishment that the First Lady was over eight months pregnant. He proved the most assiduous courtier, attentive, courteous, charming. He took care of everything, including arrangements with the clinic where she would give birth. During which period he looked after Ramfis, aged ten and now a brigadier general who in the republic was attended by several staff officers and a negro shoeshine boy singer, become his personal minstrel. Ramfis was a monster, a miniature despot, easily bored and used to demanding instant gratification. His tantrums were uncontrollable and no one dared to try to discipline him, but only to appease. It is evidence of Rubi's diplomatic subtlety that, by treating the boy not as a child but an adult and a male like himself, he created a mentor role which would stand him in good stead in the years to come, when Trujillo himself became certifiably unstable. It was a very astute move.

To Dona Maria he was the *cavaliere* to dream of, sensitive to her moods and reliable for advice on fashion and what best suited her rather full figure. He was pathologically incapable of not flirting with any woman, whatever her situation, but here *everything* was at stake. He was generous with his time but also with gifts of jewellery. Such princely gestures became him and cost nothing; he had a drawer full of pieces he couldn't dispose of in France or Switzerland without questions about their provenance.

Dona Maria, healthy and happy with her new baby, spoke highly of Rubi in her letters to Trujillo, and was enthusiastic about the delights of Paris. So much so that the Benefactor decided to visit his wife and family in the French capital which, despite the threat of impending war, was enjoying a spell of almost feverish gaiety.

Once again Rubi was driven in the embassy's Mercedes to meet the dictator off the boat. Despite his cool, he must have experienced some trepidation; his rupture with Trujillo had not been pretty, for a while he'd feared for his life. But, 'in place of a furious father-in-law and an autocrat exasperated by my impertinence, I found a friendly and agreeable man.'

He took care of him in the same diligent manner as he'd looked after Dona Maria and Ramfis. He was an excellent guide to the city: he could recommend tailors, shoemakers, gunsmiths. He possessed equal familiarity with nightclubs and the demi-monde. It turned out the dictator had particular interest in the demi-monde, which back home didn't amount to much. The scope of Rubi's services effortlessly expanded to include the role of pimp. He took pleasure in the job, he had an eye for excellence. Indeed the capability he displayed in performing every task required of him convinced Trujillo what an indispensable fellow he was, how well-connected and what an elegant and worthy ambassador for his country. Before the Benefactor sailed for home, followed by his family, Rubi had been reappointed to his post at the Paris embassy.

❧

In the winter of 1938–39 (six months before Rubi will meet Danielle), Nazi troops marched into Austria to annex the country in the Anschluss and occupied the Sudetenland, the German-speaking area of Czechoslovakia. Conditions for Jews and the restrictions on Jewish businesses had long been oppressive. In Germany they were banned from public swimming pools, sports stadiums, parks, cafés, theatres and restaurants. Now occurred the infamous *Kristallnacht* (night of broken glass) when the windows of more than 7,000 Jewish shops were smashed and their contents looted; 400 synagogues were torched and burnt down.

The horror of the event was flashed around the globe to an outraged world, timid in its response. President Trujillo in his own country was already under censure as a result of his own atrocity, the genocide he'd inflicted on Haitian immigrants. The aid he received from the US together with the highly advantageous sugar quota favouring the island was about to be withdrawn. However, the PR company Trujillo employed in New York saw in Hitler's persecution of the Jews an opportunity for him to redeem his tarnished image. In a well-publicised gesture he announced that, small though his island was, he would be happy to accept 100,000 Jewish refugees.

This was at a time when both the US and Britain maintained strict, even cruel, quotas on whom they would admit, despite their professed condemnation of Hitler's pogrom. An article commending Trujillo appeared in the *Washington Post*; his humane offer was acknowledged, and particularly approved by the Jewish lobby in Washington.

The PR company issued the press with colour photographs of the area the Benefactor had designated to be a Jewish homeland, which lacked housing but otherwise looked to be a beachside Eden. It was not an empty gesture but a shrewd move on Trujillo's part for more than one reason. His own people were idle and feckless, and to introduce a skilled industrious group of immigrants who had particular reason to owe him loyalty could only benefit the economy. The move was uncharacteristic on his part, as it was his own land that he was bestowing – though this is somewhat less generous than it sounds for by now over half the island's habitable land personally belonged to him.

At the Paris embassy Rubi was well aware of this development; it obtained prominent exposure in French and other European newspapers. He was no businessman and had no desire to become one, but he could do basic arithmetic. One hundred thousand would-be immigrants to the republic meant that Dominican embassies and consulates in Europe would need to issue 100,000 visas to enter the island. Rubi had access to unlimited blank visas; they required only a rubber stamp and his own signature to become valid. He sold them for up to $5,000 apiece. The market was brisk, the cash flowed in. He could afford to be generous, giving them away for free to people he had only just met. He liked to please, women but also men. To dispense salvation in a casual throwaway gesture was irresistible. His brother Cesar – also working for Trujillo in the diplomatic service – after the war explained the source of

Rubi's wealth quite candidly, 'He got rich selling visas to Jews. Didn't everybody?'

The occupation of Paris put a stop to Rubi's business, bringing with it some personal inconvenience. The embassies of the neutral countries, of which the Dominican Republic was one, were obliged to relocate in Vichy in the unoccupied zone of France. It inhabited comfortable premises in the Hotel des Ambassadeurs, but social life in the little town was limited and dull. Often Rubi drove to Paris, where he retained his apartment, to look for something more to his taste. He continued to receive many invitations, one from a French diplomat still in the city, Count André de Limur…

⚜

Now, only a few weeks later, Danielle is in love with him, and he with her. Just twenty-four years old, she has played in thirty films. *Mayerling* may have turned her into an international star, but her fan base in France and Germany was already huge. Fame has not turned her head; she is firmly grounded, professional and disciplined. Married life with Henri Decoin, so much older than her, has been domestically stable and largely occupied by work. Perhaps too stable – for even in adolescence she's never had the opportunity to slip the leash. Her last picture, *Premier Rendezvous*, is now on general release in France and soon will be in Germany. It is a light romantic comedy well suited to an audience with a need to escape briefly from the realities of defeat and occupation. It is charming and upbeat with a happy ending. There are two other pictures in preparation lined up for her, but for the moment she is idle, fancy-free and in love. It is a condition she has rarely had the opportunity to enjoy.

Occupied Paris is a limbo-land with disconcerting aspects of normality. There are hardly any cars or buses, the Metro stops between 11 a.m. and 3 p.m. to save electricity. When open, its station entrances are watched over by French gendarmes, who salute every German officer with obsequious deference. Great red flags with swastikas are flying everywhere and drape the front of public buildings. There are wall posters all over town: VERBOTEN! It is forbidden to listen to foreign radio broadcasts or to refuse German currency. Notices in cafés prohibit German soldiers from dancing, *You may not while so many of our brave men are being shot down over England.* There are signs in bars and restaurants: NO JEWS. Jewish-owned shops not displaying a notice JEWISH ENTERPRISE are subject to closure and confiscation of the premises.

The German army has seized 90 per cent of the forty million tons of coal that France consumes annually and there is no gas for cooking. Often the electricity supply is switched off for hours at a time. It's been a cold hard winter. Long queues form outside food shops before they open for business in the morning, what they have to sell is scant and gone within an hour. Food is still being produced in the country, but without petrol there is no way of transporting it to the city. This restriction is evaded by Maxim's and a handful of other Michelin-starred restaurants, which have a clientele of ranking German officers and an *arrangement*; here the quality remains superb.

Elsewhere, food is so short that some people have taken to keeping chickens on the balcony of their apartments. Men are wearing scarves in place of ties, their collars are worn out and shirts not to be found. Yet the couturiers Schiaparelli, Molyneux and Coco Chanel continue to show their seasonal collections. Theatres, concert halls and cinemas are full. The show ends, the audience disperses to reach home before curfew and silence descends on the darkened city, disturbed only by the booted tramp of military patrols.

Despite the exigencies of occupation, the good life continues in parallel at another level; its infrastructure is not destroyed by defeat. It requires a little time to get to know the order of the new order, a little adjustment and rearrangement is involved but soon the invader is recognised for what he is: just another consumer, and received appropriately.

Both Danielle and Rubi own cars with Service Publique plates, but civilian autos are so few they are often stopped at road blocks. Always the scene plays the same way: a German warrant officer steps to the driver's wound-down window, asking to see their papers. Rubi hands them over. The man glances at both sets, spots Danielle's name, and bends to the window to see if it is really her. His face lights up in recognition. Excitedly he beckons up his soldiers, they crowd around. Invariably it ends with her signing autographs.

Danielle possesses the universal passport of celebrity, and as her escort so does Rubi. It's a new experience for him. He's well-known in some of the best places, a regular. But Danielle is identifiable on sight by almost everybody, they've watched this enchanting young woman grow up on screen, she's been part of their own growing-up and is almost family. *But who is he?* Most people have no idea, but the two make such a handsome couple and are so obviously in love.

Rubi returns to Vichy from time to time, to put in an appearance at the embassy, but he is more concerned with the pursuit of his new romance. When the Japanese bomb Pearl Harbor and America declares war on the Axis powers, Trujillo throws in his lot with his patron and does the same. It is only pragmatic as it requires no further contribution on his part, but it would not be the dictator's nature to declare war without a declamatory gesture so he locks up the German staff of their embassy in one of the island's ghastly prisons.

In response the Germans arrest Rubi, intern him at Bad Nauheim, and hold him as hostage to their release. Conditions in the resort in no way replicate those in Trujillo's repulsive jails, though it is unlikely the German diplomats were actually shackled in their own filth. Bad Nauheim is a spa town where rich invalids take the waters, which has become an internment centre for foreign nationals. Rubi is at liberty provided he remains within the confines of the town and, as jails go, it's not so bad. 'There were friends, women, girls, everything you would need to kill time. They organised card games and social events. You could dance … We indulged in drunken parties with white wine.'

Danielle is distraught at her lover's arrest. Others might reach for a lawyer in the circumstances, a star calls her studio. She goes to Greven at Continental, where she is under contract for her next two pictures. She is his biggest asset and he receives her warmly, giving her the stock reassurance, 'Don't worry, the studio will take care of everything.' He goes on to say that *Premier Rendezvous* is about to

70

open in Berlin; he'd like her and the cast to make a promotional tour and attend the launch. She is happy to agree, it may provide an opportunity to visit Rubi.

In all, six members of the cast fly to Berlin where they spend three days, shepherded by publicists from head office. This is the first new French movie to run in Germany since the outbreak of war, and its opening signals the trade and cultural concord between the two countries. The delegation of French artistes is received with some pomp and ceremony by the Minister of Propaganda, Joseph Goebbels, and his wife, who declares herself an ardent fan of Danielle's movies. The actress has no difficulty getting cosy with her in an intimate chat about the man she loves who has been snatched away to imprisonment. Madame Goebbels is particularly fascinated because she already knows Rubi, she met him and his then-wife, Flor, at the Olympic Games in 1936. It is a drama of the heart Danielle confides to her, the best quality of gossip. Touched by what she hears, Madame Goebbels promises to have a word with her husband.

Love conquers all. The impediments in Danielle's path are brushed away and she is granted a special pass allowing her to spend ten days in Bad Nauheim with the man she is now describing as her fiancé. The permit is easy to obtain, requiring only a token concession on her part: she agrees to sing at a concert for German troops. She stays with Rubi in the town, recognised by everyone in the overcrowded milieu of rich invalids and international diplomats interned here. Soon after, Trujillo releases the embassy staff from jail in the republic, they are repatriated to Germany shaken but unharmed. Rubi is let free. He returns to Vichy, where Danielle is waiting for him, and they are married there on 18 September 1942. In the Dominican Republic, Flor learns the fact from a newspaper.

❧

That same autumn, *Life* magazine publishes a blacklist of French entertainers who have been tried *in absentia* and convicted by the French Resistance of betraying their country by collaborating with the Nazis: Sacha Guitry, Maurice Chevalier, Mistinguett, Arletty (the mistress of German general Hanese) … and Danielle.

If she'd stayed married to Decoin, she would not have made the same mistakes. He had guided her career and would have prevented the moves which progressively put her further into danger. The initial step on that path had been taken, aged eighteen, when she made her first picture for Greven at the German company Continental. It was without political significance at the time, but her later actions built upon that foundation of suspect loyalty, together with the fact she'd shot several movies in Berlin. Now she is a star, and all she does receives coverage. She seems to lead a charmed life: she travels in her own car which has Service Publique plates and evidently petrol, she moves around France unhindered by the restrictions placed on everyone else. She'd taken a lead part in a highly visible promotional tour in Berlin, been feted by Goebbels – and, crucially, she had entertained German troops.

The initial acceptance of the Nazis in occupied France has changed now, along with the course of the Second World War. At first appeasement derived from defeat and acceptance of the fact that the Boches looked to be here forever. Now with America's entry into the war that outcome appears less likely. It is anyway remarkable that the pact of non-resistance in exchange for peaceful occupation – a condition that Ambassador Bullitt was in no position to provide, far less ensure – has lasted as long as it did. The first assassination of a German sailor took place in the summer of 1941. Then an officer was knifed at the Bastille metro station.

Everyone on the platform was arrested and all were shot next day. Other attacks followed, and in response hostages – communists, Jews, Freemasons, captured resistants or anyone held in a police station for violating curfew – were shot. In the winter of 1941–1942 fifty hostages were shot in retribution for the killing of one lieutenant-colonel.

For Danielle, Vichy no longer is a safe haven. The romantic adventure she'd entered on with Rubi in her first grown-up affair has shifted into melodrama shot through with a most unsettling menace; she cannot feel secure anywhere in France. They move to Megève in the zone occupied by the Italians. It is a small fashionable skiing resort with one good hotel and three decent restaurants. The idea of lying low here is naïve; Rubi is incapable of lying low. Danielle is outed within days.

She cannot appeal to her studio for help – her studio is part cause of this censure and ever-present threat of reprisal. She can only turn to Rubi, who is completely unreliable but in this case has the shady connections for what is necessary. He obtains new identities and new papers. Both Dominican nationals, they become Mr and Mrs Rubira. Dressed in clothes as dowdy, worn and patched as the rest of the population, they move to a farm in the country east of Paris where they hide out with Danielle's sister, her husband and their two children.

There they remain as refugees. Danielle is badly shaken by the threats and hate mail she received in Vichy. She fears for her life, and worse, if she were to be snatched by a Resistance group. She has good reason to be afraid: when Paris is finally reoccupied in 1944, it will be followed by two weeks of licensed revenge. Many are shot, but women who have slept with the enemy have their heads shaved and are exposed to public humiliation. In exemplary punishment a group of some hundred women are rounded up, stripped, shaved, force-fed paraffin oil and marched naked in column through the streets of Paris before a baying crowd of onlookers.

Danielle and Rubi wait out the war in anonymity and obscurity on the farm. It is not ideal to be sharing their accommodation with another couple and children. Both of them have previously avoided domesticity of this sort, it's not an easy adaptation. Their circumstances are inconvenient and claustrophobic, but for Danielle not to be making films is painful. It is not that she is driven by ambition for her career, but she loved to practise the art she'd become good at. It is a loss like that of hearing to a musician or sight to a painter, a death in the soul.

As for Rubi … for him life in a shared farmhouse noisy with kids in a rural nowhere three miles from the nearest bar tabac, which is frequented only by peasants, represents the seventh circle of hell. He has nothing to do, he's bored. He doesn't read books as she does, can't enjoy music except to dance to and talk above. He doesn't like being without a surrounding scene, lights, action, ambient extras, music and background noise. He's a social life-form, a fish deprived of the water in which it swims and needs to survive.

The couple has been together four years. The first act of their love affair has run its course. It was a great first act and a brilliant opening to a stylish drama with a lead cast of two. The occupation had provided an appropriately cinematic setting to their romance. A beautiful couple recognised everywhere, they had played their parts with *élan*, for they were in love. But now passion is absent along with illusion and an audience. In the cramped proximity of the farmhouse mystery is also gone – they know each other too well. For him she's not the woman he loved, the glamorous creature he married. He's been with countless women, what made Danielle so special was her stardom, the aura that embraced him too in her company. That was what had drawn him to her and might have kept him in thrall still – but now that very stardom and glamour has become a liability she cannot afford to display.

In practical matters they are to a large extent self-sufficient in their isolation. He explains, 'I became a peasant. I bought a cow to get butter, pigs to make hams, sheep to make grilled chops. I learned how to herd cattle. Danielle saw to her chickens…' She accepts the situation they are in. Her life is not rich in choices at that moment. She is weary in the confines of their self-exile, and beneath the weariness she's always aware of a chronic low-grade fear; it is debilitating.

From time to time Rubi comes up with a reason he has to be in Paris. Danielle is quite used to his infidelities by now. On each occasion he disappears for three or four days, using his false identity in a city where many know him. He is a national of a country at war with Germany, an alien with forged papers. His arrest inevitably would lead to Danielle's exposure. It does not appear to trouble him that each new dalliance puts his wife at risk.

⚜

With D-Day and the Allied invasion of Europe leading to the reoccupation of Paris, Danielle's fears of reprisal are only increased. It is reported that the Committee of National Cleansing and Purification wish to question her at a hearing. But it is the offer of the lead in a film, *Adieu Cherie*, to start shooting that autumn, that draws her and Rubi to Paris.

The US embassy has reopened. The city is full of Americans, military and civilian. Danielle and Rubi are invited to a party for William Randolph Hearst Jnr. They are given a lift home by a press attaché at the Greek embassy, Spiro Vassilopoulos, and his wife Edmée. Their car has gone only a short distance on Boulevard Malesherbes when Vassilopoulos slows down in response to a police whistle. Three men with Sten guns flag the vehicle to a stop. 'Keep driving!' Rubi tells him urgently.

He does, but the group open fire. Edmée screams. She's been hit, her seat is covered in blood.

'At the same time I felt I'd been whipped in the back,' says Rubi. 'I had the feeling that a hot object had lodged itself deeply within me ... the poor woman was shouting, bleeding everywhere ... I opened my collar, I breathed with difficulty. I had the impression that something was escaping from me – my life. I murmured, "There's no point in yelling, I'm also wounded."'

By him in the back seat, Danielle goes into a panic. She paws his slumped body demanding, 'What's wrong? What's wrong?' At the wheel of the car, Vassilopoulos is in high alarm about his wife, bleeding and shrieking beside him. He doesn't know Paris well or where to go. Rubi gathers himself sufficiently to direct him to Hospital Marmoltan. 'We made a striking entrance, Edmée didn't stop screaming.'

She is the first into surgery, followed by Rubi who undergoes a two and a half hour operation to remove a bullet from his right kidney. Hers is a flesh wound in the thigh but Rubi's condition is serious. He survives, but it is close.

Who shot them? And who were they trying to kill? Was it the French Resistance exacting sentence declared on Danielle for her collaboration? Or was Rubi the intended victim? There was a list of people who wanted to kill Rubi for various reasons. Revenge killings were tacitly accepted by the authorities at the time and armed men available at a discount price. And there may have been other players, other reasons, for by now Rubi was suspected to have worked as a German agent; Military Intelligence had a file on him. Who knows if it had basis? He was a man to whom legend attached itself. The intended assassins of Rubi/Danielle were never identified.

She nurses him back to health. The story, accompanied by a photograph of a rueful Rubi with Danielle at his bedside, runs in the *New York Times*, and on the front page of *La Nación*, the Dominican newspaper, which reports that Rubi's first thoughts 'were of his country, his relatives and his protector, Rafael Leonidas Trujillo'. The article quoted the cable sent by the injured man to his patron: 'I've been liberated from German internment by Allied forces. Find me in Paris awaiting your orders. Found in a Greek car, I was gravely wounded on September 23 by shots aimed at that car. I believe I'm out of danger after surgery. Danielle has carried herself bravely. She has been at my side night and day from the moment I was injured. Rubirosa.'

The story reads well, and for once it is not to his discredit. Despite his divorce from Flor, Rubi is back in favour with the Great Benefactor on his island kingdom, to which Rubi had no desire ever to return. He is awarded the job of Chargé d'Affaires at the embassy in Rome. Danielle is scheduled soon to start shooting on a picture in Morocco but definitely does not want to pass the wait alone in Paris, so accompanies her husband to his new post.

CHAPTER 5

DORIS DUKE, CASERTA, ITALY, JANUARY 1945

I f you lack education and are untrained in any skill, have never been employed, are thirty-three years old, are of tall slightly off-putting appearance, but happen to be the richest woman on earth ... if there's a war in progress, you've just dumped your no-good husband and are feeling the urge to save the world ... what do you go for?

Doris Duke's answer is to become a secret agent.

She has just ended a seven-year sexless marriage; she is free and has a keen desire to experience life to the full. Although socially inept, her great wealth provides connections. 'Wild Bill' Donovan, the colourful head of Overseas Strategic Services (OSS), is a friend. She is hired by the organisation at $2,000 a month and chooses the codename 'Daisy'. On 6 January 1945, she flies to Italy from Cairo aboard a converted B-25 bomber.

Tex McCrary, a former journalist now PR officer for the Mediterranean Allied Air Force, has received a cable from General Donovan, DUKE ARRIVING 0400 HOURS CAMPINO B-25. MEET EXPEDITE. He has no idea who this Duke is, 'How the hell do you meet a Duke properly? A B-25 comes in. Suddenly this long pair of legs dangles out from the bomb door. I assume it's the captain. He came over and saluted smartly and I said, "Where's the Duke?" She flipped her hood back and it was Doris.'

McCrary has dated her in New York and danced with her at the Stork Club. He's necked with her. He is dismayed by her arrival in a war zone. He tells her, 'Get your skinny blonde ass back on that plane, I'm sending you back.'

Doris Duke and Rubi © Press Association

She's not a woman to be told what she can and cannot do – not anymore she's not. She may be painfully shy but she knows her own mind and has a whim of steel. Rejecting the suggestion, she smiles sweetly at her pre-war pal, gives him a friendly kiss on the cheek, hitches a lift into bomb-damaged Caserta, checks into the only functioning hotel, and prepares for her self-appointed mission.

What precisely this consists of is not clear and, on the face of it, Doris is not a spymaster's first choice as an agent in a foreign theatre of war. She's almost six feet tall, unmistakably American, speaks only rudimentary Italian and no German. She's flown here from Cairo where she had wangled herself a job with the US Seaman Service. To obtain her present assignment and get to Italy she's unashamedly pulled wires. For a woman of such singular wealth a network of connection lies to hand. While working it she's upset a number of government and military officials who strongly resent being bypassed, particularly while running a war. Even as Doris is unpacking her one suitcase in her Caserta hotel a cable from Cairo is delivered to the Secretary of State in Washington: STRONGLY RECOMMEND WASHINGTON TAKE STEPS TO FRUSTRATE THIS FOR GOOD OF OUR AGENCY. Next day OSS field station in Caserta receives a message from the State Department saying that Doris's passport is about to be cancelled. She is not to be employed and they are to have no contact with her. Officers within the agency are livid at the special treatment awarded to this heiress spy imposed upon them. Doris's cover is blown by the ensuing row and her progress stymied.

Not a great start to a career in espionage and subversion but, as stated, her will is strong and she's not easily to be discouraged. Over dinner that evening she consults with McCrary on her next move. He's always liked her and is amused by her seigneurial attitude to life. He suggests she switch professions and become a war-correspondent. She has no qualifications but she's here, her passport may be dodgy but she's physically in possession of it. She can move around. Why not?

Doris is delighted by the idea and by the end of the meal she's decided that's what she will be. Within days she and McCrary are lovers and what he has to say about her is in flat contradiction to her husband Jimmy Cromwell's claim in the divorce court that she is frigid. 'Sex with Doris was a joy. It was wild and wonderful … I had a great deal of fun with her. It was pure, glorious sex. It was the best I've ever known because afterwards we talked and we talked and we talked … We continued the affair for years. I can say I loved her.'

Next day, Doris goes through her address book. One of her first cables is to an old friend, William Randolph Hearst's son, Bill. She is hired by Joseph Kingsbury-Smith, European general manager of International News Service (INS), and accredited to the Italian bureau. When Rome is occupied by Allied Forces, INS moves there. Doris rents a modest flat in the city and throws herself into the work. She finds the job the toughest and most satisfying of her life. Female war correspondents are almost unknown, but the role might have been created for her. She is fearless. 'Any goddam crazy idea I had, she would go along with,' says McCrary. 'She was never afraid. Never.'

During her stint with US Forces, Doris hitches a lift aboard a plane to London for a few days' leave. Kingsbury-Smith happens to be there at the same time and his account provides a glimpse into her attitude to money. 'My wife and I got to know her … the interesting thing was the discovery that she was very very tight with money… She was scared to death to lose a dollar. Her whole attitude was that somebody was out to get her.'

In Italy, many in the Press Corps take exception to Doris. They have put in years of work to obtain this assignment and resent the fact that this inexperienced young woman can walk into the job so effortlessly. She is mocked as a 'debutramp' looking for a kick, just another war-zone junkie. 'We more or less laughed at her,' says Mike Stern, then head of the American Press Association in Rome. 'We kind of victimised her.' She is sensitive. Hatred can be acceptable, there's distinction in it, but to be mocked is hard. But she doesn't react, she's long learned to control any show of emotion. *Don't get mad, get even* is the current maxim. And Doris does so in nothing less than majestic style. The war in Europe ends on 8 May. Four days later, she and a mob of correspondents are gathered at the airport at Linz, waiting for the appearance of General George S. Patton, swashbuckling commander of the Third Army, which has fought its way through Europe to meet up here with the advancing Russian forces.

Patton's plane touches down and the General comes down the ramp. Doris walks over to his staff car, 'Why Georgie, how are you?' she enquires blithely.

He looks at her in astonishment. 'Doris!' he exclaims, 'What are you doing here? Has the polo season started?'

She knows him from Hawaii, where he'd been stationed before the war. Now without a moment's hesitation she steps into the staff car and seats herself beside him. The vehicle sweeps off to the historic rendezvous, watched by the crowd of reporters in baffled rage.

The totemic meeting of Russian and US forces is celebrated at the headquarters of Soviet Marshal Feodor Tolbukhin, in a castle which once was the summer residence of Emperor Franz Joseph. Russian soldiers standing to attention line the drive; inside is a scene of barbaric splendour. Dozens of strapping female Soviet volunteers in drab ill-fitting tunics have been shipped in to staff the place without any training whatever; they have never seen a modern kitchen before, far less an indoor lavatory.

Patton, his ADC and Doris are entertained to a lavish rowdy feast. The marshal and his savage court are high on firewater and victory. A band is playing, the table is crowded with tins of caviar and bottles of vodka. Buxom Soviet workers attend the guests, spraying them with rank perfume. A stupendous showgirl, imported from Moscow, provides a spirited cabaret, stripping off all her clothes. General Patton applauds enthusiastically, then rises to inform his host that he intends to honour the dancer with a medal. Detaching one from the display on his chest he moves to pin it on her but finds only bare flesh ... The Marshal bellows his approval. Roaring drunk, he unclasps one of his own medals; he in turn wishes to honour an American working woman and fellow comrade embodying the working-class values that soon will rule the world. Lurching over to Doris Duke, the richest woman in it, he pins the decoration to her breast then kisses her on both cheeks with full wet lips.

The next four days Doris spends with Patton, sharing this continuing celebration and his bed. 'She liked older men. She was in love with her father,' McCrary observes. And Doris herself has recorded her impression of top brass as lovers. 'It is common knowledge that generals ... are usually under-endowed. That is probably what motivates them. I got it from his wife that General Douglas MacArthur was absolutely tiny. Georgie did not suffer from that problem.' In further explanation of Patton's attraction, she explains, 'He wore polished leather knee boots. I found those boots to be a marvellous turn-on.'

For his part, Patton is understandably elated just now at his place in history. 'Write something about me,' he tells her. She intends to anyway and has secretly been making notes, but now she has his sanction for a full kiss and tell. Combining epic conflict *apercus*, it's one hell of a good piece. Novice she may be, but she's a forerunner in a form of journalism that today is a staple item of redtop fare. Her interview with Patton runs in every major US paper. To the undying fury of the Press Corps, she has scored a journalistic coup.

With the end of hostilities in Europe, the Hearst-owned INS shifts to syndicating stories more suited to the peacetime mood. The film star Danielle Darrieux has just arrived in Rome, accompanied by her husband, Porfirio Rubirosa. She is not welcome in France because of past collaboration with the Nazi occupier; he is no longer acceptable there as a diplomat, having served as legate to the Vichy regime.

INS assigns a reporter to interview the film star. On the day after the couple's arrival, Doris Duke shows up at their hotel suite to do so. It takes Rubirosa only minutes to identify and place this gangling, badly dressed, pointy-chinned blonde. During the interview Danielle is cool and guarded, refusing to be drawn by Doris's questions. But Rubi, a good three inches shorter than Doris, is attentive and charming. Afterwards, they move to a restaurant for lunch. Even before the meal is served, and while the three are still declaring their mutual pleasure at finding themselves *en poste* together in this delightful city, Rubi has determined to marry her.

Doris knows his reputation; a now-professional journalist, she has done the necessary research. She knows about his part in the assassination of the dissident Dominican exile Boscome in New York, his dubious wartime activities, gem smuggling, thefts, that he worked as an Abwehr agent; she knows that he is dangerous.

A few days after that interview, while Danielle is otherwise engaged, Rubi and his prospective bride are meeting in a hotel bar. She seeks reassurance on her safety. 'I asked Rubi straight out of the blue whether he would consider killing me to get my money.'

He rises to the occasion with suave gallantry. Gently laying his hand upon hers, he looks at her with his sultry bedroom eyes and breathes, 'I have done much worse.' She finds his words irresistible. Ten days later, Danielle flies to Monaco on location, leaving Rubi in Rome, the same city as the richest woman in the *world*.

꧁ꕤ꧂

Doris's father, Buck Duke, was a man of extraordinary foresight and business acumen. Born in a shack in North Carolina, his parents grew tobacco, which as a teenager he hawked around local townships from a wagon. When his father built a factory in Durham he was already playing an active part in the newly formed company.

At this period, the late 1800s, sales were almost entirely in pipe and chewing tobacco. Buck's prescience showed in acquiring the recently invented Bonsack rolling machine and switching production to cigarettes made from paler tobacco. He also demonstrated an innovative flair for the new arts of advertising and promotion. A statuesque French actress with a racy reputation, Madame Rhea, featured on giant posters, proffering a pack together with full cleavage and come-hither smile. This first example of celebrity endorsement was followed by others. Buck was the first to sponsor baseball, basketball and roller-skating teams to display his logo, while salesmen (and, later, saucily uniformed salesgirls) peddled Duke brands to spectators at the events. His methods proved wildly successful. In 1890 he formed the American Tobacco Company, capitalised at $25 million (equivalent to $750 million today). The company controlled over 90 per cent of the cigarette business in the US.

When Doris was born in November 1912 it was in the mansion he had constructed on Fifth Avenue and East 78 Street, which was based on the Chateau Labottiere in Bordeaux. *The Times* reported, 'No child of royal blood ever came into the world amid more comfortable and luxurious surroundings … The magnificent mansion was turned into a private hospital; no expense was spared in obtaining the best physicians and nurses … The money of the tobacco king will someday belong solely to this baby.'

Another newspaper published a Rich List of her competitors'

worth: John Jacob Astor $3 million. John Nicholas Brown $10 million. Edward Vincent McLean $50 million. W. K. Vanderbilt $60 million. Doris Duke's value was set at $100 million (to calculate today's equivalent, multiply by around twenty-five).

Doris's mother, Nanaline, was Buck's second wife. His first he'd divorced for rampant infidelity. 'She was always on heat,' says Doris, who was his only child. Nanaline had been raised in genteel poverty in the Old South; her own mother had been obliged to take in boarders. But Nanaline had pretensions to grace and style. As Buck's wife, she saw it as her mission to bring background and breeding to the Duke family, and to invest her boorish husband and herself with the status and social respectability that is the perquisite of great wealth.

As a mother to Doris, Nanaline was distant and chill; but Buck was obsessed with his daughter. The publicity surrounding her birth and fortune made him nervous, kidnapping was becoming *the* characteristic American crime. He moved the family to London, leasing Crewe House in Curzon Street, now the Saudi embassy. His security was stringent as it is today at the same building. Doris was kept indoors, not allowed to mix with other children and given 25 US cents a week as an allowance.

On the outbreak of the Great War in 1914, Buck transferred the household back to the US for safety. He was a workaholic who got up at 7 a.m., breakfasted on stewed prunes and was at his office on Fifth Avenue at 45 Street by 8.30. Content to wear the same crumpled suit for days, he set no store by fancy manners. Nanaline, however, was dedicated to the family's social advancement. Her initial plan for her husband to become a tax exile in England and acquire a title had been thwarted by the war. Now she set out on the well-trodden route of ostentatious real estate and conspicuous consumption favoured by most swells of the era.

Apart from the chateau on Fifth Avenue, Buck already owned Duke Farms in New Jersey and a country estate at Charlotte, North Carolina. Now he and Nanaline bought a huge mansion overlooking the sea, Rough Point. Newport had become *the* place for the summer. In this post-war period of roaring prosperity, America's rich – new and old – berthed their yachts in Newport harbour and constructed 'summer cottages', many of breathtaking grandeur. The Breakers, owned by the Vanderbilts, had seventy-five rooms. Occupation during the season was provided by rigorous entertaining. The parties, costume balls and extravaganzas were continuous and competitive. It was quite usual for gold trinkets and unmounted jewels to be served as party favours on silver trays by liveried staff. At one particular rout, a Servants' Ball, the guests arrived costumed as their own maids and butlers.

Doris had no place in her parents' social life. She grew up on the country estate and in the New York mansion, looked after by a young French governess, Jenny Renaud. The Manhattan residence had sixteen servants and resembled an echoing museum in its vast expanse of marble floor, statues and sombre walls hung with Old Masters. It had a ballroom and a library whose shelving displayed the leather spines of what looked like books, but were only dummies. Buck had not time for reading, he said books were too slow for him.

Doris was a plain, solitary and lonely child. Not until she was enrolled in New York's Brearley School, aged ten, did she mix with other girls. She arrived dressed in her mother's hand-me-down clothes with a hat pulled down over her eyes. The other girls jeered at her, she was greeted with mockery. Tall, thin and gauche, she was nicknamed 'The Giraffe'. 'She was kind of scrawny,' one classmate recalls. 'She would have fit in better if she'd been more coordinated.' On vacation at Newport, once she went swimming from fashionable Bailey's Beach wearing a white swimsuit. It was unlined, and when she came out the water it had become transparent. 'She was pathetic,' another Brearley student remembers.

But her Daddy loved her, he still called her 'the baby'. 'He really adored her,' says a family friend. 'I recall walking into the breakfast room at the Duke mansion and seeing him kissing her and loving her and I said, "Go as far as you like. Don't bother about us." He really was devoted to her. And he admired her mind, but he said that she got that mind from him.'

Why did Buck and Nanaline not have another child? Surely he would have wished for a son to inherit his business and fortune? But Nanaline had been damaged in giving birth to Doris, emotionally and perhaps physically. She disliked her own daughter. Parturition had traumatised her, she did not care for the physical side of life and Buck was not insistent. He had needs, but he had mistresses.

His tobacco empire was growing into one of the largest businesses in the country. From the start, Buck had employed market researchers at American Tobacco and commissioned scientific studies, but now these revealed disturbing evidence that cigarette smokers were prone to heart disease and lung cancer. The implication was ominous. He forbade his wife to smoke and Doris ever to take up the habit – unsuccessfully in both cases. Most crucially, he began to transfer capital out of American Tobacco to invest in hydroelectric power in North Carolina and Piedmont, establishing Duke Power and acquiring stock in the oil company Texaco. Prompted by his wife, he increased the million-dollar grant he'd given to obscure Trinity College in Durham by a further $40 million, proposing a whole new campus. In gratitude, the board of trustees voted unanimously to change the name to Duke University.

Then, aged sixty-eight, Buck's ferocious life-force began to fail. He sickened, lost weight and spirit. In October 1925 Doris's beloved father died. On the day of his funeral the cities of Winston, Salem and Danville suspended tobacco sales for a full ten minutes in honour of their patron saint.

Doris was twelve years old.

⚜

Two weeks later, the will was read. Buck's worth was assessed at $300 million (the inexact science of historical conversion might arrive at a modern equivalent of $4 billion). The bulk of the estate was left to Doris, with Nanaline receiving an allowance of $100,000 a year and the right to live in the four houses, Manhattan, Duke Farms, Newport and North Carolina. But the will was ambiguous; Nanaline maintained that *she* was the outright owner. Doris, by now just into her teens, who had inherited her father's head for business together with his guiding maxim *trust nobody*, sued for possession and won.

The case did not improve her relationship with her mother, who remained her legal guardian. Nanaline was dismayed by her tall plain daughter, so lacking in social skills, whose only interest was playing jazz piano and learning to dance everything from tap to clog. When she became sixteen, she was packed off to a boarding school, Fermata, in South Carolina, whose students were taught flower arrangement along with the social graces of the Old South.

She loathed the place, and her fellow students loathed her back for all the reasons that can be imagined, plus the fact that her family voted Democrat and she herself was drawn to black men and *liked* them. Such sedition was anathema to them. Dyed in the wool reactionaries, they existed in a time warp, refusing to acknowledge what had become the modern era.

It was mass communication that cued the period, the explosive growth of the tabloids and commercial radio during the 1920s. In America it was a period of unparalleled prosperity. Business earnings were soaring, so was the stock market. The good times were here and here to stay – or so it felt. It was a wonderful world whose inhabitants had been transformed to include women who wore make-up, silk stockings and cropped their hair; who smoked cigarettes, drank cocktails of bootleg gin, and wisecracked; who flung their lean bodies about dancing the Charleston and Black Bottom with men in wide-shouldered suits and two-tone shoes. Life was fun in the blare of jazz, the gramophone a must-have. A rage to live possessed people, a sharp appetite for everything that was new.

Sheltered from the world though she'd been, Doris was intuitively aware of the modern ethos and in tune with it. She loved its music and she loved to dance, the only time when she could shuck off her self-consciousness and lose herself in the beat. While on vacation at Rough Point, she asked a Princeton man who was one of the Newport bloods to take her to the Cotton Club. 'I agreed, but I didn't like it. In those days nobody went to Harlem. I thought we would be murdered or something. Doris just loved it,' he said.

Though Doris chafed against the antebellum fantasy that was Fermata, she remained there until she was seventeen in December 1929. By that date the world that she and others knew had changed, changed catastrophically: Wall Street had crashed.

The havoc the Crash unloosed upon the country was devastating. On 24 October thirteen million shares had been sold in an avalanche of loss, ruining many on the instant. By 11.30 a.m. the market was in free fall, gripped by blind panic. Outside the Exchange in Broad Street groups of traumatised people gathered into a crowd. The sound coming from them penetrated the building to those within as an animal roar of baffled pain. Police were deployed to keep the peace. Those in the mob outside, and in the city and throughout the country in the days, weeks, months and weary years that followed, felt they had been betrayed. The American Dream had been blown away and exposed for what it was: a dream. In the harsh reality which replaced it they might continue to exist but they had ceased to live. Their illusions had been stripped from them along with their savings, their jobs, and their homes. The idea of a better, fuller life was unimaginable – many were pressed to live at all. Some didn't, but jumped, shot themselves or hung themselves from a beam in a mortgaged barn. Depending on charity, the rest continued somehow, but all sparkle and all joy had been drained from being, all jaunty pride and strut and hope for tomorrow. In this drab numbness of circumstance only the cinema and soap opera of celebrity provided an escape into a richer, more brightly coloured existence.

Prior to the Crash, Doris's fortune had been assessed at $400 million (circa $6 billion in today's language). The money was invested in power companies and tobacco and, so essential were these products to the US population, these stocks remained relatively unscathed. The four vast properties she owned were unsaleable and technically worthless, but, since she lived in them, this mattered nothing to her. She was still by far the richest woman in America. Compared to her, Barbara Hutton – heiress to the Woodworth fortune, known as 'The million dollar baby' and with whom she'd been at school – came a poor second.

For a young woman to make her debut into the social world (and marriage mart) at the age of seventeen was a blue-blood tradition – as was her coming-out ball.

Barbara Hutton's in Manhattan, which Doris attended, was spectacular. It outraged America in its profligacy. Her own, at Rough Point, was more restrained and in keeping with the times. She hated publicity, believed she was ugly and detested being photographed. Never was there a more reluctant celebrity. Yet there was a public *need* for women such as Barbara and her. The development of tabloid newspapers had created a requirement, a hunger for them. Walter Winchell's column was syndicated in over one thousand national papers. He wielded (and abused) an extraordinary influence in shaping public opinion. Doris was prime game for him and other rival columnists, cannon fodder to the tabloids. She hated their attention, it made her desperately uncomfortable. To see a photograph of herself reminded her she was unattractive, to be questioned was embarrassing. When she went out she wore drab clothes and a cloche hat tugged low on her forehead; she refused all requests for an interview. Nevertheless, she went to dances and parties; she was obliged to, that was what 'doing the Season' was about and a cringe-making rite she was forced to endure.

The culmination of Doris's launch on high society was a voyage to England, where she was to be presented to the King and Queen at Buckingham Palace, along with nine other US debutantes – Barbara Hutton would go through the same ritual the following year. For her and the other Americans the purpose of the Presentation, and the round of parties and dances that would follow in the days afterward, was to extend the range of their eligibility to British and other aristocracy in a trade-off between title plus stately home and American wealth, an established historical tradition which strengthened the special relationship between the two countries.

Presentation at the Court of St James did indeed ensure the exposure of both Doris and Barbara Hutton to titled European adventurers; several of Barbara's later husbands would be accomplished cosmopolitan con-men. Doris's own renown spread far into the continent's furthest and most unlettered provinces. Nanaline was approached by emissaries from King Zog of Albania – who was particularly cash-strapped at that time – seeking to negotiate a union. After locating the country in an atlas, Nanaline was tickled by the notion of her ugly duckling becoming a Queen, but Doris vetoed the idea.

She was a prime catch, but for a suitor there was a downside to accommodate. The same Ivy League date who'd escorted her to the Cotton Club describes her as 'aloof, in the clouds. She was never a very warm person … elusive. Very much into herself. And she was not physically attractive. I think she felt ill at ease. She was conscious of her looks and I think she felt unhappy about it.'

The gossip columnist Elsa Maxwell targeted Doris and would track her through the years to come. Elsa was primarily a social fixer and publicist who threw spectacular well-attended parties in New York, Paris, Venice or Rome (always paid for by someone else). A dowdy squat wide woman with the crumpled face of a toad,† Elsa briefed against Doris from the start. 'She stands five feet ten in bare feet, is unhappy, shuns people and pinches pennies. She talks in jerky, almost inaudible sentences, wears sixteen dollar dresses which look like sixteen dollar dresses, walks awkwardly … and has the appetite of a farm hand and the manners of a shy child.'

She was also without education. Nanaline had scoffed at the idea of her attending university – even though they owned one – asking, why? What was the use of a degree? She'd never have to teach in school.

Yet Doris had to be found a husband. It was the way things were for heiresses and, despite her anti-social nature – she was happiest slumming – she did not rebel. She did fall unsuitably in

---

† Machiavellian and manipulative, Elsa moved in a world of highly charged sexual liaisons but was herself sexually inactive beyond an obsessive crush on the Duchess of Windsor who, according to Wallis's persistent biographer, Michael Bloch, may or may not have been a male.

love though. She was strongly attracted to the British MP Alec Cunningham-Reid. A worldly sophisticate, he had the habit of travel and infidelity; she slept with him when he visited the US. Alec was thirty-seven, a war hero, handsome, charming and desirably louche – but he was already married to an heiress, the sister of Countess Mountbatten.

Jimmy Cromwell, however, was husband material, 100 per cent American and available. Step-son to the fabulously wealthy market speculator, Edward Statesbury, he was sixteen years older than Doris and had just been divorced from auto heiress Delphine Dodge, but remained very much a mamma's boy in thrall to Eva Statesbury. Like Cunningham-Reid, Jimmy enjoyed a somewhat tarnished reputation, having been involved in a dubious scheme to transform a tract of swamp between Miami and Palm Beach into a plushy residential estate for the very rich, which had cost its investors a lot of money. Failing as a developer, he had converted from Republicanism to become a New Dealer under Roosevelt. Although not generally known, the Statesbury fortune had been wiped out by the Crash and he had need of a rich wife to back him in his newly chosen political career. With a strong if unsubstantiated belief in his own ability, he had conceived the ambition to become a Senator, and one day President of the United States.

The union between Doris and Jimmy Cromwell was an arranged marriage, set up by his mother Eva with the collusion of Nanaline. It took place in 1935 in what had been Buck Duke's library in the Fifth Avenue mansion. The ceremony lasted only five minutes and, at Doris's insistence, the word 'obey' was omitted from her vows, and it was reported that in reciting the rite what Jimmy actually muttered was, 'With all thy worldly goods I *me* endow.'

CHAPTER 6

DORIS DUKE, PARIS, SEPTEMBER 1947

The last chapter closed at the unpropitious start to Doris Duke's first marriage. Her *second* takes place twelve years later. Her new husband is Porfirio Rubirosa and on this occasion 'obey' remains in place in the marriage rite but an embarrassing hitch occurs, causing discord and mistrust between the couple before they even reach the crucial point where each is supposed to say, 'I do.'

The event takes place in the late summer of 1947, when Doris is working for *Harper's Bazaar* and staying at the Paris Ritz with the magazine's editor, Carmel Snow. Carmel informs her that tomorrow they will be photographing the designer's collection at Balenciaga. Regretfully Doris begs off from the shoot; she has an engagement at the Dominican Legation, where she is scheduled to wed Rubi.

Since their first meeting two years ago, she has continued working for INS in Rome, Paris and London. Meanwhile Doris has maintained a sexual liaison with Rubi, meeting whenever and wherever convenient to both. He is assiduous as a lover and she appreciates his perfect manners. When she – or any woman – reaches for a cigarette, he will already have drawn his gold lighter and be offering flame. Eileen Kingsbury-Smith (wife of INS bureau chief) and some others did not care for him. 'He was a dreadful creature. When he danced with a woman, it was like paper to a wall. He did everything but make love on the dance floor.' Some men disparage him, claiming he's no more than a cliché Latino creep – perhaps that's jealousy.

But Doris, while fully aware that Rubi is only after her fortune, has remained enraptured by him. She likes black men – she formed a taste for them in Hawaii. Rubi is not black but – despite his claim to Spanish ancestry – a mulatto quadroon, who's had his hair straightened and his wide nose fixed by the very best. The result is an accessory to be envied by every woman. Rubi is expensive, the best *is* expensive, but for Doris he is a prize cockerel to be proud of. 'It was the most legendary penis I have ever seen, there has never been anything like it. It was eleven inches long and thick as a beer can.' Pony Duke, her godson, describes it as 'six inches in circumference … much like the last foot of a Louisville Slugger baseball bat'.

But, in the words of a song current at that time, *It ain't what you do, it's the way that you do it*. Doris explains,

His purpose was to satisfy women. He was sterile and possibly impotent but his prick was so large that it seemed to be in a state of eternal erection … he was able to do whatever I wanted for endless hours. I was always the focus during sex. All that mattered was that I be satisfied. He simply wanted to make every woman on earth experience the ultimate climax. He would even fake an orgasm. Women have had to fake orgasms for centuries to make men think they were better than they were, but Rubi's dry runs were absolutely charming. The world would be a better place if more men were capable of faking an orgasm but all other males I have ever known have been basically interested in only satisfying themselves. There is nothing so useless as a man who has just climaxed.

⁂

In Paris, Carmel Snow is appalled to learn of Doris's wedding plans for next day. She fears not just her fortune and safety, but that she may forfeit her US citizenship by marrying on what is legally Dominican soil. 'It was nearly five o'clock on Friday afternoon and I barely had time to get hold of our French lawyer. He said, "This wedding mustn't go on unless the girl is represented by counsel." He got on the phone to America and received his instructions.'

Despite Doris's aversion to publicity, the press has been tipped off – probably by Rubi himself. The Legation is staked out by reporters and photographers. The room where the ceremony is due to take place has the impersonal décor of an hotel. The guests are few: Carmel Snow, the Kingsbury-Smiths, the racing driver Jean Pierre Wimille. They are not enough to generate a party atmosphere and stand around self-consciously. There is champagne and canapés, but the atmosphere is tense. Rubi is seen to fortify himself with a stiff highball, followed by a second.

All are assembled at the venue and the Dominican consul general is about to start the ceremony when there is an interruption. Two uninvited male guests enter, sombrely dressed in suits, carrying briefcases and walking with intent. Going directly to the groom, they identify themselves as attorneys from the distinguished law firm Condert, with a prenuptial agreement. The legal document is remarkably brief; it is an agreement for Rubi to sign, stating that in marrying Doris he renounces any claim to her fortune.

'His face was quite a picture when the lawyers walked in,' says

Kingsbury-Smith. 'He looked like one of those fierce black Miura bulls about to charge a black cape. I've never seen anyone madder. But he signed. There wasn't much else he could do.'

But Rubi is rattled by the incident. When he does sign, his handwriting is wobbly. He's noticeably drunk by now, and as the service starts, he lights a cigarette with a shaky hand. He smokes it during the ceremony, extinguishing it only so that he and Doris can exchange rings. Then, as the brief rite ends, Rubi collapses. There will be speculation later that someone, not unconnected with the proceedings, spiked his drink in an attempt to derail the marriage. Whatever the reason, he folds. 'Big Boy passed out in my arms,' Doris explains.

He comes to in their honeymoon suite in the Hotel du Cap with no memory of how he has got to Antibes. He is furious about the pre-nup; he can hardly bring himself to speak to his wife.

'I thought it was funny,' Doris says. 'Big Boy was so upset he just paced around the suite smoking cigarettes.' 'He was one pissed playboy,' says Pony Duke.

He is indeed. He's incensed at his public humiliation. He withdraws his favours, refusing to come to his wife's bed. But there is no scene, no violence; Doris has him and she knows it. Of course it takes contrition and a little wooing on her part before he starts lighting her cigarettes again. She gives him a make-up present, a seventeenth-century townhouse in Paris, for which she pays $100,000 plus a half million to a decorator to do it up according to Rubi's wishes as a personal expression of his questionable taste.

The mansion is well-chosen. It is protected by a high wall and has the privacy and security of a stronghold; Doris envisages living here herself. And Rubi is made very happy by the gift. Mr Nasty becomes Mr Nice and Big Boy is back again, quick on the draw with his solid gold lighter. Recovering from his pique, he takes up his role and marital obligations as husband to the richest woman in the world.

⚜

As had Jimmy Cromwell twelve years earlier in New York. Both marriages were equally unpromising, and both grooms motivated by desire for her money. In Rubi's case the discord between bride and husband was soon resolved by great sex. With Jimmy it was not. He was a bit of a limp rag in the sack and, though he'd slept with a number of women, had learned nothing about foreplay.

Doris and Jimmy had embarked on their honeymoon that same afternoon of their wedding to sail for Europe. Doris was nervous, she'd been agitated by the mob of photographers and reporters who had chased after them to the ship. And she was apprehensive of the wedding night ahead.

But Jimmy was cock-a-hoop with joy. In dire straits financially, he'd landed the world's top-ranking heiress. He reported, 'We got tremendous publicity when she and I were married. That's considered something you need in order to be successful in politics.'

He was thirty-eight (she was twenty-two) and strung tight with anticipation. His mother had warned him, she'd told him to wait until they were several days at sea and the marriage well consummated before mentioning money. But Jimmy was impatient and could not restrain himself. That very evening, when Doris had slipped into a negligee, climbed between the sheets and smiled shyly toward him, he lit a cigarette, came to sit on the edge of the bed and leaned ardently toward his bride to say, 'My darling, what might I expect my annual income to be?'

On the second day of the crossing an embarrassed purser accosted Doris to apologise, but was something being done about the matter of the cheque? It seemed the one her husband gave to Thomas Cook to pay for their tickets had been refused.

Doris was baffled. 'Why would the bank refuse a cheque?' When it was explained to her what a bounced cheque was, she was incensed. Furious, she kicked her husband in the shins, he kicked her back. Apart from that, the honeymoon was not attended by much passion. Doris explains, 'The truth of the matter was that we did try to have sex but there was not much to him. He was small where it would have been nice had he been larger. My experience was very limited so I thought this must be the way all men are. You can imagine my disappointment. But you cannot believe my relief when I learned that some men were far more gifted.'

Jimmy saw it differently. 'I was as patient as I could be and tried hard to go halfway, make it easier for her if I could. But it was very simple, she was frigid.'

Doris nicknamed her husband 'The Pope', because of his pomposity and habit of wearing a small hat to conceal his bald spot. 'He was very grand and very expensive but he did nothing in bed.' Under-endowed, yet in every other way stereotypically male, Jimmy attributed the problem to Doris. He called her 'the Fridgidairess'.

The couple's honeymoon took in India, Thailand, Bali, the Philippines and Japan, while they bickered continuously. In August they arrived in Hawaii. And here, free of the press photographers in this lush paradise Doris found the secluded spot upon the globe where she would make her spiritual and physical home. Deciding to build a dream house on the island, she rented a cottage and cased the island for the perfect site.

Great wealth confers a magic wand upon its owner, a power not far short of God's when He decreed, *Let there be land*. In Hawaii there was already land and beach aplenty; Doris required a location she could restructure to her own design.

She loved beach life. She was a strong swimmer and now she learned to surf. It was a new sport, unknown except in Hawaii. Her instructor was Sam Kahanamoku, and through him she got to know his brother Duke, an Olympic swimming champion, 6ft 3in in height and sheriff of Honolulu. 'She liked dark people,' says Jimmy Cromwell. While riding a surfboard Doris discovered a freedom and co-ordinated body rhythm she'd known only in dancing. First she took Sam Kahanamoku to be her lover then, more enduringly, his brother. 'My father, Duke, was the only person I was sure really loved me, but another man named Duke would teach me how to make love.'

Jimmy Cromwell, fretful at his exclusion and cross that his allowance was only 'a measly $10,000 a month', went home to mother. Eva sent him back quickly, but not before Doris had bought four and a half acres of land near Diamond Head for $100,000. She hired a local architect to draw up plans for a fortress, impregnable to the outside world, a perfect Shangri La.

Then the Jimmy Cromwells returned to the US, for him to pursue his political career. By now Doris knew – she'd known from the first night of their honeymoon – that he was a mistake. But a husband was thought to be a necessary accessory for an heiress, conveying a respectability that made it possible for the partners in the marriage to live as they chose. She didn't *need* Jimmy, she was admirably independent by nature and, with the assurance of great wealth, genuinely did not care a hoot what others thought.

Yet, very generously, she donated $50,000 to the Democrats' campaign, enabling Jimmy to take up cards in this new game. He started work upon a book, *In Defense of Capitalism*, designed to secure him the reputation of a political pundit. Doris flew between the East Coast and Hawaii to supervise construction of her house. The two led separate lives, covering 500,000 miles in the first two years of their marriage. Jimmy would have liked to have a son, if only to secure their union, but Doris had no wish for a child.

In 1938 the couple sailed together to England to attend the Coronation of George VI on 12 May. Barbara Hutton was there, together with a set of people Doris knew; among them Alec Cunningham-Reid. Doris and he resumed their affair. 'Oh, I knew he was a lizard,' she says, 'but he was the most exciting and best-looking lizard I have ever seen. The best part was that he made Jimmy nervous so I gave him a lot of attention.'

But Jimmy was complaisant about his wife's affairs, so long as they did not embarrass him or damage his political reputation. Many husbands felt the same way and a line of colluding cuckolds stretches back in history. It was a civilised arrangement, a couple could follow individual lives without rancour. To some husbands it provided sexual stimulus. Others, whose wives dallied with princes, were rewarded with honours or advancement.

Jimmy did not object to Doris's infidelity, while it remained discreet. Egotistical and firmly self-centred, he took himself seriously, mistakenly believing he was an original political thinker. He wrote to an aide to Roosevelt at the White House: 'I should like to have ten or perhaps fifteen minutes of his time in order to point out certain errors in his recent fireside chat...' Money may prattle foolishly, still money talks. The Cromwells were invited to cocktails at the White House, Jimmy's name was announced as contender for a seat in the Senate. Then, to his enormous gratification, Doris was asked to accompany Eleanor Roosevelt, the President's wife, on a visit to a deprived mining community in West Virginia.

What Doris chose to wear for this opportune occasion at the side of the First Lady was obviously important. She was normally uninterested in how she dressed. The columnist, Cobina Wright, recalls, 'One day she came back with a nightgown which she converted into an evening gown. She had a maid take off the flowers. She said it was a bargain.'

Clothes meant nothing to her, yet what she wore at the First Lady's side to visit impoverished miners and their hungry families in their uninsulated shacks was a statement. Upon the day, she chose to appear in a full-length Russian mink coat and custom-made English walking boots. Eleanor Roosevelt was appalled, so incensed she refused to speak one word to her.

Jimmy was mortified. 'Why would you dress better for some coal miners in wherever that place was, and wear a made-over nightgown to my parents' ball in Palm Beach?' he demanded. 'It does not make any sense.'

It made perfect sense. She disliked parties and a crush of people, was repelled by the political class. By a single aptly styled appearance she ensured that she would never be asked again.

Jimmy's next move was to use Doris's money to produce a film, *Of Men and Money*. He spoke of buying a newspaper and throwing it behind the Democrats' cause. 'I don't think they took him too seriously,' says a Washington editor. 'I don't think people had a great deal of respect for him.' He was behaving impetuously because he was under the gun; he needed to secure nomination to the New Jersey Senate seat, while maintaining the impression that his wealthy wife was happy in funding his bid from her enormous fortune.

Meanwhile, Doris was following an independent life in Hawaii, where her house was starting to take shape, but also visiting Paris, Athens and London to meet with Alec Cunningham-Reid, who was waiting for the divorce from his second heiress-wife, Ruth Ashley, to become final. Doris seldom read a newspaper, yet not only friends but her business manager, William Baldwin, and lawyer, Tom Perkins, had made her fully aware of Alec's reputation. She depended on them for advice, which she seldom opposed in any business affair. Yet in this matter of the heart she was impregnable to counsel. She was not blind about Alec, she knew him to be a rat. But the rat came sleekly packaged. He could pass for a respectable establishment figure, while in fact he was an opportunistic chancer. Chancers are attractive, there is an exhilaration in their company. Many women thought so about Alec. Doris knew herself to be physically unattractive; Alec was a validation of her worth. Besides, her advisers were warning her against him and there is a keen thrill in transgressive love.

In the winter of 1939, Jimmy – one of five candidates for the New Jersey seat – was given by Roosevelt the job of US Minister to Canada. And it was at this crucial moment that Doris told him she wanted a divorce, before flying to join Alec on a winter sports vacation. She then left for Hawaii, to await him there when his divorce became final, omitting to mention to either man that she was pregnant.

❧

In Honolulu Doris found her fortress was nearing completion.

Protected by a high white wall the garden contained its own grove of relocated full-grown palm trees. A sand-bottom stream wound its way through the garden and interior of the house. Closed-off on its landward side, the property opened onto its own beach and the sea beyond. It was a dream setting.

Duke's brother and his wife lived in the grounds as caretakers, and Duke had his own room in the house. Now Doris moved in. She made no effort to entertain or be invited by the resident white community and, piqued, its members gossiped and bad-mouthed her in return.

Doris cared not a fig, but she was concerned about her pregnancy. The baby might be Duke's or Alec's, but could not be Jimmy's, whom she had not slept with for two years.

On 11 July, while Alec was in a plane on his way to join her, Doris went surfing for several hours with Duke. Afterward, she went into premature labour. In Honolulu's hospital she gave birth to a three-pound dark-skinned baby girl. Unable to sustain life, the infant died less than twenty-four hours later. Doris learned that she could never have another child, went through a minor breakdown, and was comforted by Alec.

Jimmy Cromwell learned of the birth from newspapers. When he called her she forbad him to come to Hawaii, saying if he did she would refuse to see him. He had received a lot of bad publicity of late and now the press shredded him for not being at his wife's side when she most needed him. In New Jersey, Mayor Hague became aware that Jimmy was no longer funded by the Duke millions, refusing to see him or return his telephone calls. 'My whole organisation actually turned up their toes and quit,' he says.

It was the end of Jimmy Cromwell's career, and he exits this narrative, leaving his own pitiful epitaph:

I was a ladies' man. I was extremely good-looking. I used to have a perfect physique ... But I didn't have a decent break of luck ... Fate has decreed that I will never be a financial success. Mine has been a really weird life in that I have always been connected with great fortunes ... but never have I ever had any capital of my own.

Alec Cunningham-Reid was a very different kettle of fish to poor dimwitted Jimmy. It's true he was a hero, a Conservative MP, a popular figure in London and other capitals. He had wit, charm, looks and upper-crust background. But, as Doris had figured early in their relationship, he was unquestionably a rat.

He lived in England, where he was somewhat idle in his parliamentary duties, and his habit of jaunting off to international social destinations had been curtailed by the war. Britain was a particularly bleak place to live in at that time. The country was governed by emergency restrictions. Black-out and food rationing were in place, food was short, petrol rationed and British subjects were not permitted to travel abroad.

Alec cooked up an ingenious scheme not only to evade these constraints but to secure himself a nice little earner to see out the conflict and provide a safe haven for his family at no cost to himself. Doris, who wanted him with her and wished to marry him, was happy to go along with the racket under his direction. She wrote to old Joe Kennedy, US ambassador in London. She'd known his sons, Jack, Bobby and Ted, since childhood. Through Kennedy she donated $25,000 to the Red Cross to assist British child refugees. Alec created the Children's Overseas Reception Board, naming himself its chief representative. It was a worthy cause; he experienced no difficulty in obtaining exit permits and US visas for himself, his mother, and his two sons, aged twelve and ten.

At the height of the Blitz, with bombs falling nightly upon London, Alec fled the country with his personal brood of evacuees, travelling First Class to America, where they took up residence in their luxurious refugee camp, Duke Farms. The two boys were enrolled in a nearby private school. His timely flight did not go unnoticed. The war was going badly, and that a Conservative MP should choose to run away with his family to the States was repugnant to everyone. The press vilified him and there were repeated calls for him to resign from Parliament. Eventually he was forced to return. When he slunk back a newspaper named him The Most Hated Man in Britain and, on turning up at the House of Commons, another MP punched him in the face.

᙭᙭᙭

In December 1941 the Japanese bombed Pearl Harbor, only a few miles down the coast from Doris's house by Diamond Head.

As a civilian, she was unable to leave mainland America. Duke Kahanamoku was in Hawaii, Alec back in London, and in New York Jimmy Cromwell was proving difficult about the divorce. He wanted $7 million to go quietly. He threatened to write a tell-all book; he was an embittered disappointed man and he'd go as low as it took. Nanaline and Doris's advisers begged her to pay but she jibbed at the price, she hated anyone to cheat her.

In November 1942 Doris turned thirty, then in December won a divorce in Reno, Nevada. It was the best Christmas present she could imagine. On that birthday she came into the last slab of her fortune of over $450 million (around $7 billion in today's value). She had total control over how she used it; she was guided only by William Baldwin, Tom Perkins and her own good sense. For the first time in her life she was truly free and now in possession of a mature knowledge of what she wanted and – even more important – what she did *not* want. She was at liberty to act as she liked. This was an epic moment in history. America had entered the war and she wished to make her own contribution to victory – but what? As the reader will recall, she elected to become a secret agent … which led to her marrying Rubirosa.

CHAPTER 7

DORIS DUKE, PARIS, 1947–48

Doris Duke's rocky honeymoon on Cap d'Antibes with her sulky groom Rubi pacing the floor, chain smoking and glaring at her in ruffled pique, is assuaged and made smooth by her gift of the Paris house. Reconciled, the newly-weds return to the city to put up at the George V while the property is redecorated and made ready for them.

Rubi is overjoyed with the house – he's never owned his own home before. He is without a job as he is still unacceptable to the French authorities, so has ample leisure to oversee the building's redecoration. Doris has given him the title deeds and *carte blanche* to do as he likes.

The mansion formerly belonged to Princess Chavchavadze, an American heiress. The place is already elegant but Rubi is seeking a tone of swanky opulence. He installs rosewood panelling, and silk hangings on the walls. The house is decorated in the style of a high-class brothel of the Belle Époque, offset by manly touches. He wants a gymnasium, a boxing ring, a sauna. In the secluded courtyard he installs two exercise bicycles and a mechanical bull, which Doris rides while wearing the tiniest of shorts. Her long legs are quite her best physical feature.

Rubi is excited as a child with his new toy and Doris is happy to indulge him. He is good company. He possesses unlimited energy and appetite for life; he loves to eat, to drink, to party and to dance. He's stimulating, witty and makes her laugh. She seems to have overcome her natural stinginess and enjoys spending her money – though not as much as Rubi does. He delights in throwing it around to create a good time for all.

Things are well between the newly married couple and Doris is happy to be seen about with her husband, who represented a must-have to so many women in the past and still does. She watches him closely, there are warning signs. On one occasion while passing a few days in Cannes, Doris asked him to get her a pack of cigarettes. In the lobby of the hotel he ran into Manouche, a lover in his past, who suggested a coffee.

She provides her own slant on his widely discussed apparatus: 'It was long and pointed and it hurt … It was nothing for *ce cher* Rubi to take on two or three women in a night. By late at night, when he was good and drunk, he didn't give a damn what kind of legs were opening.'

Three days later, Rubi returned with Doris's cigarettes.

She is at first forgiving of these lapses and conceals the discomfort they occasion in her. They are both worldly, though Doris is much less jaded than he. But the couple are aware of the strains imposed by constant togetherness. Deliberately, they take up individual pursuits. For Rubi it is polo, for Doris jazz. Rubi's sport, which he played before in the Dominican Republic, is a great deal more costly than his wife's. He has ridden since infancy, he has an affinity with horses, and polo ponies are the princelings of horseflesh. At their mettlesome best, he reveres and loves them. Although he drinks heavily and goes to bed late, by 10 a.m. Rubi is at the Bagatelle Club in the Bois de Boulogne, where the French champion Pierre

Dobadie is coaching him in the game. Though now forty, his body is fit and hard. He is quick and recklessly brave. Courage is necessary, it is a dangerous sport and it suits him perfectly.

It is while Rubi is absorbed in this rediscovered passion that he receives a letter from Ramfis Trujillo in the Dominican Republic. The dictator's eldest son, and Rubi's ex-brother-in-law, is heir to his father's fortune and dominion. Created an army colonel when he was six, he's been looked after by servants and bodyguards all his life, indulged and spoilt rotten. He is now a teenager, and pining for a wider life than the island can provide. Alert as ever to the main chance, Rubi invites him to stay with them in Paris, where he introduces him to polo and much else. He becomes once again the youth's mentor, showing him the scene and teaching him the moves.

It is an expedient exercise. Rubi is a glamorous figure to Ramfis, a model of how he'd like to be himself. His letters to Papa speak well of his hosts and his guided entrée to a sophisticated European côterie. In the twenty years Rubi has worked for Trujillo the dictator more than once has come close to firing him, he has sacked and banished many of his court. But, among the several devils that possess Trujillo, one is a particular idiosyncrasy: however displeased he is with someone, he hates for them to leave *him*. It bothers him not to control them. However, he's elated by Rubi's marriage to such a wealthy woman and wishes to make use of the connection. He offers Rubi the post of ambassador to Argentina, heading up the Dominican embassy in Buenos Aires.

Trujillo's desire to be seen as a significant global figure has prompted him to set up embassies in several capitals, though, apart from maintaining secret files on key individuals, their function is slight. Buenos Aires is one of the larger of these establishments. Trujillo fancies himself to have much in common with Juan Perón, the strongman ruling Argentina. The problems they both face in dealing with the USA, their near-neighbour, are similar, though Argentina is a very much bigger and richer country than the Dominican Republic, and its profile is higher in the world. This is largely due to Perón's charismatic wife, Eva. Born illegitimate into provincial poverty, a bastard child in a strictly Catholic country, she was marked down from the start. Uneducated, she is intuitively acute to a very sharp edge. Highly attractive and an aspiring actress, she has climbed to the position she now enjoys on a ladder formed by ascending rungs of men. First Lady, married to the man who came to power eighteen months ago, she's as dedicated to politics as her husband and has embraced as her cause the country's poor, who venerate her as an almost saintly figure.

Trujillo's reasoning is that appointing an ambassador to Argentina whose own wife is an international celebrity, will generate coverage that will raise the prestige of the republic, in both the host country and globally. Whether he has sufficiently considered the snags inherent in having two big-time female personalities sharing the same stage is doubtful.

Trujillo wants to secure Doris as an ally, to draw her close. By marrying Rubi on Dominican soil she's become a citizen of his country, he believes, though she's retained her US passport. Trujillo is perennially in need of hard currency, but just now especially so. He is aware of the prenuptial agreement Rubi was obliged to sign but is confident he will in time obtain control of her fortune. Possibly he will get her to revoke the agreement and even if he doesn't Doris is mortal, is she not? Life is uncertain; she might meet with an accident. In the moral universe Trujillo inhabits, accidents happen quite often. And if Doris dies, her millions will go to her husband.

Rubi flies to Buenos Aires to take up his new appointment, but Doris cannot accompany him. The State Department has stepped in to deny her a diplomatic visa. Both the CIA and J. Edgar Hoover, head of the FBI, have a fat file on Rubi – his goes way back – and another on Doris. Hers is one of the most substantial stockholdings in the US. Duke Power provides electricity to millions of homes, factories and government buildings across the land. The possibility that an unstable despot on a remote tropical island might be in a position to shut down supply is a worst-case nightmare. A newspaper reports, 'She has let her country down and faces a life-and-death fight with Washington, which may refuse to let her go to Buenos Aires. It may even use its influence to have Rubi refused accreditation.'

Nevertheless with her usual ingenuity, she finds a way to get to Buenos Aires and moves into the well-appointed residence that goes with the post. Rubi is now 'His Excellency' and she gives him a present to mark the appointment. He receives his own B-25 twin-engined bomber, which Doris has had upholstered in leather and fitted out as a luxurious private plane to accommodate a handful of passengers. Rubi is overjoyed by the gift and loves to fly it with his wife and others. He can't be bothered to learn navigation, sometimes gets lost and runs out of petrol, so the number of willing passengers declines, but Doris enjoys the ride with its casual risk and doesn't mind in the least.

Rubi's job involves almost no actual work, but his and his wife's social duties are demanding. Curiosity about Doris is high, very many people want to say they know her; the couple are stars of the diplomatic community. She finds its company superficial and bland as she did politicians'. She has never enjoyed parties and only likes bohemians, musicians or artistes of some kind. She loved talent and creativity in individuals and was herself classless and devoid of prejudice – except against pretension, as displayed here. The diplomatic wives are competitive and dressy, preoccupied by fashion and gossip; the men guarded and insincere. She has no talent in social nicety and little patience.

But Rubi enjoys his job hugely. His prodigious energy enables him to party all night and still get up to ride in the morning, but Doris flags on the remorseless circuit. Often he goes out alone at night, and there is always a professional reason to do so. Such gatherings, when she does attend them, can be embarrassing. Women glance at her then at one another, and whisper behind their hands. She wonders which and how many of them Rubi has slept with. There is one particular rival Doris is very conscious of: Eva Perón.

Eva understood Rubi from the instant she first met him. She has considerable experience of macho Latin American males, and the two of them have much in common. He's come up by the same ladder as she, manipulating the opposite sex. Both enjoy glamour and shiny toys. He likes airplanes, she likes diamonds – what's the difference? Not least in their resemblance, both have dabbled in the same swill. During the war she made her fortune from selling Argentine passports. Rubi's customers for Dominican nationality were Jews, hers were Nazis aware that Germany was going to lose.

Eva knows she can get Rubi anytime she wants but she dallies with him, making him wait until he comes up with a donation of $1,500 for her pet charity, the Shirtless Ones. A fellow ambassador observes that it is 'the only time in recorded history that a pimp ever gave money to a harlot'.

Then the wife of a senior diplomat passes a night with Rubi and loses her reason entirely, along with all discretion. She pursues him relentlessly, causing public scenes. He is obliged to fly to Paris to escape her, but she follows him, now vengeful in her incontinent passion. Newspapers get hold of the story, which becomes a scandal in BA. It is impossible for Rubi to continue in the post.

Trujillo is furious, recalling him. With great generosity of heart, Doris accompanies her errant husband on his summons to the headmaster's study. Going out of her way to soothe and flatter the dictator, she manages to preserve a relationship between the two men, fraught though it is.

Afterward, the couple return to their house in Paris – Rubi's house – but Doris is unhappy. Rubi is unemployed, though he busies himself in his usual hyper fashion, 'I find it impossible to work, there's just no time.' He sets up his own polo team, Cibao La Pampa. He and Doris resume their life in the French capital, but it is not the same as it was. She fills the house with musicians, sometimes their impromptu jazz sessions continue all night. In the early hours of the morning Rubi usually comes home with a gang of hangers-on picked up in the last nightclub, rousing the servants and calling for food. Ramfis Trujillo arrives for an extended stay. Thanks to Rubi, he's familiar with this city, particularly its seamy side which offers opportunity unavailable at home. He's already a drinker, now he discovers drugs. Then Rubi's shady brother Cesar and nephew Gilberto turn up to stay. They bring girls back to the house, which becomes a ritzy *garçonnière* with Doris as its reluctant chatelaine.

Sometimes Rubi does not return until the next morning, and she senses the jagged edge of a previously unknown torment. Her first love and model of masculinity was her father, who loved and valued her but died when she was twelve. Buck had been dominant and forceful, sometimes tyrannical. He was larger than life, he had an aura. He was a hard act to follow and none of her lovers – certainly not her husband Jimmy Cromwell – have matched up to him.

Rubi has an aura. Rubi equals her father in these dominant-male characteristics but he has no regard for marriage – none. In result, Doris suffers. She was raised as a loner. In childhood she was awkward, plain, too tall, at school mocked. Yet, armoured by wealth, she developed into a mature and self-confident, if wary, woman. She knows to hold off, to give little of herself, never to show vulnerability. She controlled her marriage to Jimmy, she controlled all her relationships. At the start with Rubi the reins were firmly in her grasp and it had been a great ride, she'd enjoyed life as she never had before. She's overcome her stinginess and found pleasure in spending and pleasure in Rubi's pleasure.

She'd been in charge. She isn't now. She had gone into this with her eyes wide open. She'd had no illusions about Rubi from the start. But she was a big girl – she thought she could handle it. And now she finds she can't.

To marry Rubi had been an affirmation. Rubi as a husband validated her as an attractive woman; at his side she could believe she was. She could read the envy, rivalry, hatred in other women's eyes and it thrilled her with satisfaction. But Rubi – so like her father in his brand of maleness – is utterly deficient in other crucial aspects that existed in Buck. Rubi values her, but only for her money; he does not love her, he has no interest in protecting or taking care of her.

Rubi had won her and Doris has been unable to conceal the fact that she is in thrall to him. She's lost the initiative, and with it control of the relationship.

For Rubi the thrill is in the pursuit and seduction; conquest is the climax. Afterwards, he's bored – the rest is merely maintenance and expedience. Now it is not he who has changed, but Doris. She has developed a dependency and, fatally, her need and desperation has begun to show. Her validation has been withdrawn and she is bereft. She's unable to conceal her pain, even while aware that expressing it is to drive him away. He is *programmed* to back off. He has endless experience of clingy women who, in response to a single night of lovemaking and series of knee-buckling orgasms, have pinned the entire cargo of their emotional needs upon him. He is predetermined to dump them.

⁂

Such is the unhappy state of affairs in the couple's marriage in 1948 when two events occur in swift succession. Rubi's B-25 crashes while taking off in New Jersey. He is not on board and none of the crew is injured – but Doris was scheduled to be on the flight; she'd changed her plans only hours before.

The second incident possibly has connection with the first, but if the crash is the trigger for it the cumulative reasons are already set in place and their weight is crushing her. Doris cuts her wrists in a bathroom in the Paris house. A maid finds her; the room is splashed with blood. She is rushed to hospital and given a transfusion. No word leaks to the press. Discharging herself, she checks into a sanatorium in Italy under a pseudonym to recover.

In October 1949 Doris is granted a divorce from Rubi in Reno, Nevada.

CHAPTER 8

ZSA ZSA GABOR, NEW YORK CITY, NEW YEAR'S DAY 1953

now is falling heavily and the sidewalk is a trampled froth of slush. It's only a short walk from where she's parked the car on Central Park South to the Plaza and Zsa Zsa is well wrapped up in furs, but the hike through the melting sludge does nothing to improve her mood. The drive to Idlewild, where she put her husband George Sanders on a plane to Rome, and the journey back into the city through a blizzard was a nightmare.

Zsa Zsa is often discontent, her full lips set into a sulky pout – part of her charm, she's been told – but just now she is seriously furious with George. *Such disrespect and lack of consideration.*

It's true though that George has never pretended to be a dutiful husband. At the marriage ceremony on April Fools' Day three years ago he'd forgotten to buy a ring, they'd had to use one given her by a previous husband – now aged thirty-four, already she's got through two. George is neglectful and stingy, he even makes her buy her own cigarettes. He kept his own apartment when he moved in with her. All he brought to the marriage were two suits, a painting she'd given him and his own ashtray; when he moved out following a row – and there were many – he took these with him. He dislikes possessions, he feels trapped by them, he claims.

But the reasons for Zsa Zsa's discontent as she crosses the Plaza's ornate lobby – which is a busy hive of activity rimmed by elderly female residents perched on gilt chairs observing those who sashay in and out, in lieu of a life of their own – is more specific than general dissatisfaction with her husband. The movie she's recently completed, *Moulin Rouge* directed by John Huston, is about to open in Manhattan but George has chosen to leave for Italy to work on a picture with Rossellini. It's not the first of such slights; more than once she's been driven to fury by lipstick on his handkerchief or coming upon a scrap of paper with a scribbled telephone number. Once, hysterical with jealousy, she'd yelled, 'I hate you, I'll get even with you! I'm going to have an affair with Rubirosa!'

Zsa Zsa Gabor with Rubirosa

But, although Rubi was notorious for his sexual exploits, George knew she'd never met him and only laughed.

Zsa Zsa stands at the bank of elevators with flecks of snow melting on her fur coat as she waits impatiently for one to arrive. She'd begged George to take her with him to Rome but he'd refused, 'No, my dear, you'll spoil my fun.' Awaiting the elevator, blonde, beautiful, exquisitely dressed though glittering with specks of moisture, Zsa Zsa is seething with resentment.

Ping ... the door to one of the elevators draws open. The passengers get out and she steps into the interior, aware that someone has followed her in. The door closes and the cabin lifts off. A man's voice enquires, 'Madame, what are you doing in New York?'

Zsa Zsa turns to look at him. Captive with her in the small space, he smiles. It is Rubirosa.

She is tired and overwrought, for a moment uncharacteristically speechless. He repeats the question.

'Why, to open my picture *Moulin Rouge*...'

'A pleasant coincidence, is it not? I am here with my President, General Trujillo. It would be an honour if you would join us for a drink...'

She's wrong-footed by the suggestion. She's slept little the night before, is tired and out of sorts, and the slick riposte which normally comes so easily to her is lacking.

'I really don't know...' The elevator brakes to a stop on the tenth floor. She steps out and the door slides shut behind her. She continues to her room, throws herself fully dressed upon the bed and is asleep in moments.

When she wakes the room is filled with red roses, dozens of them, arranged by the maid while she slept. She examines the small card engraved:

Don Porfirio Rubirosa
Minister Plenipotentiary The Dominican Republic

on which is written, *For a most beautiful lady – Rubi*.

She's seated at the dressing table twenty minutes later, face smeared with cold cream while blow-drying her hair, when the telephone rings. It is Rubirosa, 'May I come over for a drink?'

She is flustered, 'No, no. It's impossible.'

'Perhaps later?'

'Perhaps. The roses are beautiful.'

'A strange coincidence, we have adjoining suites. You have only to open your door, and I mine…'

Had he changed his room to be next to her? She says hurriedly, 'If you will call me tomorrow, monsieur…'

❦

Now it *is* tomorrow, the day of the premiere and *Moulin Rouge* is due to open at the Capitol on Broadway in two hours' time. Velvet ropes are already in place slung on brass posts, and a small crowd has started to gather, watching news crews set up lights and their bulky cameras on rostrums outside the theatre, where Walter Winchell will greet the stars and celebs as they descend from their limos to cross the red carpet to attend the performance.

In her suite at the Plaza, Zsa Zsa is struggling to do up her form-fitting black dress, with a train of broadtail mink and a zip up the back. The telephone rings, it is Rubirosa. She has an inspiration, 'It's so silly but I can't do up my dress and there's no maid. If you will be good enough…'

Seconds later he steps through the inter-connecting door into her suite. He zips up the dress deftly. She turns around to face him and they stand for a moment, smiling almost sheepishly at one another. Then he helps her into her coat and escorts her down to the lobby and the waiting limo.

The premiere receives a rapturous reception; the audience stands to applaud Zsa Zsa's performance. It's a triumph but also a vindication; her husband George Sanders has done all he can to stop her going into movies: 'You'd be hopeless at acting, darling. You're just too dumb. Don't be silly.'

Afterward she returns to the Plaza, goes to her room, still heavy with the scent of roses. She sits there exultant at her success and brimming with emotion ... but she is alone, there is no one to share it. On cue the telephone rings: Rubi. 'I'm in the Persian Room downstairs with a party of friends. Won't you join us?'

She touches up her make-up, brushes her hair, and does so. He pulls out a chair for her at the crowded table. 'I believe you already know Prince Bernadotte...'

She chats to the Prince, whom she's met in Paris, all the while covertly observing Rubirosa. George spoke of him disparagingly but he does not seem absurd to her, far from it. He looked

> solemn, almost tortured. His hair was black, eyebrows heavy and black, almost glowering over sombre dark eyes, and on either side of his mouth deep furrows formed ... a man, I thought, who always has himself under control. He sat almost as if by himself, remote, detached... He drank steadily, quietly, responding to others' questions with little more than a monosyllable. At one point he rose and walked to the bar. He moved with a kind of catlike grace... When he came back, he took the chair next to me...

They talk but she's hardly aware of his words. 'Through the haze of champagne I saw him, a dark man with glowing eyes, watching me, enveloping me in a gaze of such naked intensity that everyone else at the table seemed to melt away … I thought uneasily, fighting for my own calm: *this man is a primitive, he is all purpose.*'

He fills her glass. 'You must drink,' he says. 'It is your night.'

The evening ends. Rubi escorts her upstairs and to her door. He asks, 'May I come in?'

Zsa Zsa says, 'I was drunk at that moment – drunk with power, drunk with achievement, drunk with yearning for George. I was in a daze, so over-miserable, so overexcited … because here was Rubirosa, the only man whose name could make George grow pale … I said yes. So it all began…'

❧

Zsa Zsa invariably lied about her age, and lied so inconsistently it is impossible to determine the date of her birth in Hungary; the best guess is circa 1917. Her mother, Jolie, had given up her ambitions of a stage career at the age of seventeen to marry a man eighteen years older. Zsa Zsa's father, Vilmos, was an autocrat who ruled his household in the old-style imperial tradition, his temper was ungovernable.

His own family had been rather grand, though the Great War had reduced his and many aristocratic fortunes. Nevertheless, home was a large over-furnished apartment in Budapest and there was a holiday house on Lake Balaton; their car was a Mercedes. Zsa Zsa and her sisters, Magda and Eva, owned their own ponies and attended classes in riding, ballet, tennis, fencing, piano, and received almost nothing by way of formal education.

The sisters were never allowed to forget they were not boys. At the theatre their mother remarked, 'Ah, I would be up there now if only you hadn't been girls. I gave up my career for you.' Jolie came from a family of jewellers and through necessity her husband had been obliged to practise the same trade, déclassé though it was. It made it all the more necessary to keep up pretensions of a grander life they could no longer afford. 'Remember who you are,' Zsa Zsa was told. Appearance and performance were what mattered; that was an early lesson in behaviour.

Thwarted in her own career, Jolie was fiercely ambitious for her daughters. She was determined they would excel, though in nothing as mundane as a 'job'. They would succeed as *women*, as paragons of beauty, glamour and style. Quite contrary to the upbringing they would have received in England at that time, they were encouraged to be both *seen* and *heard*. The family environment promoted performance. Jolie was volatile in her emotions, theatrical in her expression; Vilmos given to bouts of jealousy and rage, flinging china at the wall. He had affairs himself – he could not believe his much-younger wife did not do the same. The atmosphere at home was fraught with drama and a free range of emotions; calm was seldom permitted to intrude.

None of his daughters was cowed by their father's behaviour. They spoke back to him boldly, raising their voices to the level required. In their tempestuous mittel-European household, rows blew out as suddenly as they erupted. And they were lavished with attention from both parents, indulged, bought clothes and always beautifully dressed in identical outfits. *Presentation* was the other fundamental lesson.

'I wanted to be beautiful,' says Zsa Zsa. 'I delighted in wearing the Tyrolean leather shorts and flowered braces Father bought me.' She wore it to the all-in wrestling matches he took her to.

> I would sit proudly with him, imitating him as he leaped to his feet to applaud, to shout, 'Give it to him!' … Father was, what we

in Hungary call a *big style man* … intensely masculine, passionate and powerful, and extremely loving toward me … I adored my mother, but it was Father I admired. He was unreasonable, he was jealous, he was violent, he was overwhelming – he was a *man*.

⁂

'Sooner or later there had to come a day when I filled out my leather shorts too well,' Zsa Zsa says.

At the age of thirteen she was sent to Madame Sabilia's School for young ladies in Lausanne. She was not bookish, but she was smart and quick. She possessed a sharp eye and a ready tongue. She was precociously representative of that between-the-wars period in which young women bobbed their hair, shortened their skirts, drank cocktails, smoked and transformed their traditional image beyond recognition. She was not without anxieties but she kept this to herself. 'To show fear, to admit that I was hurt, to reveal my true feelings, to be *pitied* – this I could not bear.' To protect herself she cultivated the bold over-the-top persona that would become her image, fashioning an individual style that would remain hers throughout her life.

At school, 'I adored the English girls, especially a tall languid brunette … her calm, her indifference to argument, her cool disdain seemed to me the height of all that was elegant.'

Zsa Zsa's first letter home flags the priorities she would retain:

I'm the only Hungarian girl here, all the rest are English … They think all Hungarian girls are gypsies and are amazed I know how to use a knife and fork … Mamika, I want you to burn this letter as soon as you finish it so Father won't see it – but Mama dear, I'd love to have a garter belt. All the English girls have them…

Such values, accompanied by her vivacity, looks and talent to play the strumpet with a carnal swagger, would take her a long way; eventually, and not surprisingly, to Hollywood.

❧

Zsa Zsa's first theatrical break occurred when she was fifteen and in Vienna with her mother. She was spotted in a café by Richard Tauber, the operatic tenor and matinee idol. In 1935, he cast her as an ingénue in a musical, *The Singing Dream*. To Zsa Zsa the stage and grown-up independent life in the sophisticated city was an intoxicating experience. She was crushed when the run ended and she had to go home. 'After Vienna, how could I return to long black stockings, penances and psalms before dinner?'

Her mother understood her disappointment. 'I know, darling. But what else is there for you to do?'

A month later Zsa Zsa married Burham Belge, a Turk twenty years older than herself who had already divorced two wives. She'd met him often at her grandmother's house, finding him then to be 'a dour sinister-looking man ... who looked world-weary and bored.' Despite that impression, on her forced return from Vienna, learning Burham was in town, she telephoned him at the Turkish embassy. They made an assignation at the Ritz, where she set out to seduce him, taking with her a portfolio of glamour shots done by a theatrical photographer. In one she wore a tight red sweater as she bit into an apple; in another her blouse was open as she teased a dangling cherry with the tip of her tongue. She says Monsieur Belge regarded the shots with interest. 'He continued to look at them, then at me, then back at them.'

'Will you marry me?' she asked him.

He choked on his drink and she went on hastily, 'I'll be a good wife to you, Excellency. You need someone like me, anyway. You are always so solemn.'

'May I have a little time to think this over?' he asked. It did not take him long.

Vilmos approved the match after a show of outrage; he had three daughters to dispose of, all without dowries. He came up with the gift of a ten-carat diamond, along with the advice that Zsa Zsa should never accept a smaller diamond from any man – she says she always did her best to follow his injunction.

Her mother's counsel was equally worldly: 'My darling, it does not have to be forever. You can always come back to me if you don't like him.'

⁂

The oddly matched couple moved to live in Ankara, where Burham was Director of Press and Propaganda in Kemal Ataturk's government. The charismatic fifty-year-old President had instituted a secular state in the region, abolishing the veil and fez along with links to Islam. Burham, who had studied at Cambridge and Heidelberg, was a leading member of the Young Turks helping to shape the new modern republic. The group had formed between the two world wars; he and they were supporters of Hitler and Nazi Germany.

Zsa Zsa's social life consisted in accompanying her husband on the diplomatic circuit and as token hostess at home, where politics formed the only subject and conversation took place in Turkish – which she did not speak. She was however learning to play bridge, and at those parties was the preferred partner of the Russian ambassador. The two never failed to lose money. Asked why he always chose to play with her, he explained, 'Because she had such a delicious décolletage.'

Zsa Zsa's several memoirs convey a breezy insouciance, but are short on self-examination. However she does reflect that it might perhaps have been wiser to get to know at least *something* about her husband and his work before she married him. Now, 'as Burham talked I would find myself yawning. He would stand up suddenly and walk away, I could not help it. At first I'd been terribly intrigued. How exciting I thought to be married to a man of such intelligence … But now as his wife he made me feel like a silly girl called before a schoolmaster.'

Zsa Zsa claims – not entirely convincingly – that she never slept with Burham and the marriage remained unconsummated. In her telling it is Ataturk who took her virginity. She saw him only once before this event, when she was dining with her husband and others at Ankara's best restaurant. Suddenly the orchestra ceased playing, the dancing couples froze, everyone in the place stood up. The President had entered the room, followed by a retinue of elegant women and police guards. 'He stood, framed in the entrance … impeccably dressed, surveying the room as if from a great distance utterly indifferent to what he saw … Until he sat down no one else moved. It was odd to see a man seated while women stood.'

Ataturk's reputation was mythic. He was the saviour of his country, and founder of the Republic, a man credited with almost supernatural powers, who slept no more than four hours a night. His voracious appetites were legendary, he could outsmart, outfight, outdrink and outfuck any rival – and he would die of cirrhosis within a year.

On that night Zsa Zsa first glimpsed him. 'I stole a glance at him again. Our eyes met; I felt the blood rush up to my face and I turned swiftly away. Yet I knew what would happen next.'

The next occasion was a few days later when she arrived for the first of what became regular afternoon meetings following her Wednesday lesson at the Riding Academy, at a house he kept expressly for assignations. They never lasted longer than one hour as she had to be home by 5.30.

> In his secret hideaway we were locked in each other's arms, while he dazzled me with his sexual prowess and seduced me with his perversion. Ataturk was very wicked. He knew exactly how to please a young girl... Mesmerised, I complied. He offered me his pipe – I took it. Then he passed me a gold-and-emerald cup... I sipped from the cup... Sometimes I think I was in an opium daze, all I know is that Ataturk, the conqueror of Turkey, the idol of a million women took my virginity.

⁂

When the Second World War broke out in 1939 Zsa Zsa was desperate to escape from her marriage and had determined to join her sister Eva in Los Angeles, where she was unhappily married to an American and under contract to Paramount for $75 a week. Within two months of Zsa Zsa's arrival Eva had left her husband and the sisters were sharing a small house in the Hollywood Hills.

Neither had any money. They lived on the abundant capital of their wits and looks. Both were ultra glamorous, their accent was captivating, and to the sunlit capital of Moviedom they brought an exotic whiff of sophisticated European decadence. Every night they were invited. They slotted deftly into the international A-list, meeting Clark Gable, Douglas Fairbanks, Jack Warner, Louis B. Mayer, David O. Selznick, Cole Porter, Chaplin; also Cary Grant and his wife Barbara Hutton, whom Zsa Zsa would cross with thirteen years later as a rival for Rubirosa.

Among the non-movie 'civilians' she met was Conrad Hilton, the 55-year-old self-made hotel tycoon. 'Ignoring his tacky necktie (with pictures of his three hotels embroidered on it), all I could see was his similarity to Father … he was Father, Ataturk and even more. The words were out before I could stop myself: "I think I'm going to marry you".'

Conrad, married already and a practising Catholic, took it as a joke and roared with laughter. 'Why don't you do that!' he said.

Four months later she did, at Easter 1942. The civil ceremony was conducted by a judge in Santa Fé, New Mexico (both had only just become divorced). Immediately afterward they flew to Chicago, where Conrad was negotiating to buy the Blackstone Hotel. He took Zsa Zsa to view it on the way to where they were to stay for their wedding night.

'I was afraid of Conrad and knew that the main reason he had married me was because I had refused to go to bed with him, that he was obsessed by me and by my body…' Zsa Zsa believed him when he said, 'Anyone who double-crosses me, I kill.' But it would seem the marital transaction went smoothly, 'He was a wonderful lover, virile, well-endowed and masterful.'

Post-coitum, lying beside him, Zsa Zsa gazed into her husband's wide blue eyes and whispered, 'What are you thinking?'

'By golly!' said Conrad, 'I'm thinking of that Blackstone deal.'[†]

⁂

[†]   He later bought the Plaza and the Roosevelt in New York City. Hilton's financing at this time came from Woolworth funds controlled by E. F. Hutton, Barbara's father.

The couple took up residence at Conrad's house in Bel Air. His sons Nicky (sixteen) and Barron (fourteen) shared a separate apartment in one of the wings; the youngest boy, Eric, lived with his mother.

Marriage meant the end to Zsa Zsa's freedom. Conrad was a workaholic, breakfasting at 6 a.m. and flying off to another city to cut a deal at a moment's notice. Arbitrarily she'd be summoned to join him. 'I would be shipped across the country like a piece of Louis Vuitton luggage that its owner had suddenly decided was indispensable and sent for. My own needs were completely ignored; I belonged to Conrad … Conrad, however, did not always want me.'

Money was his god, she says, and not just Catholicism but white supremacy his religion. He struck her as a Nazi. By contrast, he could be both thoughtful and generous. When Zsa Zsa's parents succeeded in escaping Hungary to land in America destitute, he gave them a suite at the Plaza and loaned Jolie the money to open a jewellery shop on Madison Avenue. It proved very successful.

Conrad, the son of immigrant pioneers, who had worked his way up from the most humble of beginnings and was pathologically stingy, remained convinced that Zsa Zsa had married him only for his money. Now he found himself surrounded by an environment of wanton extravagance, shopping, partying and party-giving. This and the fact that, as a divorcée, he could not receive Holy Communion, troubled him greatly. Zsa Zsa was beautiful, charming, funny and possessed of an insouciant recklessness. These were the qualities that attracted him to her. Now, having married her, he followed the pattern of many husbands and set out to change her.

He attempted to limit her spending on clothes. This was entirely unsuccessful. He was irritated, often angry with her, but she could still make him laugh. She wanted a Cadillac convertible, he bought her a Chrysler sedan. Blue, 'the colour of a kitchen stove', she complained. She was an appalling driver, then and always; she could rarely take to the road without causing an accident. She crashed the Chrysler into the rear of the actress Rosemary Lane's car, halted at a stop light. Conrad, who was away on business, was apprised of the accident and sent her a note: 'Is it true that you damaged Rosemary Lane's car?' She replied by return: 'Dear Connie, I never, never damaged Rosemary Lane's car, but if yes let the insurance pay.'

All of Zsa Zsa's nine marriages were contracted so swiftly there was little opportunity to acquaint herself with the groom prior to the event. Now, 'I began to learn more … [Conrad] was not a man to be controlled by a woman, he sought no approval from me; he went his own way. I remembered what Ataturk had told me, "Yes, I divorced my wife. She began questioning me – where I had been, where I was going. I will not be answerable to a woman."' The way Conrad put it was different: 'Don't fence me in,' he told her.

He liked to retire to bed at 9 p.m. Sometimes she would suggest a movie. He'd say, 'I'm tired. Why don't you go with the boys.' She, Nicky and Barron would sit together munching popcorn and candy, then come straight home like three obedient children. The boys disappeared into their apartment; she – at first – went down the long corridor to her husband's room. She learned not to. '"Conrad?" I whispered. There was no answer. I tried the knob – the door was locked.'

She bought a dog for company, a German shepherd that had been mistreated. She lavished love on the beast: 'She would nudge her nose into my palm as though she sensed my loneliness.' At a premiere she met a European producer to whom she felt an instant attraction. She and Eva went to several lunch parties at his beach house and, while casing the joint on the pretext of visiting the bathroom, found a riding whip of beige leather on his dressing table. 'I saw myself turn crimson with shame… This type of man

I knew. One little thing I might say – one word – and he would hate me and beat me. But whatever it was, I understood this man. I knew his reactions, I understood them as he understood mine… But with Conrad I never knew where I was.'

After two years of marriage the couple was still technically together but under stress. Zsa Zsa explains their estrangement as due to the familiar characteristic of alpha-male achievers: their buzz comes from conquest. Having achieved what they want, it loses its appeal and they no longer continue to want it. But in his memoirs Conrad provides a deeper reason for his unhappiness. His failure to obtain a Papal annulment to his first marriage meant that his union with Zsa Zsa was not recognised by the Church. Catholic faith together with the work ethic formed the foundation to his character. Now, though attending church regularly, he was excluded from Mass. 'I stayed on my knees in the pew, chained as it were to the side of my beautiful wife … to be deprived of the sacraments was a price I had not fully understood … I felt adrift, cut off, spiritually forlorn. In the end it was more than I could pay.'

Despite her performance at parties and outward show of bravado, Zsa Zsa was already in a fragile state of mind when a series of mishaps fell upon her. Then she was held up at knifepoint and robbed. While she and Conrad were out, the house in Bel Air caught fire and burnt down. Her dog, locked inside, could be heard howling by the crowd in the street but could not be saved.

She was distraught at the loss. She could not sleep and was prescribed barbiturates. They fogged her brain and slowed her speech. She was prescribed amphetamines to function. They sent her manic. Obtaining a legal separation from Conrad, at Christmas 1944, she quit the marital home to move into a suite on the Plaza in NYC, which she redecorated at a cost of $15,000 (around $250,000 today). She spent $5,000 on a bed reputed to have belonged to

Josephine Bonaparte. Her weight went down to eighty pounds. She bought entire collections of clothes, had a nose job; in El Morocco she slapped the face of the club's owner, John Perona; she woke up one morning to find her step-son, Nicky, sharing her bed. She was sliding further and further out of control and filled with guilt, tormented by her own selfishness. One morning she flung all her jewellery out the window. Conrad had her committed to a sanatorium.

After seven weeks' incarceration, she escaped only with the help of an attorney who obtained a writ of *habeas corpus*. A friend, Hamlin Turner, who'd succeeded in visiting her swore an affidavit:

> She was in shocking physical condition. She'd been brutally assaulted about the face, nose and body; she had been given insulin shock treatments tri-weekly and, as a result of the hypo-dermic injections, she displayed to me two large infected areas on both thighs which resisted healing and which were open and festering.

The writ was sustained by a judge and Zsa Zsa walked free. She was five months pregnant by Conrad when she petitioned for divorce. She was awarded $35,000 in cash and $2,000 per month for ten years, unless she remarried.

The money restored her confidence. Hormonal change brought about by pregnancy lifted her mood and helped her overcome dependency on drugs, which she achieved without therapeu-tic counselling. She possessed the national characteristic of all Hungarians: she was adaptable and resilient, a survivor. Beneath the elaborately confected exterior, she was quite some cookie.

Zsa Zsa's daughter Francesca was born in 1947 into her own trust fund. 'When I held her in my arms it was one of the happiest days I've ever known … when I looked into Francesca's little face I felt complete … All at once there was purpose in my life.'

❦

Six weeks after her daughter's birth, Zsa Zsa spotted George Sanders across the room at a party in the St Regis Hotel. 'Aware that I was dressed to kill, I opted for a spontaneous approach and walked over. I said, "Mr Sanders, I'm madly in love with you."'

Raising a trademark eyebrow he murmured, 'How very well I understand you, my dear.'

He'd won the Academy Award for his performance in *All About Eve*, but he was a character actor before he became a star. Born in Russia, educated at a second-rate English public school, he'd drifted into acting, a profession he despised throughout his career. 'For a time I was considered the ideal actor to play sneering, arrogant, bull-necked Nazi brutes. Nobody, it seems, could enunciate the word *Schweinehund!* quite as feelingly as I.' His first American film was *Lloyds of London*, when 'a major movie villain was born'. In *The Moon and Sixpence*, where he plays a character based on Gauguin, the artist says, 'Women are strange little beasts. You can treat them like dogs, you can beat them until your arm aches, and still they love you. Of course it's an absurd illusion that they have souls.' Women were outraged, which only encouraged him to appropriate the role of a woman-hater. It led him to express extreme attitudes that sound almost quaint today. 'Mr Sanders, what do you think of intellectual women?' *Are there any?* In a notorious interview for *Photoplay* he said, 'Women should remain where they belong, in the boudoir and the parlour. Men should keep women subjugated. When they are subjugated they are happy.' He always acted the same character: the smooth sardonic cad. He had *become* that character and in real life – so far as actors ever inhabit real life – he was always 'in character'. Except, that is, during daily fifty-minute sessions with his analyst, when the mask could be set aside and he might disintegrate into an insecure bundle of raging neuroses spilled across the couch. The session over, he got up, smoothed down his lapels, donned the mask and left, once again an urbane schizo and man of the world.

Zsa Zsa adored indifferent, unapproachable men. 'They were the great challenge of my life.' She and George were married in Las Vegas on 1 April 1949. That evening he admitted, 'I don't know if I can ever make love to you ever again. Yesterday you were the glamorous Mrs Conrad Hilton now you are just plain Mrs George Sanders.' Instead, they spent the night playing chess.

An actor may succeed in remaining in character while in public; it is another matter to maintain the role with a spouse. On their honeymoon in Mallorca George revealed himself to be both jealous and physically abusive. Suspecting Zsa Zsa to be attracted to the guitarist in the hotel band, he created a row in their bedroom, accusing her of having slept with the youth. Grabbing her by the collar of her dress, he hung her out the window demanding she confess.

She was not particularly shocked by the assault; this was the way she expected, even liked, men to behave. Her perception of the event is blithe. 'George pulled me back into the room. I thanked my lucky stars … for the expensive Balenciaga model I was wearing. A cheaper dress might have ripped apart, sending me hurtling into eternity.'

George was not an easy man to live with. He abhorred responsibility, commitment, emotional ties, was happiest alone in his workshop making furniture and inventing gadgets nobody wanted. He was even stingier than Conrad. He moved into her house, where she continued to pay the bills. Though she filled his cigarette case each morning he refused to give her one when she asked. 'I can't afford it, buy your own.'

Moody and difficult, nevertheless he had style. He could be charming, wonderfully witty – and she loved him. And he her, in his fashion. In *Memoirs of a Professional Cad*, he writes:

> Not for her the conventional mask of studied behaviour, she is spontaneous and genuine… No one is a better date than Zsa Zsa. No one is a better companion on a trip even if it involves roughing it… Every age has its Madame Pompadour, its Lady Hamilton, its Queen of Sheba, its Cleopatra, and I wouldn't be surprised if history singles out Zsa Zsa as the Twentieth Century prototype of this exclusive côterie.

In 1951 when George was filming *Ivanhoe* in England, she was invited as guest on a TV show, *Bachelor's Heaven*. Hosted by Tom Conway (George's elder brother) and networked on CBS, it provided advice to viewers on relationship and marriage. The programme went out live in prime time; on the drive to the studio she was shaking with stage fright. Conway tried to calm her, 'Do what you always do, *yak-yak*,' he told her. Gorgeously dressed, sporting a diamond bracelet, with a twenty-carat diamond solitaire ring blazing in the lights, she made her entrance on the set, causing one of the jurors to shade his eyes and let out a whistle. 'Oh darling,' she drawled, 'These are just my *working* diamonds.'

The studio audience cracked up. From that moment she could do no wrong. To a viewer's question, 'I'm breaking my engagement to a very wealthy man. He gave me a beautiful home, a mink coat, diamonds, a stove, and an expensive car. What shall I do?' She answered, 'Give back the stove.' To another, 'Do you think large families are a good idea?' She replied, 'Oh yes. Every woman should have at least three husbands.' Another, 'My husband is a travelling salesman but I know he strays, even when he's home. How can I stop him?' brought the advice, 'Shoot him in the legs.' The audience hooted with laughter, they adored her.

Overnight she became a celebrity. She was booked as a regular on the show, saluted by Winchell, acclaimed by Hedda Hopper and Louella Parsons, the bitch-columnists who both made and destroyed Hollywood reputations. 'I was handed my career on a silver plate.' In fifty minutes she accomplished what her sister Eva had failed to achieve in twelve years.

'Part of me was a woman who wanted to be dominated by a man like George. But now there was also in me a restless, driving, ambitious woman who *had* to have a career.' By the time her husband returned home she was a TV star. Over the next months she played in her first movie, *Lovely To Look At*, and featured on the covers of *Collier's*, *Paris Match*, *Look*, *Picture Post* ... and John Huston cast her for his forthcoming film about Toulouse Lautrec, *Moulin Rouge*...

CHAPTER 9

ZSA ZSA GABOR, NEW YORK CITY, JANUARY 1953

On the morning after *Moulin Rouge*'s premiere, Rubi rises from Zsa Zsa's bed at 6 a.m., whispers, 'You'll hear from me, *mon amour*,' and goes through into his own suite to get ready to fly to the Dominican Republic with his President, Trujillo.

Zsa Zsa says, 'In the morning I knew that I never wanted to leave him again. I was madly in love with George, but after one night with Rubi I lost all sense of reality. He was exciting, sensual, passionate, primitive yet incredibly sophisticated...'

Later that same day she takes the train to Philadelphia, first city in a coast-to-coast tour promoting *Moulin Rouge*. On checking into her hotel, she is handed two cables. One reads, I MISS YOU TERRIBLY. I LOVE YOU I LOVE YOU. GEORGE. The other is from his Hollywood agent: IMPORTANT YOU GO SOONEST ROME. GEORGE UNHAPPY NEEDS YOU DESPERATELY. 'If George was not psychic, I have no other way to account for it,' she says.

Stricken by remorse, Zsa Zsa cancels the scheduled tour despite the damage to her career, and flies obediently to Italy. On arrival in Rome, she soothes George, who is in a highly agitated state due to problems with his director, Rossellini, who expects him to improvise his scenes; he's at a loss without scripted dialogue. He's seriously unnerved. 'Don't leave me,' he begs her. She promises not to, she truly loves him.

Their reconciliation is destroyed by another cable. Addressed to Zsa Zsa, this is delivered to their room by a bellboy. George snatches it from him, saying, 'There should be no secrets between a husband and wife.' Watching Zsa Zsa's face while he does so, he opens the envelope with sadistic deliberation – the scene could have been scripted for him. He reads the text aloud: 'No word from you. Miss and love you much. Wire me 46 Rue de Bellechasse. Rubi.'

Flustered, she protests, 'George, it doesn't mean anything. It's over.'

He tosses the cable at her in disdain, 'Rubirosa,' he sneers. 'What a conquest. You must reply, my dear.'

'No!' She's panic-stricken. 'It's over, I'm finished with him.'

'That would not be courteous. You must answer.'

'Oh no, no!' she begs him.

'Then I will,' he says.

On the back of the form he prints: MON CHERI I LOVE YOU AND CANNOT WAIT TO SEE YOU AGAIN. ZSA ZSA. He gives it to the bellboy to dispatch.

❧

Zsa Zsa writes,

> I meant it when I said I was finished with Rubi. I was not yet deeply involved … I fought again and again to free myself. I needed George to help keep me away from Rubi; and George,

for whatever complex, self-punishing, self-mocking reasons, was throwing me into Rubi's arms.

Only a few days later Zsa Zsa is offered a part in a movie about to start filming in Paris with the donkey-faced comedian, Fernandel, then at the height of his popular success. She hears the news by telephone, then hurries to tell George, who is seated on the hotel terrace among a group of men including John Huston.

George tells her, 'Don't take it, my dear. Stay here with me.'

Huston turns on him, 'But this is a terrific break for her. You're not going to stop her, are you?'

Zsa Zsa writes, 'Suddenly I was sick of being toyed with. "No," I said. "He won't stop me."'

When she lands at Orly a week later, Rubi is at the airport to meet her.

Rubi and Zsa Zsa

She lives at the Plaza Athénée while filming, but spends almost every night with Rubi at his house in Rue Bellechasse. In this opulent residence Rubi is attended by his giant Russian valet (who also serves as sparring partner), an Iberian chef, and two Spanish maids dressed in white aprons and lace caps. The house is opulently decorated and furnished and everywhere are trophies to Rubi's sporting success: silver cups gained in fencing, at polo, and in the Ferrari and Mercedes he races on European and South American circuits. Discreetly absent are photographs of the women he has won, he is no braggart about his conquests.

How do you explain Rubi… What is his appeal? Zsa Zsa asks. She goes on to provide the answer, 'He is everything a woman can want in a man – if she does not think, if she asks herself no questions of today or tomorrow. He is all male … thinking of you always as a woman to be taken and possessed and kept away from all other men because, being so feminine and desirable, you are their natural prey… He knows what goes on in your mind every moment – he has the instinct of a wild animal to sense your every mood.'

She says,

> We were like two children: pleasure-seeking, hedonistic, perhaps spoiled and selfish, but full of an unquenchable lust for life and an insatiably strong appetite for excitement. For Rubi and I both suffered from the same curse … we were too greedy for life and too greedy for each other. Rubi understood me … which made him irresistible … He was like a sickness to me.

During the months that follow Zsa Zsa swings between the two men in her life. 'I found myself rushing from George to Rubi –

tears in my eyes because I was leaving my husband; then, a few weeks later, rushing from Rubi back to George – tears in my eyes because I was leaving Rubi.'

> On the one hand there was my husband – indifferent, supercili-
> ous, and hurting me more than anyone knew… Then there was
> Rubi, one of the most jealous men I ever met. He resented even
> the time it took me to go to the powder room. After George's
> take-it-or-leave-it attitude, Rubi was a gift sent from heaven to
> make me feel a woman again.

Why do women marry shits? Although they became fiancés, Zsa Zsa never married him but her reasons for hanging out with this particular shit are compelling on an emotional scale. However it is not long before she encounters the violence in Rubi's nature. The two are dining out with the couturier Genevieve Fath and her lover, a Portuguese prince. Afterwards, Rubi drops them off outside Genevieve's house, where Zsa Zsa kisses the prince goodnight too warmly for Rubi's taste. As the couple go toward the front door, he turns on her and slaps her around the face. She screams … Genevieve runs back and helps her out the car and into the house. Rubi drives off with a squeal of tyres.

Genevieve is outraged – 'How can he do this to you?' – and wants to call the police. She cleans up Zsa Zsa's bloody face, while the victim begs her not to and dissuades the prince from going after Rubi to kill him. The three are still absorbed in the drama when the front doorbell rings.

> It was three in the morning. Genevieve … begged me not to let
> him in. But I had no choice. Rubi owned me, I had lost my will,

I was a part of him and no longer belonged to myself… He knelt in front of me and asked for my forgiveness. Then the next minute we were making love…

In the autumn of that year George Sanders files for divorce.

CHAPTER 10

BARBARA HUTTON
DEAUVILLE, AUGUST 1953

The day sparkles bright, the warm breeze smells of the sea. The sun shines on fresh green turf and crisply laundered young men, glossy ponies and the colourful clothes of the spectators as Barbara Hutton, wearing a Chanel suit, wide-brimmed hat and very dark glasses, watches her son Lance playing polo this summer afternoon in Deauville. She looks delicate, even fragile; what you can see of her face is wan. She has been named one of the ten best-dressed women in the world, her suit comes from this spring's collection, yet she does not seem really to be a part of the animated crowd talking and laughing in the stand. There is a separateness about her as she sits with her stoned gaze turned toward the game, glassed-off, composed and still. Calm – as she can be when the mix of speed, barbiturates, codeine and alcohol circulating in her bloodstream is exactly right. She is in Deauville because of Lance, she is performing her duty as a mother. This is his summer vacation. While with her here he is studying for his college entrance – that anyway is the theory. Aged sixteen, blond, burly-handsome, owner of a sports coupé and already dating starlets, he is aiming to be a racing driver. What need has he for academic qualifications?

Barbara Hutton © Press Association

Deauville is a favoured stopover for the international set in season. The town has classy chic and a handful of good hotels, but bars and nightclubs are few. Lance has with him his roommate Leland Rosenberg, and one evening while the two are trawling this limited circuit they are befriended by a stranger here to compete in the international polo tournament; indeed his team is favoured to win the Coupe d'Or prize. And not exactly a stranger, for though the boys haven't met him before they well know who he is. They have watched him playing and are aware of his reputation, as is anyone who reads a newspaper.

Rubi is now forty-four, and for a couple of teenagers hanging out in a bar to be picked up by a well-known (and unequivocally heterosexual) playboy who is a six-handicap polo player, boxer, fencer, racing driver and lover of famous women (including currently the showgirl Zsa Zsa Gabor, with him in Deauville) who buys them drinks, listens to what they have to say and treats them as equals is an exhilarating and flattering experience. They are at the heart of the action in a sexy adult milieu.

Leland Rosenberg, who is unrich and hasn't been around so much as Lance, is particularly warmed by Rubirosa's friendship. And friendship it seems to be not merely a casual encounter, for next day, by pure chance – oh yes? – Leland runs into Rubi again, who is as amiable as the night before. They chat. Rubi gives good chat, he causes the sixteen-year-old to feel hip and experienced as himself as he speaks about a world the boy has glimpsed through Lance but which otherwise is unknown to him. Leland is thrilled by the lifestyle Rubi reveals and especially impressed by his casual mention of the people he mixes with: Errol Flynn, Sinatra, Dean Martin, Aly Khan, King Farouk, the Kennedys, the Citroëns, the Rothschilds, the Peróns… It sounds to Leland the sort of life he'd like to lead himself.

And then, as though the notion has just occurred to him, Rubi mentions how curiously opportune it is that he and Leland should encounter each other so fortuitously when they are in a position to perform a personal service for one another. Lightly but quite specifically he proposes a devil's contract. He will sponsor the young man as a protégé in that glitzy world he knows; Leland's part in the deal is to set up a date for him with Barbara Hutton.

⚜

Barbara had been launched upon the world aged eighteen at her debut ball in December 1930, one year after the Wall Street Crash. A blizzard was howling down Madison Avenue that evening, snatching at the clothes of poorly dressed people, most of them women, who stood in a crowd of several thousand outside the entrance to the Ritz-Carlton hotel. It was the worst winter in America anyone had known. In Manhattan a third of the city's working population was unemployed. Banks had failed, factories closed, dockyards shut down; farms had been repossessed across the country and families evicted from their homes. In bleak city streets men with slack expressionless faces shivered in soup-lines in the bitter cold while old women bundled up against the driving snow grubbed for food in garbage cans.

This was a singular moment to choose to throw so magnificent a party, or one so conspicuously visible. Black limousines coasted through the slush-covered Madison Avenue to draw up before the Ritz-Carlton, as police held back the crowd. Men in tailcoats partnered by women in ball gowns stepped from the cars onto the red carpet which led into the building. The guests were a pampered bunch accustomed to the best, yet many would recall this evening as the most spectacular junket they had ever attended. The shouting and abuse which greeted them on arrival was upsetting, of course, but their disquiet lasted only for an instant before it was magicked away by the hallucinatory impact of the domain they had stepped into. Father Christmas was there to welcome them – Maurice Chevalier inside the scarlet tunic. Costumed dwarfs swarmed merrily around his thighs, distributing small gold caskets containing a diamond, emerald or ruby as amuse-bouches to set the tone. And then the guests moved on...

It was like entering an enchanted forest, a scene from fairy-tale. Teams of men had been working in shifts day and night to transform the hotel into a winter wonderland. Snow lay deep upon the ground but it wasn't the sort to make your feet wet. The air was warm and fragrant with perfume and cigarette smoke, and the strains of dance music drifted from the ballroom which was roofed by a sky of dark blue gauze glittering with stars and a lustrous moon. There were four orchestras, 1,000 guests and – though this was Prohibition and America was dry – 2,000 bottles of champagne.

In the storm of real snow outside, a Cadillac limousine emerged from the murk to pull up at the kerb. The crowd stirred, pressing closer to the barriers while those in front fought to keep their position. A doorman opened the car's door and a girl emerged wearing a fur coat over her white silk dress, a plump blonde kewpie doll with pink cheeks and big curiously blank blue eyes. For a moment the crowd fell silent at the sight of her, then as she started up the red carpet came the first catcall to cue the jeering and abuse that accompanied her walk into the hotel as the photographers ducked and crouched, firing off their pictures while the mob shrieked insults and waved their fists.

This was Barbara Hutton's introduction to the public; its response to her was established then. Here was the image, with various shadings, that would remain with her all her life. It was celebrity for sure, but in the guise of infamy. To achieve public fame through admiration and love takes time, hatred delivers the goods on the nose.

She was cast in melodrama while still an infant, and it was the press who cast her. Her mother Edna had been driven to frenzy by her husband's flagrant infidelity, over the years her humiliation had grown unbearable. The terminal insult came when a photograph of Franklyn appeared in the New York *Sun*. Snapped at a party, he was dancing with his latest flame, the Swedish actress Monica von Fursten. Edna dressed carefully for her parting gesture, then swallowed strychnine. She was wearing a white lace dress and a double strand of pearls when her body was found sprawled on the red carpet of the family suite at the Plaza Hotel. The one to find her was her daughter Barbara. She was four years old.

Such was, such is, the power of vast wealth, there followed no autopsy, no inquest, no stories in the press beyond the bare announcement of her passing and the coroner's verdict: cerebral thrombosis. Barbara was sent to live at Grandpa Woolworth's gloomy country house on Long Island, from which a car drove her every morning to school in Manhattan where she made friends with Doris Duke, the same age as her, whose future life would intersect often with her own. But at weekends and on vacation Barbara had no friend. The sombre mansion echoed with the sound of organ music as Grandpa crouched at his Wurlitzer flashing with coloured lights, playing up a storm while Grandma rocked in her chair, lost to the world and mewing softly in the fog of dementia.

Grandpa was the workaholic farm boy who had opened America's first 5-cent store with $400 worth of borrowed goods. At his death Barbara's share of the estate was $28 million (equivalent to $400 million today) when she inherited it, aged twelve. The money was held in a trust fund administered by her father until she was twenty-one. She was enrolled in a boarding school in northern California. 'She was a lovely little girl,' her school house-mother recalls, 'but she just never seemed to have a chance. She had so much money but no one to guide or listen to her. She was lonely and very shy... No one ever came to see her at the school, not even at Christmas.' After one year there she was taken in by her rackety Aunt Jessie Donahue (her mother's sister) and her hard-drinking husband. They had two sons around her own age, one of them, Jimmy, who became her dangerous lifelong playmate.

At her new boarding school in Connecticut other girls were distrustful of her aloofness and expensive clothes. It took her a while to identify the barrier that separated her from other people. 'Can't we give it all away?' she asked her father but was told that was not possible. Even before his remarriage she saw him rarely. Their encounters were fraught with bullying incomprehension on his part, and on hers naked hostility. She could not forgive him for her mother's death; she hated him and wanted to make him suffer. And she would.

The Donahues, with whom Barbara was billeted during vacations, were – thanks to Grandpa Woolworth – good and loaded. Life with them was untrammelled by restraint, and Barbara's adolescence accustomed her to luxury and a habit of travel which would remain with her always. At the age of seventeen she was in Biarritz with her father's friends the Fiskes when she first came to the notice of the notorious fixer and publicist Elsa Maxwell. Barbara was discarded as inadequate material. 'I saw a short, plump girl whose hands and feet were too small for a rather clumsy body and whose dress was a trifle too tight.' Another acquaintance of the time describes her as a 'butterball'.

Biarritz then was a resort as fashionable as Cannes, the smart set was there in force. Despite her inarticulacy, awkwardness and shyness, Barbara was invited to lunches and parties. At one of these she ran into a man she knew. Prince Alexis Mdivani was a polo-playing adventurer engaged to her friend Louise van Alen. Barbara had been writing to him throughout the past year, pouring out her feelings, her hopes, her fears. 'And I had the most wonderful letters from him. There wasn't even the suggestion of a love affair … he was in love with Louise. But he made himself the only person I could trust with my thoughts. He was kind, he was gentle, and he listened to me without being bored…' Alex wasn't in the least bored. He was about to get married, but heiresses were his revealed vocation and Barbara was an investment.

She and Tiki, her maid, left Biarritz to join Franklyn and her stepmother Irene at the Carlton in Cannes. There she lost her virginity to the tennis coach. 'It was my first experience with a man who devoured me… It is like being captured and drained. It is not altogether pleasant, and it certainly isn't very graceful.' Back in New York at the end of summer Franklyn hired a bodyguard to watch over his increasingly wayward daughter. She seduced the man. 'He was rampant as a bull… We made love repeatedly for hours. I was black and blue and torn and tattered and covered with stickiness.' By telling her stepmother Barbara made sure her father got to know of it. 'At first he said nothing at all to me, he just looked at me as if I were an insect of some kind. Then he wanted to know if I'd ever been with a man before, and of course I lied and said I hadn't. "Why a security guard?" he said. "Why not a chimney sweep or a garbage collector or the husband of the chambermaid? You have such elegant taste, my dear."'

One day Barbara went into a music store on 57th Street to choose some gramophone records. A young clerk came up to serve her. The selection and purchase of the discs involved a few minutes of talk at the end of which Barbara asked, 'Tell me, what do people like you do when you go out in the evening?'

The clerk, who had recognised her, was outraged by such conde-scension. But he was trained for deference and answered in a tight voice, 'Well, we do what most ordinary people do. We can't afford to go to the Central Park Casino, but we go to smaller places we know, and we dance and walk through Central Park.'

But it was clear that he was angry. 'Don't be cross, please,' Barbara said, 'I really wanted to know. I've got a date with a young man who works in a garage, and he doesn't know who I am. I just honestly wanted to know what to say when he asks me what I want to do tonight. That's all.'

She had no understanding at all of the real world. How could she, she'd never lived in it. The only advice she received was from her father – a toxic source she automatically rejected. Yet the media's treatment of her from the start must have taught her something. If she had wished, her debut at the Ritz-Carlton could have been staged elsewhere, at very least could have been cloaked by discretion and some restraint as was Doris Duke's. No – she wanted it how it was, and she must not only have foreseen the consequences but *chosen* them. She *invited* punishment: *smack me, I'm bad!*

That December evening in 1930, when she reigned as princess over the enchanted winter wonderland while a shivering mob shrieked abuse in the trampled slush outside, made news. Barbara was a story, and from that moment the press would not leave her alone. She would spend the rest of her life exposed to public view, she would never have privacy. She had become a symbol of riches, self-indulgence and excess, an image calibrated to make people detest her. And – here was the wonder of it, the modern marvel – all this plus the emotion it aroused *could be conveyed in a newspaper photograph*. The caption below it was hardly necessary, merely an add-on to the established story.

Most articles written about Barbara then and later were hostile. Yet because of the extravagance of her behaviour and opulence of her settings these pieces had an undertone of unwilling awe. Her life looked and sounded so very glamorous. She thought it so herself when reading of it. Despite the cruel remarks some journalists made about her, she found the attention profoundly gratifying. She'd never received attention from her father or anyone else while growing up, never been acknowledged or listened to; never had the chance to develop her identity through relationship with others. Now she had found these opportunities with the press. She recognised that the woman who lived so fully on the page was *her*.

Celebrity is a drug. For some, the first line sets the taste. It was so for Barbara. In the months that followed she acquired an addiction contracted by all who yearn for publicity, the taste for a transaction giving both pleasure and torment but without which they do not, cannot live. Hurt comes with the experience, anger, shame, the pain of denial and suffering of withdrawal, yet an addict will *always* pay the price. It is better to be written about with malice than not at all.

She loved to see her photograph and read about herself; it confirmed her identity – *that* was the person she was. She needed an audience in order properly to exist; the spotlight of public attention transfigured her. She was – she remains still – an archetype of value-free celebrity, famous not for any accomplishment but simply for being *there*. Celebrity was her destiny … and, despite the competition, she will become one of its most spectacular global casualties.

CHAPTER 11

BARBARA HUTTON, DEAUVILLE, 1953

I t is 2.30 a.m. on a summer morning in Deauville and Barbara Hutton is asleep alone in her suite in the Hotel Normandie, overlooking the sea.

The small dinner party set up by Leland Rosenberg duly has taken place two days ago, where Porfirio Rubirosa was seated next to Barbara. She's met him before when he was married to Doris Duke, but never alone – Doris was quite careful of that. She knows a lot about him, as does everyone, from her daily study of newspapers, magazines and gossip columns. He's recently featured as co-respondent in two high-profile divorces, in one of which Barbara's earlier suitor Robert Sweeny cited him in his split from Joanne Connelly, the Texas Oil heiress. Barbara is also well aware that Rubi has had affairs with Tina Onassis, Eva Perón, Joan Crawford, Jayne Mansfield and Marilyn Monroe, and is currently involved in a tempestuous romance with Zsa Zsa Gabor. What she does not know is that the adverse publicity resulting from the two divorces and his own from Doris Duke has so displeased President Trujillo that once again he's fired Rubi from his diplomatic post and cut off his salary. He's unemployed, low on funds and operating on credit.

Barbara finds Rubi to be charming and attentive; he demonstrates an almost feminine sensibility. He gives no sign of the flamboyant party animal he is reputed to be, instead shows himself quiet and solicitous. He makes no move on her but remains faultless in consideration and, rather irritatingly, in restraint.

Barbara always sleeps poorly and never without pills. It is so tonight, but in the early hours of the morning the sound of pounding music seeps through her stupor to rouse her. Groggily she comes awake – and the music is still there, loud and raucous with a driving beat. Irritated, puzzled, at last she is impelled to get out of the bed, go to the French window and step out on her balcony to establish its origin.

On the night-time promenade above the beach and expanse of moonlit sea, a mariachi band is grouped beneath her window. Extravagantly costumed as Mexican bandits and fired up on tequila, its membership is swollen by a handful of revellers in evening dress, including Baron Elie de Rothschild, dragged on from the same nightclub as the band. Guitars, bongo drums and castanets are pounding out a deafening rhythm, disrupting the tranquillity of the dormant town, and every window in the hotel is occupied by bewildered guests staring down at the disturbance. The upturned faces of the rackety group below show ghost white in the lamplight, all raised toward Barbara upon her balcony. At their centre stands the figure of Rubi, arms spread wide, serenading her in full-throated song.

By the extravagance of the gesture he wins her fragile heart and spell of tenure in her bed plus, quite soon, her hand in marriage.

Zsa Zsa Gabor has left Deauville to return to Los Angeles, and during the nights that follow Barbara comes to know full well the subject of Doris Duke's incautious boast, confided while married to him:

> He loves to please women, because by pleasing them he pleases himself. He is the ultimate sorcerer ... priapic, indefatigable, grotesquely proportioned. His lovemaking secret is that he practises an Egyptian technique called *Imsak*. No matter how aroused he becomes, he doesn't allow himself to complete the act. What he enjoys about it is the sense of control he achieves over his own body while exciting the woman beyond control, beyond the threshold...

To be led by the sorcerer into fairyland always has formed Barbara's escape, though even with the aid of drugs, that elusive destination has been proving ever harder to achieve of late. Now, in a troubled time, here it is delivered to her. She's gained the world's most notorious lover and to compound her satisfaction her triumph is not private – when it would have meant little – but shared with the press. Their liaison is reported in countless column inches and she, that legend known as Barbara Hutton – aged forty-one but in appearance a raddled fifty – is back where she belongs on the front page of the tabloids.

❧

She had continued to receive unremitting press coverage ever since her debut. Her conspicuous extravagance made her loathed throughout America. On her twenty-first birthday she would come into $40 million, but until then her fortune was controlled by her father, Franklyn. Famous she might be, but the situation was frustrating.

THE IRRESTIBLE MR WRONG

In the summer of 1932 she was staying in the Paris Ritz with Franklyn and her stepmother, Irene. She had her own entourage, a chauffeur and bodyguard (both her fathers' spies), a footman, and her loyal maid Tiki. She had her own Rolls-Royce fitted out in rosewood and ivory, but she was not free. Franklyn watched over her, suspicious as a surly guard dog. He was especially suspicious of Alex Mdivani, of all the tribe of Mdivanis in Paris at that time. Father had served the Tsar as a cavalry officer; after the revolution the family escaped from Georgia to become refugees in Paris. They made it onward to America where Mother unhesitatingly registered with Immigration as Princess Mdivani. Her three sons registered as Princes, the two daughters as Princesses, but Father refused to play in the charade. He is quoted as saying, 'I'm the only man who ever inherited a title from his children.'

The siblings were close and Roussie was the brains, unscrupulous, manipulative and utterly without principle. Glamorous too, with sculpted cheekbones and bobbed black hair. A dark androgynous beauty, she could have been a boy. Striking to meet, but you sensed the vividness to be a façade, there was something hidden about her. Her brother Prince Serge married the film star Pola Negri, dumping her when she lost her fortune in the Wall Street Crash. Prince David wed the actress Mae Murray, relieving her of $3 million. Princess Nina married a lawyer specialising in pre-nuptial agreements and divorce, conveniently for all. And Prince Alexis had by now married Louise van Alen. An heiress related to the Astors and Vanderbilts, she gave him a string of polo ponies and a Rolls-Royce as wedding gifts. She was rich, but by the Mdivanis's exacting standards, not *very* rich.

In Paris Roussie set up Barbara from the start. She accompanied her mark shopping, helped her choose clothes. She offered understanding and warmth to a vulnerable girl, who was unused to both.

She became her confidante, learning her tastes and hopes and fears – then passing these on to Alex. His courtship was based on the best of information. Based also on cold-blooded sexual skill – he was immensely attractive to women. Barbara was strongly drawn to him yet did not want to betray her childhood friend Louise. But her conscience was at war with her taste for drama. A man who knew her well says, 'Barbara's interest ... was aroused by his marriage to Louise van Alen. If a man was available and offered no resistance, she lost interest ... If she saw something she wanted, she went after it.'

Alex's continuing flirtation with Barbara was galling to Louise, but she kept her cool with admirable restraint. Louise said nothing, continuing to sign the cheques funding her and Alex's extended honeymoon. But her relationship with Barbara was no longer warm.

In July 1932 Barbara was a guest of Roussie and her huband Sert at Mas Juny, the castle they had restored on the Costa Brava. Alex and Louise were members of the same house party. One day, after lunch on the shaded terrace, the clan dispersed to the poolside or their rooms to take a siesta. A couple of hours later Roussie rounded up her guests for a drive to Barcelona. As a group they strolled across the lawn to Barbara's guest cottage to collect her. Carolling blithely, Roussie threw open the door and led them in. Barbara and Alex were surprised naked in each other's arms. Or rather Barbara was though not Alex, for the scenario had been scripted by Roussie and himself. By the end of the year Alex and Louise were legally separated and Nina's husband was busy negotiating Alex's $2 million divorce settlement.

Now that he was available Barbara wasn't sure she wanted him. He arrived in New York to press his claim and presented himself at 1020 Fifth Avenue to call on Franklyn Hutton. He was made to wait. When Franklyn stomped into the room he cut short Alex's civilities to demand, 'What do you want?'

'Your daughter,' Alex answered. Barbara maintained that it was the only honest thing he'd ever said.

She played hard to get, taking off for the Far East with Tiki and a couple of friends. Seeing the quarry escaping him, Alex hurried to Roussie. His pay-off from Louise had not yet come through and he was low on funds; she staked him to the chase. Alex was lying in wait for Barbara in Thailand, when the liner docked.

Franklyn Hutton was in his office in New York when he received the radiotelephone call from the American Consul in Bangkok. 'Sorry to trouble you,' the man said, 'but your daughter is here and wants me to marry her to a Prince Mdivani. She is under age and needs your consent.'

Franklyn exploded, demanding to speak to Barbara. Instead he got Alex on the line who, still smarting from his treatment in New York, issued an ultimatum: he would marry Barbara without consent unless Franklyn announced his daughter's engagement and the family's plans for a full-scale public wedding. That same evening Alex dispatched a cable to Roussie in Paris, HAVE WON THE PRIZE. ANNOUNCE BETROTHAL.

The couple were married in a civil ceremony in Paris. This was followed by an elaborate religious wedding at the Russian Orthodox Cathedral attended by reporters, photographers and a crowd of 8,000, most of them young women hysterical with excitement.

The incomprehensible ceremony at the Russian Cathedral was followed by a launch party at the Ritz where an extra suite had been rented to display the couple's wedding gifts, many of which turned out to have been charged to Barbara's petty cash account at the hotel. They left for their honeymoon from St Lazare station accompanied by seventy pieces of luggage, each embossed with a gold crown and identified as belonging to Prince or Princess Mdivani. What happened next Barbara related to several people – but only long after the event.

Understandably so, it is not a wedding-night admission any twenty-year-old bride would be greedy to confess. It seems that in their sleeping compartment a bottle of chilled champagne stood open and Barbara had changed into a ravishing satin and lace negligee which Roussie Sert had helped her choose ... when Alexis sat down at the foot of the bed and looked her over coolly. 'Barbara,' he said, 'You're too fat.'

It is hardly surprising the remark had a traumatic effect upon her, she was devastated by it. From that moment she went on a crash diet of black coffee, cigarettes and RyKrisps which she kept to almost with variation to the end of her life. It changed her personality and wrecked her health, but it sure worked. Two months later she weighed 100 pounds and was described by Elsa Maxwell as having transformed herself into 'an astonishing exotic beauty (her husband, however, is still the same queer, ambitious, reckless character he was when married to his first wife)'.

Barbara came into the independence and freedom from her father's restraint she so long had craved – and remade herself. 'It's going to be fun being a Princess,' she told reporters. Princess and Prince Mdivani were a gift to the press. What media and public required of her was performance. It came easily to her. She and Alexis acquired an entourage of secretaries, valets, maids, chauffeurs, and set out to replicate the Grand Tour in style. They travelled – to Lake Como, Florence, Venice, Rome, Morocco, Turkey. On arrival they rented a house or a floor of the best hotel, and gave parties. It was high season, the best people were in situ and in every destination they stepped into the heart of the action.

Indeed they *were* the action, young, beautiful, excessive and inordinately rich. Alex when he wasn't sulking was delightfully high-spirited and charming; Barbara, unshackled and liberated, proved herself a brilliant hostess and extravagantly imaginative as a party-giver. They were a dazzling couple who received all the attention their looks and activities deserved.

Each morning the day's papers and periodicals were served to them with breakfast and they scanned their notices. In the US media their publicity continued scathing, but there was a lot of it. The tone in the continental press was different. The Depression lay over Europe in a stagnant cloud, shutting out the sun. In this grey world of troubled people these photographs, reports and newsreels depicted a pageant remote as fairyland yet answering to a need to believe that fairytale was real. Among the masses whose lives amounted to nothing the adventures of the Princess and her Prince were absorbing as a hit movie.

⚜

In November 1933 Barbara became twenty-one, gaining control of her fortune of $50 million (worth at least $1 billion today). She tipped her father $5 million in recognition for the way he had managed her capital, gave a million to charity – which received no acknowledgement in the press – and $1.25 million to Alexis, who had already received a dowry of a million on marrying her plus an allowance of $50,000 a year.

Alex was sitting pretty but the New Year started badly for his brothers Prince David and Prince Serge, who were charged with embezzlement and larceny in connection with an oil promotion fraud. Their wives Mae Murray and Mary McCormic (both of whom they were in the process of divorcing) had with other investors put up capital to found the Pacific Oil Company. Oil had been struck and the company was showing promise as a legitimate enterprise but the temptation to rob it blind had proved irresistible. 'The Mdivanis are suave and cosmopolitan,' said Mary McCormic 'But the Asiatic male regards himself above all as a male and his wife as a slave. When I married Serge the continental veneer soon wore off...' As it did from Prince David. In her divorce from him, Mae Murray testified that among other indignities she'd been socked in the face, locked up and raped. The poor woman ended up penniless, sleeping on a bench in Central Park.

The Mdivani trial promised to be messy. To escape involvement Barbara recruited her prankster cousin Jimmy Donahue and took off for Japan, with Alexis travelling separately in a false name, pursued by a bailiff with a subpoena as witness to the fraud. When husband and wife were reunited in Tokyo it is testimony to Barbara's by now international renown that they were provided with motor cycle escorts, given a royal welcome and entertained to lunch by the Emperor. At a press conference she mentioned her plan to adopt a Chinese baby during the trip because 'the Chinese have such a long and honourable civilisation'. As Japan was about to go to war with China, the remark did not go down well, nevertheless the hotel was besieged by thousands of women trying to sell her their children and had to be cordoned off by the police for five days.

Deciding against a baby, Barbara shopped extravagantly instead, while Alexis tagged along, missing polo. The party travelled on to India where they stayed with a series of maharajahs, one of whom maintained his own polo stadium. He was a man Alex could relate to and they became instant playmates. Barbara missed her husband not at all. Boredom, a disease she'd contracted young, had become a chronic affliction. She'd obtained Alex, found him to be a disappointing, unamusing match, and tired of him. There was no bond to repair, for no bond beyond desire had existed. Anyway, to Barbara it was unthinkable to *work* on a relationship, it was simpler to bin it and pick the next.

She had her interests, and Jimmy was better company. Alexis already bored her. A few months later, in Venice, she gave him a fourteenth-century palazzo on the Grand Canal as a pay-off but, irritatingly, he didn't see it that way and dug in stubbornly. She became detached, cold, barely polite, but he was tenacious. So she had to make it clear, not just to him but to the world, that the marriage was over. She threw a party for 2,000 guests at the Paris Ritz to celebrate her twenty-second birthday. Jack Harris's orchestra was flown in from London, as were the Yacht Club Boys from the US and Hoagy Carmichael, the world's most celebrated jazz pianist. Three chartered airplanes shuttled in the guests from all over.

At the white-tie dinner before the ball, Barbara's guest of honour, seated to her right, was a stranger with a lean aristocratic face and noble profile. There was avid speculation on who he was – no one seemed to know. When the music started Barbara led him onto the floor to dance. Alex, seated at another table, watched. All watched. The number ended, but the couple remained on the floor to dance the next. They danced together all that night while Alex, unable to keep still, paced behind the tables, his face contorted in fury.

Newspapers reporting on the party next day listed the names of the Beautiful People who had attended, identifying the guest of honour who had been so signally favoured as the forty-year-old Count Kurt Haugwitz-Reventlow. It was clear to her public that a new chapter in Barbara's life had opened.

The party of six and their mountain of luggage occupied a private coach hitched to the rear of the German train, which had been booked in the name of Count and Countess Haugwitz-Reventlow.

It was the summer of 1935 and, two weeks before, Barbara had divorced Alex in Reno in a ceremony taking eleven minutes that cost $100,000. Her testimony stated: 'When I got married I had no conception of love. A strong desire for independence from my family was the main reason I married Prince Mdivani. I realised it was a mistake even before the wedding ... he married me only for my money...' Unlike most divorce statements, it was an accurate characterisation of the facts. Her marriage to Count Reventlow took place the next day at 8 a.m. attended by twenty-four armed special deputies and a scratch mob of bleary-eyed pressmen who had succeeded in making it to Nevada in time for the 'secret ceremony'. 'Now at last I have found happiness,' Barbara told them. 'My search is ended. I know this is safe and sure.'

Soon after the ceremony the happy couple (plus the ever-faithful Tiki, her secretary, Reventlow's valet, and the gay jester Jimmy Donahue) sailed for Europe, where they transferred to the chartered railroad car in which they were now crossing Germany, headed for Denmark and Reventlow's family castle where they would spend their honeymoon. Their train stopped for a few minutes at a country station and, soon after, Reventlow glanced up to see a stranger beckoning him from the door of the compartment. Identifying himself as a Reuters reporter, the man showed him a press bulletin. Reventlow read it, digested the news, and took the message to his wife. 'Barbara,' he said, 'it's Alex Mdivani. He had a bad accident. Alex is dead.'

Alex's two-year marriage to Barbara had netted him rich rewards: a palazzo in Venice, a Rolls-Royce, a speedboat, a string of polo ponies and $3 million in cash. After she'd dismissed him he'd taken up with Maud, the beautiful wife of Baron Heinrich von Thyssen, the armaments and steel tycoon. He brought her to stay at his sister Roussie Sert's house in Spain. The two set out to return in Alex's Rolls. He was gunning the big car at 80 mph when outside Gerona something caused him to swerve. The Rolls struck the verge, lifted off and slammed into a tree, coming to rest upside down. Alex was decapitated and Maud Thyssen mangled and unconscious when they pried her from the wreckage.

Roussie Sert was first to hear of the accident. Jumping into her car she raced the thirty miles to Gerona, there to find the headless body of her adored brother sprawled on the hay in a peasant's cart. Maud Thyssen was badly smashed up and lost an eye. When she came to in hospital she asked for the suitcase she'd had with her, which contained $180,000 worth of jewellery. It was never recovered.

Roussie was devastated by Alex's death. They were partners in transgression, she never recovered from the horror of his end. Barbara's affection for her wanton husband was long gone, but his violent end cast a shadow on her arrival at Castle Hardenberg. Reventlow's brother Heinrich was there to welcome them to the ancestral pile, installing the just-married couple in the master bedroom which he had vacated for their greater comfort. Of which there were not that many signs, Barbara observed.

For American heiresses to acquire a European title and live in an ancestral castle had been seen as a desirable move since the Belle Époque, denoting a significant step upward into a more aristocratic level of society. At this time there were many impoverished aristos with holes in their socks and a decaying residence falling to ruin on an encumbered continental estate. Marriage suited both partners, who fully understood the terms of the contract between them. The American Dorothy di Frasso, a close friend of Barbara's then and later, wed the penniless but amiable Count Carlo, thirty years her senior, then spent the million or two dollars necessary to restore his sixteenth-century ancestral mansion outside Rome so that the dining room could accommodate a couple of hundred, and launched herself as an A-list international hostess. One of her frequent guests was Mussolini, which caused the FBI to run a file on her. 'She is notorious for her nymphomaniac propensities, lecherous parties and publicity seeking,' the Bureau noted. Dorothy's husband, the Count, was well selected as distinguished *cavaliere servente* in their chosen lifestyle. Solicitous to his wife's pleasure, he encouraged her to enjoy the more outstanding of their guests upstairs and was never happier than when in his favourite sexual position, crouched outside her bedroom door with his eye to the keyhole.

Barbara too intended to continue her career as an international hostess and the idea of a castle had great appeal to her, but the reality of Castle Hardenberg did not come up to her expectations. Set on a lonely island off the coast of Denmark, the building was a grim fortress of blackened stone, lacking not only in towers and turrets but bathrooms and mod cons. There was no heating, part of the roof had fallen in, only one wing of the place was habitable, and that was haunted. The surroundings too left a great deal to be desired. The fort presided over flat fields extending to the horizon in a wide panorama animated only by rather a lot of cows whose job it was to provide the inadequate income on which the family Reventlow subsisted. The truth which Barbara faced with gathering hysteria was that she had married a *farmer*.

After being shown over the estate and meeting the cows, there wasn't anything to do. Neither she nor Jimmy Donahue were country girls, rural pursuits held no appeal. There was a chill grey sea but no beach identifiable by parasols, *matelas* and willing *plagistes*. And there were no charming hostelries accessible for lunch. She'd had a

Rolls-Royce shipped over, but there was nowhere to visit beyond a single village and the island's narrow lanes were obstructed by columns of defecating cattle. Cousin Jimmy did his best to liven things by feeding lurid items of misinformation to the press. He'd been lodged not at the castle but in a guest cottage, where he burnt its antique furniture in the grate to keep warm. 'Man! Was he a nuisance!' said Reventlow, who detested him.

Before she cut short the honeymoon and moved the whole caravan to Paris there occurred one redeeming scene. Heinrich gave a dinner party for Barbara in the castle. Hereditary silver decorated the table and traditional Danish dishes replaced the Spartan fare which had been the rule. At the end of the meal Heinrich made a speech and presented Barbara with a bracelet of family-heirloom emeralds. She was deeply moved by the gift. She said, 'It's the first time I've ever really been given a present I didn't have to pay for myself.'

In Paris, where the group next took up residence in the suite she maintained at the Ritz, Barbara appeared depressed by the relentlessly negative press she was receiving. 'They simply won't let me alone, and I'm so tired of being followed around,' she complained to her husband.

Reventlow went to the Paris *Herald Tribune,* one of whose reporters had been assigned to her full-time and was publishing daily stories on her shopping trips and social round. Meeting with the editor Hawkins, Reventlow asked him to lay off. Barbara's next big party at the Pré Catelan went unreported, nor did her name feature in the paper's society column. Then, a few mornings later while reading the paper, Reventlow came upon a major story about Barbara and her extravagant life. Irritated, he called Hawkins to say, 'I thought you promised to forget us.'

'Don't blame me,' Hawkins told him.

'Who then?' he asked.

'Ask your wife. She phoned here yesterday. She told us all the things she has been doing for the past few weeks and said, "What's the matter with your reporters? Am I supposed to be dead?"'

Reventlow did not again attempt to interfere with Barbara's appetite for publicity. Her appetite for food was now also causing friction between the couple. She refused to consume anything except RyKrisps and coffee and Reventlow, who had a hearty appetite, found it impossible to enjoy his meals when his every mouthful was watched by her hungry eyes. She was down to less than a hundred pounds and against his will he was losing weight himself.

By now Barbara had found her husband to be a different man from the one she'd married. The aristocratic manner she'd found so attractive was less appealing in daily close-up. Haughty and intolerant, he showed a violent temper and had firm views on a wife's place, which he believed should be in the home – or rather in the castle after she'd used a slice of her fortune to restore it. He was also aggravated by the fact that she was no longer sexually responsive to him. One night he raped her.

Some while later Barbara discovered she was pregnant. She announced to the press and to friends that she was delighted and wanted a son; she told Reventlow it didn't fit with her plans. It certainly didn't fit with her body image. For an obstetrician Barbara chose the best in Paris, the society physician Dr De Gennes, *Le petit frère des riches,* as he was known. But she was defiantly resistant to his advice about diet. At a loss how to handle so intractable a patient, he recommended a change of air. She took her group – which still included Jimmy Donahue – to Rome.

It was not the best of times to visit the eternal city. Mussolini's Blackshirt thugs strutted the streets in gangs, stealing, torching cars, and giving a hard time to anyone who looked at them sideways.

At the end of September the Fascists staged a demonstration to celebrate Mussolini's invasion of Ethiopia in the piazza outside the Grand Hotel where Barbara and her entourage were staying. She was hosting a party that evening and the noise of the mob chanting political slogans and waving banners drowned conversation in the third-floor suite. Jimmy Donahue, well lit on brandy, decided to address the crowd in his own fashion.

Stepping onto the balcony he bellowed, 'Long live Ethiopia!' A sea of faces tilted up to him; momentarily the mob was silenced in outrage. Then fury seized them and they began to howl for blood. In response Jimmy picked up a potted rose bush and dropped it on them. Unbuttoning his fly, he urinated on the rabble below. They stormed the hotel and it required the police to save him from lynching. Next morning two hard-faced men came to the hotel and, deaf to his apology, bundled him to the railway station and put him on a train to Paris.

Newspaper headlines, which form the spoor charting Barbara's earthly transit, supply the end to her Italian vacation: COUNT AND COUNTESS REVENTLOW PROVOKE BLACKSHIRT FASCIST ATTACK. ASKED TO LEAVE... COUNT AND COUNTESS COMB ENGLAND FOR SUITABLE RESIDENCE.

⤞❧⤝

Five months later Barbara gave birth to her only child. Her son, THE WORLD'S RICHEST BABY, as *The Times* named him, was delivered by caesarean section in a private house in London, where a large room had been equipped as a hospital. The infant, Lance, was a 7½-pound boy with blond hair and wide blue eyes like his mother's. He was looked after by a nanny, nursemaid and team of six bodyguards, and his appearance into the world was soon followed by the arrival of his first kidnap threat. Barbara and her husband Count Reventlow had decided to make England their home. Her association with America was not happy, and she was well connected here. She knew the King and Wallis Simpson, and on the international circuit she'd become friendly with men and women who made up the country's elite. That is to say she was on invite and be-invited terms with them. The political situation in Europe was ominous – particularly in Germany where Hitler had become Chancellor, and a National Socialist government was in power – whereas England looked a stable and safe place to bring up a child.

Dunstan Lodge, which she renamed Winfield House after her grandfather's mansion on Long Island, was a Regency house standing in fourteen acres of grounds in Regent's Park; it and Buckingham Palace were the largest private estates in London. 'Of course I'll have to make a few changes,' Barbara said.

Naturally she would. To redecorate the new home you've acquired not just forms a popular genre of present-day television but represents a primal instinct. Almost our only knowledge of pre-history derives from the automatic reflex of Man and Woman on first occupying their cave: to scratch a few signature paintings on its wall. Barbara understandably had no taste for DIY or small measures, but had the house knocked down and rebuilt as a Georgian mansion of red brick with a slate roof and thirty-five rooms. Baby Lance had his own suite on the top floor and a designer nursery walled in pink calfskin. Restoration of the mansion cost $4.5 million with a further $2 million for decoration and furniture (in today's money a total of somewhat over $100 million).

But for Barbara the year had opened with a disappointment. Elsa Maxwell had published her list of the ten most fascinating women in the world – *and she was not on it*. Pregnancy had kept her out of the social swim but, now thin again, she studied the dailies, Sunday tabloids and fashion magazines closely, and when she did not come upon her own name it was disheartening. She complained to Tiki that she'd become a has-been.

Reconstruction of Winfield House took care of the problem. At a time when unemployment was high, wages low and the future threatening, stories and pictures of the palatial home being built for the girl who already had everything were a welcome diversion. Barbara's media image was a paradigm of extravagance and waste. Newspaper articles about her invariably reprised the same snide tone. She had been created by the press before she'd been able to create herself, but the way Barbara behaved toward the media throughout her life showed staggering lack of judgement. Despite countless bad experiences she remained unsuspicious of a journalist's angle when asked for an interview. She invited them to lunch or dinner, took them up, had them to parties ... then dropped them when they bored her. It was the way she treated everybody except her own staff: she was an exemplary boss. With the press she never learned when to keep her mouth shut or considered how her actions might be reported.

On St Patrick's Day the sales staff at Woolworth's on West 14 Street in New York took over the store and staged a hunger strike in protest against their pay and working conditions. They dispatched a cable to Barbara, who was on vacation with Reventlow in Egypt, asking her to intervene and help them obtain a living wage. Tabloid coverage of the strike featured alongside photographs of a party given in Barbara's honour at the imaginatively chosen venue in Tutankhamen's burial chamber, where brunch had been served out of golden dishes laid out on top of his sarcophagus. The contrast was obscene. Barbara's image could not have been worse. She was clearly in need of professional help and the Hollywood publicist

Steve Hannagan (whose clients included Sun Valley, Miami Beach and the Indianapolis 500) made a pitch to handle her PR which she was more than happy to accept.

Even today in a more cynical age it is a relatively simple matter for a skilled publicist with a healthy budget to create an image for a would-be celeb. To *change* an already existing image in order to rebrand a current personality is very much harder and often impossible. The task facing Hannagan was a tough one. To rebrand Barbara Hutton he went to Hearst's leading female feature writer, Adela Rogers St Johns, fixing for her to do a major personality profile on Barbara for *Life* magazine.

Adela's all-day interview with her subject took place with Reventlow sitting in and listening to every word. The result was published five weeks later. 'To me there has always been something fantastic, and a little useless and stupid about Barbara Hutton,' the piece began, but went on to describe her life not at all as people imagined it. She had found fulfilment in motherhood and hardly ever went out except occasionally to the cinema with her husband. It portrayed Barbara as exiled from her own country, wounded and vulnerable. But 'now at last I've found happiness ... I love my husband and he loves me. We have our son and we shall have more children. For the first time in my life I am confident of my happiness.'

In conversation with Dean Jennings twenty-five years later the columnist expanded on that interview.

There were many things I didn't say in the story ... Some girls like Barbara are meant to be fat, husky and healthy. Then they diet ... Barbara ruined her health forever when she began what she calls her coffee diet. The poor baby. You see, they kept on at her so about the fact that if she'd been a pretty girl, then somebody might have loved her for herself and not her money ... They rubbed her nose in the dirt for being so fat and they made fun of her. The story of Barbara is heart-breaking.

Whether Adela's revisionist line could be successfully marketed was never determined. Any good the story might have achieved was immediately undone by the disastrous act which followed, though this was not Barbara's own idea. She was indifferent to money; she preferred not to think about the subject, it bored her. But her father and her New York law firm, White and Case, insisted she was spending too much. The scheme put to her was designed to save the $300,000 a year she was paying in US taxes and to protect her capital which would be taxable in the event of her death. Their proposal was that she should renounce her US citizenship.

Inconstant about everything in life, Barbara was reliably consistent only in her bad judgement on men, and the lawyer she chose to represent her – who would manage her business affairs for the rest of her life – was no exception to the rule. Graham Mattison certainly read out well. A graduate of Princeton and Harvard Law School, he was a leading expert in the murky water of international tax avoidance but also – as the next three and a half decades would prove – dishonest. He was additionally an overbearing bully, a characteristic shared by most of the men in Barbara's life, including her own father. Mattison's negotiations for her to embrace Danish citizenship (which she possessed through marriage to Reventlow) and to take up British residence were conducted at an exalted level. Dealing directly with the British Treasury, Mathson got them to agree to waive both residency and income tax for the indefinite future on the promise that Barbara would transfer her capital to Britain. In another artful move he induced Reventlow to accept a million dollars to forfeit his rights under Danish law to half her property.

Reventlow had some idea of the storm that Barbara's action would create and was conspicuously not with her when she arrived in New York to sign the Act of Renunciation to her US citizenship. Having done so, Mattison smuggled her back on board the *Europa,* which sailed for England that same night. Two days later the news broke. Workers in Woolworth stores called a strike and paraded with placards BABS RENOUNCES CITIZENSHIP BUT NOT PROFITS, while chanting limericks reviling her. Newspaper editorials vilified her for diverting Grandfather Woolworth's hard-earned dollars out of the US and into the hands of European shysters. Church leaders preached sermons on her greed and treachery. People had hated her for years but women had still wanted to *be* her. Now she'd committed the ultimate betrayal, she'd rejected the country that had made her. For the media she was red meat.

❧

What Barbara sought in life was simple: a fully realised fairytale. She was twenty-five years old and at Winfield House the elements of perfection were in place, from baby to yacht to the gratification of every whim. Yet she was restless, chain-smoking and discontented. The problem was Reventlow. He was handsome, he looked the saturnine villain in a melodrama, but in no other way did he match the bill of goods he'd presented when she married him. His 'sensitivity' was a crock, his interest in her poetry did not survive the wedding; he never opened a book. He was bad-tempered, censorious and dominating. He bullied the servants and had the effrontery to fire her chauffeur. 'The man didn't know his place,' he told her.

She was incensed.

'*Know his place?* I feel sorry for you: you're still living in the Dark Ages.'

'Am I? Perhaps. In any case you should learn to appreciate the status you've attained, thanks to your title.'

'Status?'

'Yes. Today you're the Countess Haugwitz-Reventlow because of me.'

'Who cares?' she yelled at him. 'Who cares about such tripe? Do you think I care a jot about your silly title?'

He was a social climber and a galloping snob, which she, despite her fascination with titles, was not herself. She liked the company of people who interested or amused her, regardless of their background. But the milieu she moved in at this time was restricted; later her acquaintanceship would grow wider and more louche.

One day she was visited by a ghost from her past. The butler announced an unexpected guest, Roussie Sert. It was two years since Barbara had last seen her in Venice, where she and her husband were living in the Palazzo San Gregorio which Barbara had paid for. There was, it seems, a curse on the building which years before had been stolen from the Catholic Church. The first new owner had lost both his legs in a railroad accident; the next also met a violent end. Alex Mdivani had died in a car smash and the property had been inherited by his siblings. Along with the malediction for, only a few months after his marriage to Louise van Alen, his brother's widow, Serge Mdivani had been thrown from his polo pony and killed, his skull shattered by a kick to the head.

Barbara was adept at concealing her reactions, but she was shocked by Roussie's appearance. Her clothes hung limp from an emaciated frame and her once-brilliant eyes stared dull from a haggard face. She'd exploited Barbara from the start, she lived by manipulating others as had all the Mdivanis; she was treacherous and amoral – yet Barbara received her as a friend, even confided in her. There was a past they shared. Roussie was shattered by her brothers' deaths. She was by now a morphine addict and a long way down the road. And Barbara too was in a bad way, wired on caffeine, sleepless, claustrophobic and detesting Reventlow. Had she ever asked herself why she married him, Roussie enquired.

'Freud says all women are masochistic,' Barbara replied.

'And suffering is what you want?'

'I expect bad treatment from men,' Barbara said.

'Do you think you'd be bored if a man was nice to you?'

'Probably.'

'Have you ever thought of going into analysis?' Roussie asked.

'No,' Barbara replied. 'No, I'd rather stay as I am. The old me is at least familiar. Change frightens me.'

Roussie gave her some of her own pills 'to help'. They were barbiturates and they did, not just for sleep but during the day – particularly when taken with a glass of champagne. They soothed her, blunted the rough edges and double-glazed the glass wall that separated her from the world. She liked them; it was a simple matter to obtain more.

⚜

Reventlow was no easier to get rid of than Alex Mdivani and when Barbara went to Venice that summer he was still angrily attached. While there she flirted openly with the tennis player Baron von Cramm, but Reventlow hung on doggedly. When Barbara took a trip to India he insisted on accompanying her though the relationship was now so strained the two could barely manage to be polite to each other in public.

Following their return to London, Reventlow found (and pocketed for future use) a love letter to his wife which he found lying on her dressing table in front of a framed photograph of the 21-year-old Prince Mussan Jah of Hyderabad. Not only was the prince a dusky youth of unusual beauty, but his grandfather the Nizam, who dressed like a tramp, bathed infrequently, smoked the cheapest cigarettes and whose closest companion was a pet goat, was rich to an incredible degree. He had three wives, forty-two concubines, 500 dancing girls, a thousand servants and 300 Rolls-Royces, Daimlers and Cadillacs (which he seldom used, for he and the goat didn't get around much but lived simply, chewing betel nuts or turnips, each to his taste, and smoking a little opium). Having no confidence in banks, the Nizam kept his fortune of $2 billion conveniently to hand in chests of diamonds and pearls and piled up around the smelly blissed-out twosome in an untidy jumble of gold littering their rancid lair.

Barbara was charmed by the old fellow's take on life and gratified by his grandson's infatuation. The young Prince shared her love of poetry and at least she could be sure he was not interested in her money – as she remarked pointedly to Reventlow, who still would not get the message. She realised she had to make the situation clearer.

In games of the heart she played with court cards and in the spring she picked up a trump at a Mayfair party. Prince Frederick of Prussia had blond hair, slate-blue eyes and the face of the Hohenzollerns. Aged twenty-six, he was eighteen years younger than her stuffy husband – and smitten with her. 'Just think,' she mused to Reventlow over breakfast, 'I could marry the man who might someday be the Emperor of Germany.'

Reventlow was livid she'd invited the Prince to lunch. 'The man is a Nazi, you simply don't do things like that here.' He flounced into his Rolls and drove off. Prince Frederick arrived and proved as charming in daylight as the night before. He and Barbara lunched *à deux* on the terrace. Following coffee, they took a dip in the pool. While climbing out Barbara's partner suffered a slight accident. His foot slipped and he twisted his ankle. Solicitously Barbara helped him limp upstairs where he could lie down and recover. When Reventlow stormed back home that evening he found his successor installed in the master suite, occupying his bed and being seen to by his wife.

❧

Count Reventlow was angry – and he had a gun. It was obvious he was good and sore, and the press loves an angry loser. The foolish cuckold has been a staple figure of fun since hominids first learned to kindle a fire and gleefully to gossip in its warmth.

Reventlow had been ousted from his home and the marriage bed by his wife's attentions to another man; another Prussian; younger, nobler, richer than himself. He'd been publicly cuckolded and it galled him bitterly. He hated Barbara and he wanted retribution. As Europe armed for the Second World War, so did he. He occupied a strong position – or so he believed – for he knew Barbara would pay anything to avoid unpleasantness. And he had the perfect weapon – their son. Her first offer was a million bucks to take a walk. He refused. She upped her offer to two. He demanded five and custody of Lance. He was aware of her continuing dalliance: Prince Frederick's car was parked there every night. He felt deeply humiliated. One night he boiled over – perhaps he had been drinking – and called Barbara. Admitting the affair, 'What do you propose to do?' she asked.

'I'm returning on Thursday,' he told her, 'and if I see Prince Frederick around I'll shoot him like a dog.'

183

She went to the police. Informing them that Reventlow had the habit of carrying a revolver, she swore out a warrant for his arrest. She dispatched Lance with Nanny Latimer and bodyguards to a secret location, hired extra security and claimed to be in fear of her life. The press loved it.

Reventlow was arrested. His trial a week later was attended by 200 journalists and started litigation between the couple over custody of Lance which would continue for the next decade. During the hearing Prince Frederick was referred to only as 'the gentleman in London' and Reventlow's threats of violence were described as real and convincing by Barbara's bagman, who said he'd 'known husbands who've killed their wives for far less than sleeping around'.

Sir Patrick Hastings, Barbara's eminent attorney, seized upon the phrase. *'Sleeping around?'* he boomed. 'Sleeping around, Mr Birkett, is not the appropriate term in this instance. According to the Countess her husband is a wife-beater, a sexual deviate, and a sado-masochist. Under such conditions adultery is hardly a luxury, it is a necessity.'

Barbara, who was altogether accustomed to luxury, found her necessities where and how they occurred. Prince Frederick discreetly quit the field at the threat of publicity, slinking back into the bosom of his Imperial family who had their own problems in the Nazi Fatherland at this time. With Reventlow gone, Barbara was free and unencumbered by a relationship, but she felt unsettled and redundant without a man; it was an unnatural condition for her and she was restive. Her dream of the gracious life in England was over, Reventlow had turned into a homicidal stuffed-shirt, Winfield House bored her and she was ready to move on.

Soon after the Second World War broke out in 1939, the American ambassador in London, Joseph Kennedy, asked Barbara to the US embassy to inform her that Britain was about to be defeated; she should abandon London with her infant son for the safety of America.

Barbara took his advice, deciding to close up Winfield House. However there was a problem awaiting her in the States, and although she must have anticipated trouble she made no attempt to avert it. Her return to America was scarcely low profile for she travelled with Bob Sweeny, her current lover, Lance, his nanny, Tiki and six servants, and her reception in New York was lively if not warm. Woolworth's demonstrators chanting and waving placards paraded outside the Pierre Hotel where the group was staying, and flung rocks at her car. She received more than one hundred hate letters each day, women hissed, spat and shouted at her whenever she appeared in public.

So disastrous was the shambles of her homecoming it dismayed even Jimmy Donahue and his mother Jessie, inured though they were to bad publicity. Both entreated her to make an effort to improve her image. In response to their prompting she spoke to Steve Hannagan, who had proved effective before in putting a favourable spin upon her appalling public image. Highly regarded by his clients, he was a veteran in PR, which had become a professional business only after the advent of mass media in the mid-1920s. At first it was only movie and show business stars – or, rather, their producers – who availed themselves of these self-declared experts in the field, in which chutzpah and rampant imagination composed the only basic skills. Public relations advisers were a new life-form created in response to global communication, a fresh species in a radically changed environment. Their ability to change perception rapidly became apparent. In his book *Intimate Strangers*, the critic

Richard Schickel identifies a seminal moment in social history when a movie actress, Florence Lawrence, was created an instant celebrity by means of a public relations stunt. To coincide with the opening in St Louis of her latest movie, its producer planted a story about her in a local paper. The item stated that she'd been involved in a horrific disaster and had been mangled and killed in a trolley car accident. Immediately the story broke he denounced it as a fake, a malicious invention by his rivals to wreck the movie and her career. Florence made a well-publicised visit to St Louis to expose the 'fraud', where she was set upon by a hysterical crowd of fans who tore her dress to pieces for relics. Shredded but blush-pink and radiant as Venus on the half-shell, a star was revealed.

Steve Hannagan's fee to Barbara Hutton this time was $65,000 a year plus expenses – the first item a personal cheque for $10,000 to Maury Paul, who edited the syndicated Cholly Knickerbocker column and set the tone in the Hearst press. 'She's terribly pro-American these days. And humble as pie. From now on she'll go in rags and give her money to the poor.' Newspapers were fed a continuing stream of items. The public learned of her gift of Winfield House to the US Government, of the transfer of her yacht to the British navy, her present of ten ambulances to the Red Cross, of her $50,000 to the War Relief Fund. She was photographed wearing little make-up and no jewellery demurely knitting sweaters for the French Relief Fund.

She knitted very well, Hannagan's employee Ned Moss noted, but her ignorance of the real world caused him problems. One day Barbara summoned one of the hotel bellboys and gave him an envelope, asking him to take it to the bank and get change. The boy did as asked, handing the envelope to a teller. It excited a buzz of interest followed by a considerable delay before one of the bank's vice-presidents emerged lugging a heavy canvas moneybag. 'Hey, what's this?' the boy asked. Barbara had given him a ten thousand-dollar bill.

Of course the story was splashed in the press and Barbara was mortified. She couldn't understand the fuss; she needed change and it seemed to her a perfectly normal thing to do.

Another setback in this fresh campaign to rebrand Barbara as a goodie was occasioned by the death of her father. On learning he was mortally ill she did not want to see him and had to be persuaded to do so. She felt no tenderness at his passing. 'Think of that man dying like that! Think of him dying in splendour, luxury, surrounded by servants and hangers-on when millions of people die alone, forgotten in hovels and tenements.'

Franklyn's own sentiments for Barbara were expressed in his will. 'I realise that my beloved daughter Barbara is possessed in her own right of worldly goods… Therefore, I will to her a loving father's blessing for her future happiness.' His beloved daughter's response was to sue her dad's estate for $530,000 she'd lent him, plus interest. She collected, but the story did not warm the public heart.

The next read better. In the summer of 1942 Barbara married Cary Grant in the shade of an oak tree at Lake Arrowhead. The half-dozen guests included the actor's agent, his secretary, and Barbara's now elderly maid Tiki who'd been with her since childhood. No press attended and only one photographer. Cary had a hatred of publicity. Only a single photograph of the wedding couple was ever released, invariably captioned 'Cash and Cary'.

The marriage surprised everyone, not least Bob Sweeny, her English suitor, who had no inkling of Barbara's romance. But he was a true sportsman and took his dismissal well, along with a cheque for $350,000. Following the wedding the happy couple, plus Lance, moved into Westridge, a twelve-acre estate in Pacific Palisades belonging to Douglas Fairbanks Jnr, Barbara's friend since adolescence, who was serving in the navy. Three other houses in the neighbourhood had to be rented to accommodate Barbara's staff which numbered twenty-nine, though she had to make do without the services of her butler who'd been hit on the head by a hammer while serving at a party at Errol Flynn's place.

This was the plushy if not trouble-free habitat in which the newly wed pair settled down to their marital routine. Cary left home for the studio soon after dawn. In his absence Barbara played tennis, didn't drink or use barbiturates, dieted, and filled the role of dutiful wife. Inevitably they entertained. Their friends were of two sorts. His were in the film business, hers were civilians. And civilians of Barbara's sort there were aplenty in Los Angeles at that time; the war had washed them up here. They were refugees with bogus backgrounds living on their wits, but they knew how to sing for their supper and were the kind of louche company Barbara liked.

In starving Europe the Nazi advance continued until France was occupied but in southern California war provided a fine excuse for big-scale junkets, it was only necessary to call them not parties but 'bond drives'. The potential guest list was vastly enlarged by the mixed flotsam of socialites, deposed royalty, adventurers, rich divorcées, gigolos and crooks who had found asylum here. Another strain had come to infect the capital of moviedom – the decadence of original Eurotrash.

At the start of her three-year marriage to Cary, Barbara exercised an uncharacteristic restraint in her normal pattern of behaviour. Her need to be constantly in company was satisfied in part by war work, intermittently also by her son. Under the custody arrangement he spent half the year with her, the other half with his father who now had married a replacement heiress, Peggy Astor Drayton. When Lance arrived to stay with the Reventlows in Pasadena, Peggy unpacked his luggage to find the seven-year-old boy had with him fifty shirts, a range of custom-made suits, and a gold box of personal jewellery. At the bottom of one of his suitcases she came upon a scrunched-up ball of banknotes amounting to several thousand dollars. At Christmas the boy received fifty separately wrapped presents from Barbara, and the Reventlows sneakily intercepted his coded letter to her in which they deciphered the seasonal message: TO HELL WITH MY FATHER I WOULD LIKE IT IF HE DIED.

⚜

Stars marry stars and celebs marry celebs, according to the same Darwinian law that requires Brazilian macaws to mate with Brazilian macaws. But, apart from fame and no instinctive love for children, Barbara and Cary had nothing whatever in common. Predictably, they decided to have a baby. She was quoted by Hedda Hopper as saying, 'We talk about it all the time. We'd like to have at least three.' They tried, took medical advice, but failed. 'Barbara was cut to ribbons long before I knew her,' said Cary. 'There's no surgeon or doctor who ever approached her who didn't want to cut immediately... Those scars were all from her bankroll.' The couple had no shared tastes or interests. Cary was single-minded in dedication to his craft; in two years he made five movies. He worked throughout each day and at night he came home tired. He wanted a simple meal, time to learn his lines for next morning, and sleep. The schedule did not suit Barbara, who did not like her husbands to have a job. She grew bored and restless and turned to booze. Liquor never had been important to her, now she began to drink with deliberation. She insisted on going out at night, and when Cary was unwilling she went alone. There were parties galore: this was the golden age in Hollywood and never since has it matched the gaudy splendour of that Belle Époque.

Barbara also entertained at home. A friend of Cary's is quoted by David Heymann describing the scene: 'What was on the table was sometimes different, but what was on the chairs was always the same. Barbara surrounded herself with a consortium of fawning parasites – European titles, broken-down Hollywood types, a maharajah or two, a sheikh, the military, several English press, a few tennis bums and a throng of faggots.' Cary said, 'If one more phoney earl had entered the house, I'd have suffocated.'

Yet shady company did not satisfy Barbara any more than had motherhood. She was bored of these people, bored by Hollywood, bored by Cary. Once again she was captive, suffocating in a marriage with no one to understand her. She longed for liberation, for a prince in shining armour trotting out of the forest's dappled shade on his prancing steed to rescue her.

And, though she did not know it, her Prince was already briefed and standing to. The script for Barbara's next fairytale romance had already been plotted and the part cast.

❧

Unusually, Prince Igor Troubetzskoy was a little prince who, unlike other little princes Barbara had come across, did not want a palazzo on the Grand Canal or even a string of polo ponies. All he'd ever wanted was to ride his bicycle. While other princes were playing chukkas and chasing heiresses he spent his days pedalling his bike. He pedalled and pedalled until he became champion amateur bicyclist in France. During the war he served as a soldier, but the moment it ended he changed into shorts and climbed back on his bicycle. But though he pedalled as hard as he could he didn't win any races because he was too old. So Igor came to realise sadly that he'd have to find something else to do in life.

He was thirty-five, which is not the best age to find a job, particularly if you are rather dim. But he was nice-looking, with a Byronic profile and gentle manners. Everyone said what a delightful chap he was, not a drop of guile in his sunny nature, and he was welcome everywhere.

His parents had left Lithuania almost penniless in 1906 to settle among the expat Russian colony in Nice. His older brother Youka moved to Hollywood, becoming a leading man to both Pola Negri and Norma Shearer while Igor was still pedalling around France. Youka was doing fine, but when war ended in 1945 and Igor started looking for work he was not so lucky.

Fortunately he had a friend in Freddie McEvoy, an American conman more worldly wise than himself who was based in Paris running a black-market in currency. Igor moved to live in his apartment and became his bagman, pedalling around Paris with bundles of hot money.

At this point Freddie was two years into an affair with Barbara Hutton, who had left Cary Grant and moved to Paris soon after the Second World War ended, installing herself and her staff (and intermittently son Lance) in her old suite at the Ritz. It was generally assumed by her friends, as well as Elsa Maxwell and other columnists, that Freddie was preparing the ground to become her fourth husband. But no, Freddie was smart enough to recognise that his own role in Barbara's dream was nearing its end and handled the situation pragmatically. He replaced himself in the part with his protégé Igor.

His interview, set up by Freddie, at the Ritz went well, Igor clearly passed, Barbara asked for his number. A couple of days later she called to say, 'Hello, this is Barbara Grant. I was wondering if you'd care to have dinner with me?'

Startled by her forwardness yet flattered by her interest, Igor put on his only suit and pedalled over to the Ritz. 'She phoned,' he explained later, 'We had dinner and – my God – how fast!'

His brother Youka thought he was just the right man for her. 'He does not suffer from any of the anxieties that beset most of us… His mind is clear enough to reject the idea that her money could be an obstacle.'

Igor regarded the world Barbara inhabited with the wide-eyed wonder of a child. Growing up in Nice had been anything but grand. Nothing before had provided vistas into the plushy ambience he now found himself a part of. Barbara's suite was the most luxurious at the Ritz. Its pale grey, gilt and mirrored walls were hung with her paintings, including a Botticelli, and a Cezanne; gold bibelots, Chinese porcelain and jade crowded every surface; diamonds and emeralds spilled from jewel cases upon her dressing table. Igor wandered through the glittering scene astounded as a boy who has stumbled into Aladdin's cave. He was so ingenuous, so artless, Barbara called him her Pixie.

They got married quietly in the small town of Chur, in Switzerland. Only two friends, the Sorines, attended the ceremony. The wedding breakfast was celebrated in the Maron Tea Room where Barbara was persuaded reluctantly to eat two slices of sponge cake and drink a glass of milk. She tried to give her husband a million dollars as a present, but he refused it, saying he had no need of the money. But Freddie McEvoy received a cheque for $100,000 together with a note: 'To Freddie, for everything. But especially for Pixie. Love, Barbara.'

The marriage, which remained secret for all of thirty minutes, was seized on by the US press. *Another phoney European Prince …* Cary Grant was surprised, Reventlow outraged, but Lance, who was staying with his father and stepmother in Newport, took the news phlegmatically. A few months earlier Barbara had attempted to explain the failure of her three marriages to her son. 'I was quite frank with him. I told Lance that I had been a very foolish woman, but that I hoped I was going to be wiser from then on. I told him everything. I was frightened to death of what he would think.'

Dean Jennings records the boy's reaction. There happened to be a plane passing high overhead as his mother made her confession and when she ended he looked up at it and said, 'I know what that is. It's a B-17.'

✻

Igor moved into the Ritz, where he was apportioned his own room. He did not see Barbara until she sent for him after she woke, usually around lunchtime. Not that lunch or other meals figured in the schedule. He slipped out to get something to eat in a brasserie while Barbara pursued what had become her regimen. On waking she swallowed amphetamines to suppress her appetite, but these made her so wired she took barbiturates with a glass of champagne to smooth her out. In the course of her day, which ran from 1 p.m. until 4 a.m. or 5 a.m. next morning, she got through fifteen to twenty cups of coffee, a dozen Cokes, and pack after pack of Chesterfields. At night she couldn't sleep but walked the streets or paced her room while the same record played over and over again. Sometimes she retired to bed for days at a stretch and wrote poetry. She was in poor shape physically, but when the drugs balanced out she could function socially. She gave a dinner party for the Duke and Duchess of Windsor; one of the guests said, 'The cuisine was incredibly well prepared but Barbara didn't touch a thing. She just drank black coffee and smoked cigarettes.'

As the spring of 1947 turned into summer Barbara's face grew gaunt and strained, her mood swings became more erratic. The sexual relief she'd found with Igor had not lasted, he could no longer comfort her. 'When everything is sustained by stimulants and emotions then it is alright, but otherwise no,' he explained. 'But our life together is not a physical life. Barbara, you see, is in love with love.'

She became convinced that she was seriously ill. A procession of doctors was summoned to the Ritz. Finding no evidence of physical disease, they were well rewarded for prescriptions for the drugs she needed. 'It killed everything,' said Igor. 'Her appetite, her sleep patterns, her sex drive.'

Abruptly deciding on a change of scene, Barbara moved her husband and staff of six to the Côte d'Azur. There the weather was muggy; she transferred the party to the Swiss Alps and sent for Lance to join them. For a while the change seemed to revive her, then one morning she collapsed in excruciating pain. Wrapping her in a rug, Igor drove her to a hospital in Bern. In the months that followed she went through four major operations. During one of them her remaining ovary was removed; the first had been taken out in her illness after Lance's birth. Now her convalescence in Switzerland, attended by the patient Igor, was long and slow, but when she was well enough they returned to Paris and the Ritz.

She was nearing forty. Loss of her ovary brought on symptoms of the menopause. To deal with them she drank and swallowed pills. While Igor paced the silent corridors of the Ritz, waiting to be summoned, she kept to her room playing Russian music and writing poetry. He was miserable with hotel life. On sudden impulse Barbara sailed to New York without him, and checked herself into a private clinic. Worried, Igor flew over to discover how she was. He located her at a suite in the Hotel Pierre, but it was three days before she would see him. Barbara was wasting away. The couture clothes filling her closets, the jewellery locked in the hotel safe or scattered carelessly across her dressing table, the riches and luxury surrounding her, the invitations she received and infinite possibilities on offer failed to give her pleasure. She was sick in body, sick in the head and expiring beneath a crushing weight of futility and boredom. 'All the unhappiness in my life has been because of men, including my father ... But I'm also too timid to live alone, and life doesn't make any sense without men.'

Weakened by sickness, by drugs, by drink, emaciated by her punitive regimen, somehow Barbara roused herself to re-enter the lists of life – and to reappear in the society pages, which reported its essential aspects. She started a highly publicised affair with thirty-year-old Prince Henri de la Tour d'Auvergne.

Her liaison was headlined in all the papers and Igor was mortally humiliated. His patience and extraordinary restraint reached its limit in a final outburst.

> Everything in life is like a fine string. There comes a moment when it is drawn too tightly and suddenly *crack!* I told her what I thought and felt. I talked for twenty minutes without a stop. She didn't say a word. I went to my room, closed the door, took all my things and left.

Unlike earlier husbands he had little to show for his period of tenure. No palazzo, horses, jewellery or wardrobe of clothes. He flung his two suitcases into the back of his car and headed south. He reached the Côte d'Azur unshaved, weary, with no idea what to do. And in Cannes he ran slap into Errol Flynn, who was not hobbled by Igor's scruples. It so happened that with him was the American lawyer Melvin Belli, later to become notorious in high-profile divorce cases. He was persuaded to let Belli act for him.

In Paris Belli met with Barbara's lawyer Graham Mattison,

demanding a million dollars as the price of a divorce. Getting rid of Mdivani and Reventlow had proved much more costly, but surprisingly she refused to pay up. David Heymann reports a sighting of her at a party during this period: 'There she was dancing moodily with one of the forgotten gigolos, the two of them trembling slowly in the middle of the floor. She can't have weighed sixty pounds and her ... eyes oozed like black wounds from beneath an enormous hat.'

Barbara and Igor were finally divorced in October 1951.

CHAPTER 12

BARBARA HUTTON, NEW YORK CITY, NOVEMBER 1953

R ubi's noisy wooing of Barbara Hutton with a mariachi band outside her hotel at 2.30 a.m. had made their romance public from its start. The raucous spectacle had occurred in high season when hotels on the front were full. Everyone with seaward-facing rooms had been woken by the racket, and next morning it was all people talked about.

In the days following, gossip columns speculated on their relationship. Tabloids published photographs of them and ran sidebars recycling their colourful backstories. The press dogged them. When Rubi left to fly to Los Angeles, they met his plane on arrival to question him on his plans. He was evasive but, shortly after, an item reported him dining *à deux* with Zsa Zsa Gabor. Journalists also trailed Barbara when she quit Deauville for Paris, where she retired to her suite in the Ritz and remained incommunicado. It was frustrating for everyone following the story.

It is November before she emerges from seclusion. The Statue of Liberty is veiled in fog and the waters of New York harbour wreathed in mist as the SS *United States*, newest and fastest of the transatlantic liners, docks at the West Side pier with Barbara on board.

The paparazzi are waiting and when a frail thin woman wrapped in furs steps carefully down the gangway on the arm of a walker, followed by her maid, a firestorm of flash dazzles around her as she steps ashore. Microphones are thrust into her face: 'Why are you here? Where is Rubi? Why isn't he meeting you? What are your plans?' She is bombarded by questions.

She is fragile and wan, unable even under the stimulus of attention to rise to the occasion. 'I'm so tired, so very tired. I'm sick, they don't know what it is,' is all she can manage to reply.

She checks into the Hotel Pierre with her extensive baggage to occupy suite 39. It's a familiar surrogate home she's lived in before, where she's looked after by 24-hour room service and cared for by the ever-watchful Tiki while the switchboard refuses all calls.

Doctors visit her several times a day. They write prescriptions for her mystery illness, but still Barbara continues to sicken. No remedies prove effective, she cannot sleep. She is moved to Doctors Hospital. Ten days later Rubi flies in from Zsa Zsa in Hollywood to visit her, bearing an enormous bouquet of red roses. Suave and sophisticated as ever, he soothes and woos her with practised words. A light rekindles, restoring her will to live. A few days later when she checks out of hospital he is there for her – as are a pack of photographers – to escort her home. Later that same afternoon he visits his tailor, informing him that he is going to marry her, and orders twenty-five suits in varied shades of lightweight cloth at $300 apiece – telling him to send the bill to Barbara at the Hotel Pierre.

CHAPTER 13

ZSA ZSA GABOR, LOS ANGELES, CHRISTMAS EVE 1953

In Zsa Zsa's house in Bel Air every window is ablaze with light. And noise: the sound of women's voices raised in excited competitive chatter in Hungarian. Zsa Zsa's two sisters, their mother Jolie, and her daughter Francesca are gathered together for the holiday.

It is more than just Christmas they are celebrating. The Gabor sisters are about to open in their own cabaret show in Las Vegas, on Boxing Day. It's a fabulous deal. It was Jolie who took over the negotiations together with their wardrobe; each sister will have her own suite and personal entourage of maids, make-up, hairdresser and publicist. There's already been a lot of pre-publicity about the show in the press.

Carols are playing in the Bel Air living room which is decorated in tinsel and gold. Beneath a Christmas tree the six-year-old Francesca plays among the mound of colourfully wrapped presents. One of them for George Sanders; Zsa Zsa had hoped he would drop in before the holiday. Although she knows her husband is currently involved in an affair with Rubi's ex, Doris Duke, she does not believe he really wants to divorce her. She thinks he is bluffing.

Rubirosa is also part of this Gabor family gathering. He's flown from New York to be here, bringing an elaborate train set for Francesca. Despite her delight in the present, he is not his usual party self but appears depressed. The atmosphere is not helped by Jolie, who considers him a bad influence upon Zsa Zsa, though he has recently proposed to her, and regards him with deep suspicion.

Alone with Zsa Zsa in her bedroom later that evening, Rubi confides that he has been seeing Barbara Hutton. 'She wants to marry me, but I love only you.' But, he adds, if Zsa Zsa won't marry him, he will marry Barbara. 'I need money and she has offered me $5 million if I do,' he explains.

Zsa Zsa is stunned by the ultimatum. 'We talked endlessly. He unburdened himself as he had never before…'

Their conversation is interrupted by a crash. A gift-wrapped brick comes sailing through the French window, followed by George Sanders carolling, 'Merry Christmas, darlings' as he clambers into the room. After him scramble a photographer with a flash camera and a private detective.

The surprised couple jump out of bed in panic. Zsa Zsa is wearing only her diamond earrings and Rubi less; deciding discretion the better part, he locks himself in the bathroom.

Zsa Zsa says, 'I had not seen my husband in months … he wore a blue turtleneck sweater I had bought him in Naples and faded blue jeans, and he looked beautiful. When I was able to speak I said, "Oh George, why did you have to do this?"' She knows the scandal will be all over Hollywood in hours.

'I had to,' George says. He sits down on the bed, winded and breathing heavily.

'What's the matter with you?' she asks in alarm.

'My dear, I'm an old man. I have no business climbing ladders,' he explains.

But George's mission is complete. The compromising photograph he will produce in court if Zsa Zsa asks for alimony is in the can. He leaves her room and goes to walk downstairs, followed by his team.

'George, don't go without your present. It's under the Christmas tree,' Zsa Zsa calls after him.

CHAPTER 14

ZSA ZSA GABOR, LAS VEGAS, CHRISTMAS DAY 1953

On Christmas Day Zsa Zsa flies from Los Angeles to Las Vegas accompanied by her two sisters, each with her own entourage. Mother Jolie comes too. The party comes with its baggage of multiple costume changes, and Jolie insists they are too fragile to travel in the hold; they take up an entire section of the aircraft. Rubi follows in pursuit on a later flight.

The Fabulous Gabors are a little late for dress rehearsal at the Last Frontier, closed for the holiday. The rehearsal is constantly interrupted by calls from Rubi, asking Zsa Zsa if she will marry him. The sisters' routines are complex, the technicians are on double-time; everyone is irritated by the breaks and soon she refuses to take his calls.

Rehearsals are strenuous and emotional, each of the sisters has her own idea of how the act should play and so does the producer. At 2 a.m., after the final run-through, Zsa Zsa returns to her hotel suite. Rubi, who has bribed his way in, is there waiting for her. He has been drinking and is in foul mood. 'So, are you going to marry me?' he demands.

Both are sleepless and on edge, but hardly has this interrogation begun when it is interrupted by the telephone. It is Igor Cassini, the gossip columnist who now writes 'Cholly Knickerbocker' for the Hearst press, calling from New York. He is trying to contact Rubi. 'Have you any idea where he is?'

Beside her, Rubi shakes his head.

'None at all,' Zsa Zsa answers.

There is a brief silence, then Cassini asks, 'Is it true he's going to marry Barbara Hutton?'

'I don't know anything about it,' she snaps and hangs up.

She stands up. With the instinctive theatricality that comes so naturally to her she marches to the door and flings it wide. 'Get out,' she tells Rubi. 'I never want to see you again.'

He moves to the door, glowering at her. 'Just tell me one thing. Why don't you marry me?'

She is livid with fury. 'Because I love George!' she yells and tries to push him out the door.

He slugs her in the face. The blow throws her across the room. She cannons into the wall and falls. She's up at once running to the mirror. The flesh is already swelling above her right eye. My God, she thinks, I open tomorrow!

⚜

This is Boxing Day and Zsa Zsa sits in her dressing room in the Last Frontier, staring into the make-up mirror in despair. Her eye looks tiny; the tissue around it inflamed, bruised and purple.

A huge bunch of roses dominates the many good luck bouquets of flowers arranged around the room. They've been sent by Rubi from the airport before taking off for New York. A card accompanied them: *À bientôt, Rubi.*

The door opens and Marlene Dietrich sweeps in, dressed in white leather trousers tight as a second skin. She is playing in cabaret at The Sahara further down the strip. She's heard of the assault from Eva and examines Zsa Zsa's black eye with the interest of a connoisseur.

'Darling,' she says, 'he must love you very much to strike you like that.'

❧

Zsa Zsa's publicist is Russell Birdwell, one of the best. The Gabor sisters' act opens in three hours' time, and it is clearly futile to try to conceal her swollen and part closed eye with pancake. He comes up with the idea of an eye-patch.

The show – with the three sisters dressed in identical sequinned gowns, one white, one red, one black – is a huge success. Photographers and hacks are there as a tribe. The shot of Zsa Zsa in a black eye-patch goes around the world. The photograph and story that runs with it twitches a nerve of farce. The following night at The Sahara all of Marlene Dietrich's chorus girls are wearing black eye-patches.

When Zsa Zsa flies to New York a few days later, the score of reporters who greet her at the airport are all in black eye-patches. Within a week a jewelled version of the accessory is on sale in Manhattan stores. She has started a craze.

CHAPTER 15

BARBARA HUTTON, NEW YORK CITY, 30 DECEMBER 1953

Five days after Christmas a tree still stands in a corner of Barbara's suite in the Hotel Pierre. The room is decorated with festive baubles, a log fire burns in the hearth and there's a hint of Floris's *Essence des Pins* to brace the warm conditioned air.

Barbara in Balenciaga and diamonds is posed on a settee with her fifteen-year-old son Lance as she receives the press on this, her wedding day. Her hair is up, her back straight, but there's an underwater slowness to her movements. She is now wholly dependent on drugs and can't live without their help. They fill the vacuum of boredom and hold reality at bay, allowing her to inhabit an artificial paradise. But she might as well be sleepwalking: her perfectly made-up face is blank of expression, her eyes glazed, they look like boiled sweets. The mask is held in place by astringent lotion and willpower alone. Pilled-up and fortified by champagne, she maintains poise but it's precarious and risks cracking at any moment. Beside her, the teenage boy is desperately uncomfortable at being here; his body language is painful to watch.

The door to the suit opens and Rubi comes in, accompanied by Leland Rosenberg. Lithe, suave, perfectly groomed, a storm of flash surrounds him as he enters.

Barbara waves a languid hand, 'Rubi darling, here we are.'

He takes his place on the sofa beside Lance and the questions start. 'Barbara, are you legally *free* to marry? Is it true you've refused a blood test? Are you marrying under NY State law?'

The wedding will take place in the office of the Dominican Consul, she tells them. She is marrying under Dominican law.

'Does that mean your property belongs to your husband?'

She is vague, 'I don't know, I don't think so, legally I'm still a Danish subject.'

Rubi interrupts to resolve the point, 'In my country her money belongs to her and my money belongs to me. Anyway, I don't need her money; I have enough of my own.'

'Barbara, are you aware Zsa Zsa Gabor plans to sue Rubi for assault? That she says he's now worth suing, but without you he's not worth the shirt on his back. What is your comment?'

Even within the hazed cavern of her mind she will not be drawn, 'I'm terribly sorry. I don't know the lady.' She can still manage a put-down.

'When did Rubi propose to you?'

'When we were in Deauville he told me that he loved me. I didn't believe him, it's awful to have money. I could never give anyone credit for loving me for myself…' Then her voice cracks, 'I hate to look at myself in the mirror because I'm so ugly. I used to be beautiful, but I'm not anymore…'

Rubi takes it on himself to protest, 'Barbara is beautiful. She will always be beautiful.'

She stares at him blankly then rises unsteadily to her feet. She stumbles … one of the journalists catches her before she falls.

Shrugging him off she heads for her bedroom, there to pop another pill, repair her face and put on a full-length black velvet coat and hat for the ceremony.

All her friends had been appalled when they'd learned from the columns of her intention to marry Rubi. Graham Mattison, Cary Grant, Aunt Jessie, even Jimmy Donahue had done their utmost to dissuade her. But nothing can deflect Barbara from her disastrous impulse, she is as she has ever been – wilfully self-destructive. To marry in New York State requires a licence and a blood test – which Barbara knew she must avoid for sound reason: drugs. Rubi has helpfully suggested that to marry in the Dominican consulate would solve the difficulty. He has flatly refused to sign a prenuptial agreement for less than $5 million. Graham Mattison negotiated with him, assisted by Jimmy Donahue, who, despite his love of mischief, is truly concerned about the catastrophe Barbara is headed into. Working together, they got Rubi down to $2.5 million, payable up-front: his bottom price for making the earth move for Barbara.

<hr />

She emerges from her bedroom in the Pierre with a black picture hat framing her pallid face. The wedding group descends to two limos waiting outside the hotel and, followed by the press, the caravan moves on to 1100 Park Avenue and the nominal Dominican soil of its Consul General's office on the seventeenth floor.

Rubi's best man is Ramfis Trujillo. Close friends are absent from the ceremony but Barbara has invited all the media in New York and the place is heaving. The rite is conducted in Spanish and the couple exchange rings. Then it's back to the reception at the Pierre and more champagne. At the ceremony she was hardly able to stand up, now she sits swaying gently on the sofa beside her husband.

THE IRRESTIBLE MR WRONG

Few fail to report the sound of ice cubes rattling against the rim of the highball glass she clutches in her trembling hand. She slurs her words as she speaks, 'I feel as though I've been hit over the head. I'm so tired I could die.'

Very soon she has to be put to bed. Rubi goes out, leaving the party to continue without its hosts. He spends the night on the town celebrating with Leland Rosenberg, who has joined his staff as PA – a pay-off for his role as the sly cupid who brought bride and groom together. They end the night with two showgirls in Rosenberg's apartment on East 38th street.

CHAPTER 16

BARBARA HUTTON, NEW YORK CITY, NEW YEAR'S EVE 1953

T his is day two of Barbara's marriage to Rubirosa. When she wakes in their suite in the Pierre it is past noon; she is alone in bed. She rings for her maid, already reaching for the bottle of pills on the night table.

Tiki comes in. Quiet and caring, she rearranges the pillows, sits her up and orders breakfast. Barbara tries a sip of black coffee. The cloying sweetness makes her retch. She lies there trying not to throw up, waiting for the pills to kick in while Tiki lays out her clothes.

Barbara is on a lot of pills by now: for her health, to restore her beauty, amphetamines to wake her up and keep her functioning, valium to calm her nerves, barbiturates to sleep; all invariably taken with alcohol.

In twenty minutes the speed has entered her bloodstream, and a delusive spasm of energy quickens through her veins. She swings her match-thin naked legs from the bed, pauses then pushes upright to walk a slow deliberate line to the bathroom. Closing the door, she starts for the lit-up vanity console. She falters, the leg muscle fails. With a cry she goes down hard on the marble floor.

The Rubirosas are scheduled to host a select group of guests to supper at the Pierre to see in the New Year, but for the second evening in a row Barbara is unable to attend the occasion. Her ankle is broken and has to be set in plaster.

Did she fall … or was she pushed? For the press there is no option. RUBI BIFFS BABS is the tabloids' greeting to 1954.

❧

Barbara embarks on her honeymoon with Rubi in a wheelchair. Her fall in the Pierre – if fall it was – has broken her ankle. Rubi is depicted in the press as a wife beater; the tabloids rerun photographs of Zsa Zsa's black eye. 'A man only beats a woman if he loves her,' Zsa Zsa is quoted as saying, adding that her husband George Sanders 'beat me like a gong'.

For the honeymoon Barbara has taken a three-month lease on the Maharajah of Baroda's house in Palm Beach. The newly-weds fly there in a chartered Super Constellation with a staff which includes Rosenberg, the elderly Tiki plus another maid and a medical nurse. Barbara's leg is encased in plaster from foot to hip.

In Palm Beach the nurse sleeps in her room. Rubi has his own bedroom in another part of the house and rents an apartment in town where he can entertain his dates. He is out every evening and seen in all the trendy night-spots, always with a different girl. He makes no attempt to conceal his activities. Discretion does not enter into it, and Barbara has report of these sightings both in the columns and from her friends.

When not playing polo or womanising, Rubi is out shopping. David Heymann reports that while in Palm Beach he acquired sixty suits, twenty pairs of shoes, fifty pairs of silk pyjamas, dozens of sweaters, shirts, pants, sports jackets... And made it into the Best

212

Dressed Men's list of 1954. Meanwhile, despite the way he is behaving, Barbara dowers him with gifts, including a twin-motor B25 converted bomber – he'd broken the one Doris Duke gave him – which cost her the inflated price of $250,000 (the real price was $200,000). On his forty-fifth birthday she asks him what his heart desires; he tells her a 400-acre orange plantation in the Dominican Republic. The price is $500,000 and she gives him the money to buy it.

Why did she continue to reward him while he was behaving so vilely and presents made him no more agreeable? That she was compulsively generous is hardly an adequate answer. And why for heaven's sake did she marry him?

Because he knew how to do it right? But she didn't have to *marry* him for that, she could have had him on hire and retained control. He was broke and open to an expedient transaction. Was it part of a necessary delusion she was loved and wanted, a fantasy sustainable only with drugs? In effect, wedding him put an end to sex. So what was Barbara's motive for marriage? Dean Jennings lists some answers to the question. 'Because it was her own damn business and she felt like it,' said Cary Grant. 'Because he seemed like a terribly nice guy,' said Lance. 'Because I jilted him and he was available,' said Zsa Zsa. But the most insightful answer is provided by the physician, Dr Randolph, who looked after her for years in Hollywood.

It seems simple to me, it is merely a question of Barbara wanting to take something from someone else. Zsa Zsa had him. Barbara wanted him. Doris Duke had had Rubirosa once, and that made him a catch. Barbara has always envied Doris Duke. She's jealous, and if Doris had him Barbara wanted him too. She would want the best that money could buy.

The 'best' in this case represents spectacular bad value. The honey-moon, the details of which are gleefully relayed by columnists, is lampooned on radio and television. Rubi is caricatured as a Hispanic conman, but she is mocked as a loopy self-chosen victim. The expensive campaign to rebrand her as a mature caring human being has served for nothing. Her image in the eyes of the public has been stripped of all dignity. Her marriage is a farce and she has become a laughing-stock to the world.

It's bad as it can get. Rubi is the worst disaster yet in a chain of marital disasters and it's a sorry chapter that is now ending, but she brings it to a close with style. Her ankle has mended and she is walking without crutches when she gives a dinner at the Moulin Rouge for a dozen friends. She and Rubi are barely on speaking terms by now. They sit at opposite ends of the table in the lively restaurant and the atmosphere between them is frigid. Rubi has invited his guitar-playing Dominican buddy Chago and instructs him to sing. The musician strums a chord and obligingly strikes up the number 'Just a Gigolo'. Barbara is very silent at the end but Rubi rocks back in his seat and roars with pleasure. 'Play it again!' he calls to Chago.

When he's finished the number Barbara remains sitting in silence. After a long wait she gets up and, moving with slow delib-erate gait, walks the distance separating her from her husband. Drawing back her fist, she swings at him and socks him so hard in the face she knocks him off his chair. Total silence falls upon the crowded room. She does not pause, but in the same unhur-ried trance-like pace continues to the exit and walks out on her marriage.

Next day she moves to the Everglades Club and surrenders the lease to Baroda's house. And Rubi shrugs, tells his valet to pack his extensive wardrobe, and clambers into the pilot's seat of the B-25 she has given him and takes off to join Zsa Zsa in New York in an aircraft he can pilot but still has not bothered to learn how to navigate. The marriage has lasted just fifty-three days.

⁂

To relate and, I hope, to read Barbara Hutton's life story to its end – which it has not yet reached, though it doesn't promise well – is fascinating, because it represents so exemplary a case study. She is a prototype of value-free celebrity, now a common species. The sums of money she flung around in the course of a useless life are breathtaking when translated into their present-day equivalent. Her excesses grab the attention – how *we* might have used them if dealt such opportunities – but as her story declines toward its sad close our feeling ultimately is depression. *What misuse of life.*

Perhaps she was destined to be as she was, so needy, so bored, so desperate. Conditioned not genetically but by her upbringing. She felt abandoned when her father died. She craved attention. She received it aplenty, mostly expressed in fury and censure, yet still she needed it. Without it, she did not believe she existed. She did so only because she saw on the page that she was *there*. She had a role in people's lives because she was the coin of their daily gossip. She was under pressure to deliver in an ongoing drama. Meanwhile her own need for an affirming audience was unrelenting, for media exposure required continuing exposure to validate itself and fill the hole of incompleteness that she'd sought to fill with celebrity from the beginning. But recognition did not bring peace, the satisfaction was only momentary before the need resumed. In Barbara's case the analogy of celebrity to a drug holds good through her entire life cycle. But what a desolate epitaph it provides: *What waste.*

CHAPTER 17

ODILE RODIN, PARIS, JUNE–OCTOBER 1956

P aris, which suffered no bomb damage or wholesale looting, was the first European city to recover fully after the Second World War. It had always been possible to obtain an excellent dinner in a first-class restaurant, even during the worst of times, but with peace, food, entertainment and pleasure were freely available to anyone with the cash to pay for them.

The city had never lost its rating as the capital of chic – the leading couturiers had continued to show their new collections throughout the war. Paris contained the most luxurious hotels, finest restaurants, smartest clubs, widest range of high-end boutiques and the best-dressed women ... but now a new caste has asserted its presence on the scene. More than a caste, perhaps a new species, for they have reinvented themselves wholly different from their parents, even in appearance. They are the post-war student young.

All are thin. The males dress in black shirts open at the neck, and narrow trousers; they smoke *gitanes*, drink a great deal of coffee, hang out in jazz clubs and talk earnestly into the night. The pale slender girls with them wear no make-up except for dusky eyes, straight hair, casual clothes and never heels, but otherwise behave exactly as the boys. They are existentialists, followers of the philosophy preached by Jean-Paul Sartre. Rejecting the pieties and conventions of their parents, they have defined themselves in opposition to their values: *I am – and it is I who determine how I act.* They sleep with each other freely and apparently without jealousy, but they are rather serious in their pleasures and don't laugh a lot.

Albert Camus, the writer who has voiced their alienation, can be seen dining in the Brasserie Lippe, as can their high priest Sartre, whose lizard skin is stained sepia by nicotine. There he reigns surrounded by disciples, among them invariably a special one being groomed to share their marriage bed by his wife, Simone de Beauvoir, herself a prophet of the intellectual and sexual liberation which is now the attitude *du jour.*

These, the students' mentors, are middle-aged, yet exempted from that unfashionable crime by the reverence in which they are held. The defining characteristic of the existentialists is their disdain for those older than themselves: *Never trust anyone over thirty.* They feel scorn for the old and all they represent. The old are put out by such disrespect, hurt and bewildered that these, their children, show nothing but contempt for the bourgeois values they hold dear. Parents have gone through the deprivation and suffering of a war to resist Nazi tyranny and pass on to their children a civilised world … and the kids don't give a toss. They think the old, together with all they stand for, ridiculous. They're something else, this upcoming generation: highly visible, loudly audible, so sure of themselves many of their seniors regard them as a hostile tribe.

As for the flagrant sexuality displayed by the young, the old are outraged – particularly by the girls. They form an upstart breed, these young women. Confident, contemptuous, and impregnable in their youth, they can be daunting. They make no effort to please. Spurning coquetry and fashion, they have created their own mode. They are candid, artless, clear-eyed and unimpressed. They're not prepared to do anything that bores them and unafraid to be frankly rude.

❧

Odile Rodin is nineteen, with blonde hair, liquid brown eyes, generous mouth and a cheeky smile. She is studying drama at the Conservatoire National d'Art Dramatique, as are fellow students Jean-Paul Belmondo and Claude Brialy. She has already played small parts in two films, one with Brigitte Bardot, the other starring Danielle Darrieux.

© Press Association

She is introduced to Rubi at a party in Paris in 1956. He is forty-seven years old and incapacitated. While leading his team Cibao La Pampa in a polo match he'd taken a bad fall. His neck and shoulder are encased in a surgical brace; he cannot move his left arm.

He takes her hand, bows and kisses it in an old-fashioned way that makes her smile. 'I've heard much about you, monsieur,' she tells him. 'None of it good.'

She has, she's well aware of his history and has had the opportunity of studying one of his previous wives, who emerged from the experience to remake a successful career. Now here he stands smiling at her, greying at the temples, a little heavier than before, only marginally taller than herself and disabled by a cast. She is not overwhelmed. 'I found him attractive, but I was not completely fascinated like the other ladies. He wasn't good-looking, but he had charisma. He was not very tall, not very perfect. He had a magnetism.'

If you can disregard his back-story – though who can? – Rubi at this moment represents something of a catch. He owns the splendid Paris townhouse in Rue Bellechasse Doris Duke gave him, with the furniture and paintings she bought for it. There he lives in some style, for he has not scaled down on staff, personal pugilist etc. He has the status of an international diplomat. He possesses an official car and chauffeur plus his own Ferrari and the plane Barbara Hutton gave him; he's still cash rich on money obtained from her. He has not modified his lifestyle with middle age. He plays polo, races his sports car, parties, drinks hard, screws around indiscriminately. He's still a rake and an established legend in the columns. Whoever his new liaison, it's good for an item, and there have been plenty of women to provide the accompanying photograph beside him in restaurant, club or ski resort, many of whom rate tabloid mention of their own: Eartha Kitt, Ava Gardner, Rita Hayworth,

Queen Soraya of Persia. In the glitzy jungle which forms their mutual habitat he is as much the prey as they. Both there to score, each collects a scalp and ticks a box. By now his reputation is such that he needs make little effort to score. His friend Igor Cassini (the columnist Cholly Knickerbocker, who soon will be appointed public relations consultant to Trujillo) reports on his technique at this period:

> Rubi had his own special way to conquer a lady. Certainly not the intellectual or even the romantic type, he didn't waste much time in conversation. He went right to the point, or perhaps it would be more correct to say that he made the lady get to it. An attractive English fashion lady told me of her first and unusual encounter with the famous Dominican lover. It was during a Paris dinner party and Rubi was seated next to her. They had hardly exchanged a few words when Rubi grabbed her hand under the table, and without preamble placed it on his hard cock. As she relates it, she was so stunned that she sat there frozen with that thing in her hand. It was a while, she guesses, before she politely withdrew. Rubi had made his move. From then on it was up to the lady, take it or leave it! He performed the same trick on the dance floor; no wonder he'd only dance slow numbers. His secret weapon, of course, was the perpetual hard-on.

On the face of it Rubi is doing good in the mid-1950s. But he does have certain problems of which Odile and the public are unaware. These centre on his patron and employer, Trujillo. The Dominican Republic under his continued reign has become a pariah state; his blatant misrule is now an open scandal. The genocide he inflicted on Haitian immigrants, his refusal to acknowledge the atrocity or pay reparations has resulted in world-wide ostracism. At home his despotic regime has no regard for human rights, which are not recognised to exist. Dissenters and political opponents are eliminated at source. Under his head of secret police, Johnny Garcia, snatch squads operate in countries providing refuge to Trujillo's enemies. These are either assassinated or, if their crime is seen as particularly heinous by the Benefactor, especially rendited for interrogation in the notorious torture chamber of La Cuarenta in the capital, where ultimate punishment is dispensed either by electric chair or stringing up the offender by block and tackle over a vat of boiling oil.

In particular affront to Trujillo's patron the US, Dominican agents have kidnapped Jesus Galindez, a Spanish professor teaching at Columbia who was about to publish a book exposing the bloody history of Trujillo's regime. He was snatched in broad daylight in mid-town Manhattan after lecturing at the university. Police established that his unconscious body, strapped to a stretcher, was loaded onto a plane at Amityville, NY, and flown to Ciudad Trujillo by a 22-year-old American charter pilot, Gerald Murphy. Some days later Murphy's car was found abandoned near an abattoir outside the capital; he himself had disappeared. His parents in Oregon, aware of his 'hospital' flight, were understandably suspicious, obtaining the support of their Congressman, Charles Porter, who took up the cause and instituted an enquiry.

Due to its sensational nature, the case results in a great deal of publicity. Trujillo is already in the dock, his country under sanctions imposed by the US. Now his bank loans are cancelled and his funding cut off by Congress. The Dominican Republic's sugar exports have lost their market and Trujillo's dream of turning the island into a swanky resort has come to nothing. No cruise liners with free-spending passengers berth at the new deepwater port, the marina for the yachts of the rich lies abandoned and incomplete, reeking with effluent. The island's investors have been scared off by corruption and extortion and the treasury is empty.

In Ciudad Trujillo the Benefactor rules from the heavily guarded presidential compound high above the town, where the air is sweeter. Despite the efforts of numerous contractors, the sewage problem has not been solved. Now no one will attempt it for fear of the price of failure.

He is fully informed on his situation. Internally by the creepy but ruthlessly effective Johnny Garcia, externally by his embassies – particularly those in Washington and New York. His lobby of suborned politicians and staffers has proved ineffectual in white-washing his regime; some are under investigation themselves due to their links with him. Yet the US Government has been his supporter from the start, and his extreme right-wing dictatorship is a bastion against Communism in the area. America maintains a missile base and high-tech listening station on the island. The government might have been prepared to continue to turn a blind eye to tyranny within his own country but the kidnapping of a Columbia professor in the heart of the Big Apple and blatant murder of a US citizen cannot be ignored.

Trujillo is isolated and friendless, except for his cabal of cronies, whose lives depend on his continued rule. He is moreover a disap-pointed and embittered man. His donation of a Jewish homeland has gone unrewarded; no Jewish investment resulted from the benefaction. Worse, much worse, his pride has been damaged by a gross insult to his person only last year, in 1955. He'd conceived a grandiose scheme to mark the twenty-fifth anniversary of his rule with a Jubilee, a giant fair celebrating his achievements, which would be attended by world dignitaries and crowds of overseas visitors. Millions of dollars were spent on the site and its various pavilions. The elaborate spectacle was staged under his personal direction, assisted by his PR advisers from New York … and it was a total flop. The pageant attracted no notice, nobody came.

The Benefactor does not take setbacks well. Someone else is always to blame and must be punished. By now his moods have become particularly unstable. At any hour of the day or night an order can go out to his cabal of generals, police honchos and spymasters to report within the hour to the presidential Palace. He is driven down the hill in armed convoy, wearing full uniform. His court awaits him, some roused from bed and hastily dressed, some drunk – but woe betide any who are absent. He harangues them while they tremble in his presence, trying not to attract attention. He can shift from icy control to towering rage in an instant. The sagging face swells red, his eyes bulge in fury. The least misunderstanding can produce a spitting torrent of insult and abuse. His tempers are uncontrollable.

In Paris Rubi is distant from Trujillo's levées by 3,000 miles, but word of the Benefactor's alarming behaviour has reached his brother the ambassador, Rubi, and the rest of the embassy staff – though of course it cannot be discussed. Any incautious remark risks to be reported. Rubi is well informed on his employer's erratic conduct but it does not affect him personally until he receives a cable instructing him in the dictator's latest whim. He is ordered to take the necessary steps to ensure that Trujillo is awarded the Nobel Prize for Peace. Rubi is obliged to confront the disturbing fact that the boss has gone mad.

⚜

'I've heard a lot about you, monsieur, none of it good,' Odile remarks on meeting Rubi for the first time.

He grins. His reputation has never proved a disadvantage in the past, though at the moment with a quarter of his body sealed in a cast he scarcely represents a sexual threat.

He is instantly struck by her, 'She was so young, so fresh, so pretty.' She is still a teenager; her bearing and manner are very unlike the sort of women he's gone with in the past. There's a frankness and boldness to her, an absence of pretension. She's not expensively dressed and she's neither rich nor famous. But there's an unconformity and individuality about her, and she stands in awe of no one.

He invites her to dinner and she accepts, not because she's physically attracted but she's amused by the idea, and why not? He's well-practised in the ritual of dinner, the whole choreography of choosing, ordering, discussion with the *sommelier* about the wine... Top restaurants are his stage, one among his several stages. He doesn't hit on her – he's in no shape to in his cast. For the first time in his life he's physically vulnerable. Instead they talk.

'I spoke of my country, the sun beating down on the coral, the coconut groves. She listened to me smiling... When I asked her questions she spoke gently.'

He's charmed by her. He asks her out again while still in his cast, and again when he's free of it. He too is gentle with her, he doesn't act in the gross fashion described by Igor Cassini. He's every inch the gentleman. Those impressive inches remain decently contained, dormant within his trousers, but Odile's mother is aware of the legend, as is everyone who scans the tabloids. Odile may be an existentialist but she comes of solid bourgeois stock; her father who died when she was young was a surgeon, as is her stepfather. Mother objects strongly to the liaison.

Rubi invites both mother and daughter to dinner, an uncharacteristic move on his part. He's never before sought to meet the parents of his conquests; there are already quite enough people in the world who want to shoot him.

Mother is forthright: 'Odile is in the springtime of her life. You, on the other hand, are past your prime. You will never be able to keep up with her, and you will be made most unhappy in the end.'

Then Odile – still at drama school – is offered a leading part in a new play by Marcel Pagnol, to open in Paris in September. Before rehearsals start, she goes to stay at the St Tropez villa of wealthy industrialist Paul-Louis Weiller, as one of a large party that includes Charlie Chaplin and his family. At a bar in town she learns that Rubi is also on the Côte d'Azur, staying at the Dubonnet house on Cap Ferrat. On impulse, Odile rents a Riva speedboat and roars off to call on him. The sea is choppy and on the high-speed ride her light summer dress is soaked by spray. Arriving at the villa's private jetty, she walks up to the terrace where the house party is assembled, with see-through wet silk clinging to the contours of her body. 'I made quite an entrance,' she says.

Odile is welcomed to the Weillers' house, where she remains a guest. A car is dispatched to St Tropez to collect her clothes.

There, her affair with Rubi blossoms. She is a teenager, as was his first wife Flor when he married her. She has a teenager's vivacity and enthusiasm, a spontaneous *joie de vivre*. She's not an innocent as Flor was, but infinitely more knowing and self-aware; in touch where Flor was naïve, both prettier and brighter. And, crucially, no history of parental bullying and domination. She is her own person.

The Weiller house is casually luxurious, its setting and the weather perfect. By the pool and at the lunch table others are always present, but some evenings they go out *à deux*. There is a rapport between them, both talk at length. Odile says, 'During those ten days he revealed how he truly is: attentive, always happy to get going as soon as he awakes, capable of going out ten days in a row… Rubi is deeply interested in the women he takes out. He isn't satisfied merely to make a date… He discovers her intimately.'

At the end of the vacation he has to return to the Dominican Republic, where his older sister is dying of cancer, but he gets back to Paris for the first night of *Fabien*. Her performance in the role of a knowing ingénue, who breaks up her sister's marriage to snare her husband, is singled out in the notices. The play looks to be a hit. She leaves its celebration party to dine alone with Rubi at Maxim's. A few days later she moves out of the family home to live with him in Rue de Bellechasse. 'I was a baby. I wanted to have fun. I didn't want to get married, I wanted a career. But by the end of one month I was totally fascinated by him.'

Less than one month into the play's run Odile and he are married at an unannounced ceremony at the *mairie* of Sonchamp, a small village just outside Paris.

CHAPTER 18

ZSA ZSA GABOR, LOS ANGELES, EASTER 1957

Zsa Zsa has always valued the big gesture. She is alive to its effect on herself and well aware of the impact it has upon the press. This party she is throwing will be simply the best. The purpose of the imminent bash is both social and political. It is to introduce Ramfis Trujillo (twenty-four) to the US media and to launch him on the A-List as heir to an independent state firmly allied to God's Own Country, and sharing its democratic values and ideals.

This is a project many PR agents might well have blanched at; the public image of the Dominican Republic is appalling. It is of course Rubi who has persuaded Zsa Zsa to work with him in this presumptuous PR venture, and to host the Hollywood party. Despite the fact that he is now married to Odile Rodin, whom Zsa Zsa has never met, and regardless of their violent past relationship, there is no resentment or barbed wire between them. Neither bore rancour, such is not their nature. So alike in character, they understand each other perfectly.

In his letter to Zsa Zsa, Rubi wrote, 'My Darling, for the sake of our wonderful memories – I cannot think of them for they still make me sad – I ask a favour...' Rubi describes Ramfis as 'my President's son and my dearest friend'. He has always made a point of nurturing Ramfis, who hero-worships him. And this relationship is now vital to Rubi, for Trujillo is not only certifiably mad but has been subject to two assassination attempts. If the next succeeds, the country will be up for grabs. Rubi has invested his starter marriage and twenty-five years of his life in the regime. Despite his fraught relationship with the President, he stands close to the centre of power. Ramfis is heir in line to the country and the only contender to back following the Benefactor's death.

Ramfis, now a tall dark-haired personable young man hold-ing the rank of general in the Air Force, is currently studying at Army Staff College, Fort Leavenworth, Texas, but now is Easter vacation and he chooses to make his entry to America in his yacht, *Angelita*, which happens to be the largest private vessel in the world. Accompanied by a party of friends, a Caribbean band and a large uniformed staff, he arrives in New Orleans for Mardi Gras.

It is a conspicuous advent, but the image that captures the front page next day is a shot of Zsa Zsa, snapped in the powder room of the Roosevelt Hotel, with the headline: ZSA ZSA IS HERE. BUT WHERE? IS SHE VISITING ON THE TRUJILLO YACHT?

The mayor of New Orleans, Chet Morrison, and his wife are invited to a lunch on board. He invites Zsa Zsa and Ramfis to attend the Carnival Ball that evening as his guests, adding, 'You would need to wear white tie or your uniform.'

Ramfis says his uniforms are in Texas.

'Then we'll rent you a white tie,' the mayor proposes.

Ramfis is incredulous at the suggestion. '*Rent me a white tie?*' He turns to the aide beside him, 'Call up Kansas. Charter a plane and have them fly my uniform to me.' Everything he's learned of style has come from Rubi.

⚜

Shortly after Mardi Gras, Ramfis flies to California (accompanied by his PA, his personal minstrel and his Alsatian dog) for a sinus operation in a Los Angeles hospital. He stays on afterward for the party Zsa Zsa is setting up to launch him on movie society. He wants to meet Kim Novak (who would be Hitchcock's star in *Vertigo*). Zsa Zsa fixes him up with a date.

Next, Ramfis wants to meet Joan Collins. Zsa Zsa says, 'Joan was always very beautiful but no one wanted to marry her ... she was a strange mix of very tough and very insecure. She was always complaining to me, "I can never hold onto a man".'

This time it is Rubi who proposes the date to Joan. Her response is, 'I only want to meet him if he gives me a beautiful present.'

Tactfully, Zsa Zsa conveys the message to Ramfis, who shrugs and says, 'OK, call up Van Cleef and Arpels and order a diamond necklace.' Zsa Zsa obliges and the date is duly arranged.

A few days afterward, Rubi asks how the date went. Ramfis's response is curt, 'I picked her up in my yacht in Miami,' he said tersely. 'She was so boring that I put her ashore in Palm Beach.'

Zsa Zsa adds, 'I concluded that the clever Miss Collins had taken the diamond necklace and then proceeded to make herself so boring she didn't have to do anything with Ramfis afterward.'

❧

The launch party for the Dominican dictator-in-waiting is sump-tuous. Zsa Zsa has transformed her Bel Air home for the event by gift-wrapping the entire property: garden, trees, flower-beds, shrubbery and swimming pool are all encased in cellophane. The house's dining room is an enormous bar, a dance floor has been laid in the library and there are two orchestras. The guests are drawn from the Rich List and the Hollywood elite: Conrad Hilton (with whom Zsa Zsa has remained on good terms), the David Selznicks, the Kirk Douglases, the Gary Coopers, the James Masons, the Charles Vidors, the Van Johnsons, Shirley MacLaine, Jeanne Crain, Beatrice Lillie, Spike Jones, Baby Pignatari; and of course the acid-tongued gossip columnists Hedda Hopper and Louella Parsons.

The guests number over one hundred and Zsa Zsa, a skilled hostess, has not omitted to include a louche refractory element there to make the evening memorable. Errol Flynn is exuberantly present, flying high on drugs, as is Robert Mitchum who enlivened a recent Hollywood party by stripping off his clothes, smothering his person in ketchup and announcing, 'I'm a hamburger – *eat me!*'

Ramfis has flown Rubi and Odile from Paris to attend. The two women exchange a swift appraising glance, then Zsa Zsa, who is assisted in the receiving line by George Sanders, finds herself introducing Rubi to him. Very correctly so, for though the two have met before when George burst in through the window to discover him naked in his wife's bed, they had not then been properly introduced. 'They shook hands so heartily that for a moment it seemed they might be joined together forever. George broke the spell by pouring his scotch down my dress. Rubi and Odile walked away. I was left talking to Conrad and George. Whereupon David

Selznick came over and whispered, "You are the only woman alive who could have two ex-husbands and a famous ex-lover to the same party."' An apt comment and probably no more than the truth.

⚜

As testimony to Zsa Zsa's worldly sophistication the party scores high; in all other respects the whole PR extravaganza is a disaster. Its timing could not have been worse judged.

Back home in the Dominican Republic, where all power is concentrated in one man, the administration is incapable of joined-up government. Ramfis has been kept ignorant of the detail of his father's wholesale embezzlement, while in Paris Rubi was too busy with his social, sexual and sporting life to stay closely in touch with events on Capitol Hill. Neither is aware that the Dominican Republic has just received $10 million in emergency aid from the US, despite objections in the Senate.

Zsa Zsa gets a call from a reporter at United Press. Is it true she received the gift of a floor-length chinchilla coat worth $80,000 from Ramfis, as well as a Mercedes convertible?

'Why yes,' she answers.

And did Kim Novak also get a Mercedes roadster from the same donor?

Again she answers yes. Ramfis bought her the car and one for himself at the same time; but why the interest?

She's always excited interest, even without meaning to, but this time it's official: the US Senate. She learns that, during a debate, Senator Wayne Hays has made a blistering attack on the manner in which the government conducts its foreign relations. He's suggested that, in order to cut down the paperwork and make it easier for everyone, emergency aid for the Dominican Republic might just as well be sent directly to Zsa Zsa and Kim Novak. He calls her 'The most expensive courtesan since Madame de Pompadour.'

Zsa Zsa's outrage last only for seconds. *Most expensive courtesan since Pompadour?* On consideration she finds the information flattering, the valuation no more than acknowledges her true worth.

CHAPTER 19

ODILE RODIN, PARIS, 1957–61

O dile Rodin's marriage to Rubi coincides with a radical advancement in her career and good fortune. The fates are generous in the dowry they bestow on her. The play she's in, *Fabien*, is received with acclaim. Her name is flagged in its reviews and her talent recognised.

It's hugely gratifying. She loves her art and is exhilarated by her own and the play's success, but she's uneasy with the fact that she is obliged to go to work every evening just when Rubi is gearing up for the night's entertainment. Constitutionally unable to be alone, he is not a homebody, nor can he be relied on for an instant not to stray. He too is dissatisfied that his wife is not available to hit the town with him. He is unquestionably in love; there was no other motive for him to marry her. She's young, pretty, unspoilt, unneurotic and smart as a whip – the perfect pal and playmate for an ageing rake.

For Rubi, the most self-centred of men, it is inconvenient that Odile should be unavailable to him because she works. But is it also possible that he is jealous of her success? And the independence that her talent gives her? Certainly that had never been the case with any of his previous wives. But he's a waning stud and no longer the fresh bull in the field. Odile recalls, 'Rubi made me cancel my contract with my impresario. He told Rubi, "You are doing the most foolish thing because she would have a great future."' Others too who had spotted her talent regretted its renunciation in such an unworthy cause.

In poor exchange for giving up her career, he takes her to the island of his birth, whose unspoilt beauty he has often described to her. There Odile is presented to the Benefactor. Evidently on one of his good days, for the meeting passes without incident. They fly on to Havana, where Rubi has had his Ferrari shipped from Paris so he can compete in the Cuban Grand Prix. The drama of the event is raised to a high pitch by the kidnapping of its pole-position driver, Juan Fangio, by bandits commanded by their till now unheard-of leader, Fidel Castro. Yet the snatch is not seen as a political state-ment but for reward. A ransom is paid and he's released unharmed after the race, in which Rubi fails to finish. The Ferrari is not the latest model and he's pushed it hard in the past. Nor are his own reflexes what they were.

From Havana the couple move on to Los Angeles to attend Ramfis's coming-out party hosted by Zsa Zsa Gabor which we are familiar with. Briefly Odile gets to examine in the flesh the 38-year-old woman of whom she's heard so much, and who in character is Rubi's closest equivalent to a female twin. Then, leaving Beverly Hills, the two continue to New York, where Odile meets with the metropolitan smart set while Rubi and Igor Cassini, now PR adviser to Trujillo, plot together on how to serve their master and themselves.

The task of obtaining the Nobel Peace Prize for the dictator is clearly impossible, but the two are committed to the job of rebranding him. After deliberation, Cassini approaches the Mutual Broadcasting System, a major news distributor in the US owned by

Alexander Guterma, who is under indictment for fraud and pressed for ready cash. Cassini obtains from him a guarantee that Mutual will transmit seven hours per month of favourable news and feature footage on the Dominican Republic and Trujillo – unedited and in the form that it is provided to them – for the next one and a half years, in return for a payment of $750,000. The deal has to be concluded quickly before Guterma is sent to jail. But Trujillo pays up. Rubi skims $50,000 for himself, Cassini takes his arrangement fee and the rest goes to Guterma, his to enjoy only for the next few weeks before incarceration.

The Benefactor is pleased with the deal and rewards Rubi and Odile with a prize. He is made up in rank and named ambassador to Cuba. The post is a delicate assignment and for once in his career Rubi is required to do some effectual work.

Cuba's President Batista – whose patron is the US, as Trujillo's had been until recently – has succeeded with his country where Trujillo has failed. Havana is a thriving resort only a short hop from Miami and attracts many American visitors for weekends and vacation. The place is not high-tone like Monte Carlo or Cannes, but instead rackety, colourful and alive. Gambling and prostitution form the main lure, but Havana possesses a louche shabby glamour and it is *hot*. Its casinos are very efficiently run by the US mafia. There is little crime and seldom any trouble. Cuba is an extreme right-wing country which has the death penalty for practically everything. The place continues to attract US investment: the sugar-cane industry, tourism and gaming have caused its economy to prosper. The other face to this coin is that a force of communist guerrillas is hid in the Sierra Maestra mountains, led by Castro and descending to carry out increasingly blatant attacks in the heart of Havana.

Rubi's instructions as ambassador are to connect with

someone close to Castro, offering to sell the rebels arms, while maintaining close relations with the reigning dictator, Batista. Most importantly, he is briefed to cosy up to the US ambassador, Earl Smith, and repair the breach between the Dominican Republic and its patron. In this Odile's a considerable asset. She is so vivacious and charming, so quick, her accent so enchanting … she and Rubi make up a most attractive couple who enliven the tone of any group around them. She becomes friendly with Smith's wife Florence and soon the Rubirosas are regular guests at the embassy. It's a convivial venue, for Havana is a favoured spot for quasi-official junkets. Among other visitors, she and Rubi strike up an acquaintance with another attractive young couple, Senator John F. Kennedy and his wife Jackie. Rubi and Kennedy get along at once. Both are instinctive womanisers and they have a rakish mutual pal in Igor Cassini. Jackie loathes Rubi on sight.

On New Year's Eve 1958 Odile and Rubi spend the evening at a party at the American embassy. When they leave to go home Earl Smith warns them, 'You are going to maybe have a problem. Be ready, something is going to happen.'

Driving away from the well-guarded compound, very quickly they find themselves in a war zone. Hysterical people are running down the street while from close by comes the sound of rapid fire and the thud of grenades. They reach the Dominican embassy to find the telephone ringing. Earl Smith is on the line saying, 'Listen, come over now to my embassy, Batista left the country and has just landed in the Dominican Republic.'

A well-armed force led by Castro's deputy, Che Guevara, has attacked the city, capturing the radio station. They have many supporters among the inhabitants. The police are demoralised by Batista's abandonment, the national army is leaderless. Very soon the rebels are in control of the capital.

Odile and Rubi stay for a week under asylum at the American embassy, which is guarded by US marines. They then return to the Dominican embassy, where their situation is more fraught. As Odile tells it, 'We went through hell. They were yelling outside that Rubi was a murderer … one night … there was this boom. They threw hand grenades. They made a hole in the patio and were shooting through all the windows…'

Castro takes over power with huge popular support. Batista's stooges have fled, are in jail or have been shot. Under the new rule the casinos are shut down and the mafia shipped out. US corporations own 80 per cent of Cuba's utilities, 90 per cent of its mining and half the sugar industry. Now Castro starts on a programme to nationalise every one of those 400 American businesses, together with all banks and industries on the island. The US withdraws its ambassador and closes its embassy. The Dominican embassy follows suit, and Odile and Rubi fly back to Paris.

<hr />

Odile is twenty-two, Rubi fifty, a significant marker for a man. He has slowed down, he takes whole days and nights off to rest his liver and catch up on his beauty sleep. He orders a new Ferrari 250 GT but makes another significant concession to a new regimen, he sells the mansion Doris Duke gave him and buys a house in the suburbs. It is a classy burb – their neighbour in Marnes-la-Coquette is Aly Khan – but Odile is not on record about what she thinks of the move from town. Some nights while Rubi stays home watching TV and drinking mineral water, she accepts invitations to go out alone. He doesn't appear to mind.

He is in good standing with Trujillo, thanks to the fact he doesn't have to deal with the deranged tyrant in the flesh. He is appointed ambassador to Belgium – an empty title since the Dominican Republic has no links, political or commercial, with the country. His job is to watch over Ramfis who is in a clinic there, undergoing detox and psychiatric treatment. He is addicted to both alcohol and drugs. After several months he is released. Emotionally dependent on Rubi, for although he has a ragged court of hangers-on he has no real friends, Ramfis buys a house at Neuilly, close to Rubi and Odile. He and Rubi play polo regularly, but in other respects his close company is not an asset. He's soon drinking again and back on drugs. But Ramfis is a necessary cross to bear for he's close to the Benefactor's throne and heir apparent when Trujillo finally gets his, as increasingly looks inevitable.

Trujillo's iron hold upon his country has not slackened but his judgement has. US sanctions against the republic deny the sugar industry its guaranteed market, the crop has been sold off piecemeal at knock-down price. No investment is coming in. American-owned businesses have been driven out by extortion; the US has closed down its embassy in Ciudad Trujillo, withdrawing its ambassador and staff. When the elderly American bishop, Thomas Reilly, issues a Pastoral Letter denouncing the abuse of human rights, ordering priests to read it to their congregations, a gang of police in civilian clothes break into his church and rectory to wreck them. Reilly narrowly escapes with his life to hide out in a convent school. Trujillo orders the island's radio station to play dance music throughout Holy Week. On the GOD AND TRUJILLO posters displayed all over the island hoardings, God's name is removed from the credits.

The Benefactor's behaviour has become a public embarrassment. He is sixty-eight and suffering prostate trouble but this has not diminished his sexual urge. He maintains several young mistresses living at home with their respectable parents who are rewarded for their complaisance; one of them only fourteen when thus honoured by his favour. These liaisons are not secret, gossip makes them the property of everyone.

Trujillo had always lived by a regimen of little and plain food, no alcohol during the day. Now that isn't so. Splendidly uniformed, on occasions he strides around the presidential compound haranguing his attendants in words that make no sense; his thoughts and meaning temporarily lose their link. Yet his pronouncements demand acknowledgement from his clique; they applaud automatically. He attends evening parties where he now drinks heavily. His enlarged prostate has resulted in incontinence. At several gatherings he's been seen to soil his pants.

❧

When John F. Kennedy is elected President in November 1960 he learns that he's inherited a specific CIA mission authorised by the previous Eisenhower administration, which by now is fully prepared and waiting only on his approval to go into action. Three foreign dictators, Castro, Patrice Lumumba of the Congo and Trujillo, have been targeted for political assassination prior to regime change. Dissident forces already exist in the Dominican Republic, as does a pirate radio state unstoppably preaching revolution to the island's listeners. The likelihood is that Trujillo will be toppled anyway, but unless this is orchestrated by Washington the country risks falling into the hands of pro-Castro communist radicals.

At this moment Igor Cassini proposes to old Joe Kennedy – the President's father whom he knows well – that the two of them open a direct line between Trujillo and the White House to effect an expedient solution to the problem.

In result, the President sends his old pal from Congress, Senator George Smathers, to sound out the possibility of Trujillo relinquishing power and moving out before it is too late. But even the prospect of an open road to retirement in Switzerland with fortune and dignity intact fails to persuade Trujillo to stand down. It would seem that power not only corrupts but possesses, its owner *cannot* renounce it. Nevertheless, Smathers testifies, 'Trujillo was a very very interesting character. He pulled out a .45 pistol and he laid it right out on the desk, pointed right at me, and we started talking…'

❧

Rubi's polo team Cibao La Pampa notches up three wins in a row at the start of the French season in 1961. Ramfis is a member, along with his brother Rhamades and Rubi's nephew Gilberto. On 30 May they win again against a private team, Les Mousequetaires. At the party afterward Rubi has only a token drink before making a date to ride with Ramfis next day, then goes home to Odile.

The following morning he arrives at Ramfis's house at 10 a.m., dressed in riding clothes. He finds the place in uproar. Ramfis had been woken by an early call from his mother in the republic. She was in hysterics, begging him to come home at once, but unable to say why. In high alarm, he put a call through to his brother-in-law, Chesty Estevez, but neither could Estevez explain the urgency, no line in Ciudad Trujillo is secure. He would only say, 'Everything is under control but your presence is absolutely necessary. Do you understand?'

When Rubi walks into the house, Ramfis is in a state close to hysteria. He says, 'They've killed my father.' It is decided to charter a plane and fly home immediately. Ramfis takes with him a party of seven, including Rubi still in riding breeches. Odile has gone to the hairdresser and her husband gets through to inform her of his departure only just before the plane takes off from Orly. Their flight is unregistered and traffic control at Puerto Rico instructs them to land, airspace over the Dominican Republic is closed. Ramfis, with Rubi by him in the cockpit, switches off the radio, ordering the charter pilot to continue or Rubi will take over. From above the airport at Ciudad Trujillo they see the runway to be lined with tanks. Switching on communication, they hear from Estevez in the control tower who assures them the army is loyal. They put down. Ramfis and Rhamades are first off the aircraft. Someone passes Rubi a pistol and he steps onto his native soil just behind them.

⚜

The evening before, Trujillo had dined with his daughter Angelita in town, leaving her house at 9.40 p.m. He was on the way to his favourite beachfront home Hacienda Fundacion when they'd got him.

He was not in one of his official cars but a Chevrolet Bel Air with fancy twin-fender horns and distinctive whitewall tyres. He sat in the back on the right, the nearside. On the seat beside him was a briefcase containing 100,000 US dollars and a loaded .45 revolver; he never went anywhere without both. At the wheel was Captain de la Cruz, his driver for the last eighteen years, by him two automatic rifles and a revolver. A Thompson sub machine gun lay hid beneath the seat.

As the Chevrolet went by the fairground on the outskirts of the capital a black sedan pulled out to follow it. The car contained seven mid-ranking army officers, who with a half-dozen others had plotted this ambush and subsequent coup. Only two days previously they had approached General Papo Roman – Secretary for the armed forces and married to Trujillo's niece – to propose he should lead the country after the Benefactor's death. His acceptance had cued this attempt.

Once clear of town and on the now-unlit expressway, the black sedan closed the distance between the two cars. It pulled out to overtake... but held steady alongside. The blast of two sawn-off shotguns shattered the side windows of the Chevy. One spray of shot disabled Trujillo's left arm, the other struck the driver in the shoulder. The car slewed sideways, skidding to halt broadside on the highway. The black sedan continued past, braking hard. It came to rest angled across the traffic lane. Four of the assassins leapt out and flattened to the ground to continue shooting. Those remaining inside the vehicle fired from the windows with machine carbines. The weapons had been provided by the CIA.

Trujillo was out of the Chevrolet, firing his revolver from cover of its open door. His left arm hung useless. His wounded driver returned fire with both the automatic rifles. The Chevy beams were full on and its police siren wailing above the gunshots. A bullet creased the driver's skull and he went down.

The assassins saw a figure coming toward them, blundering in and out of the dusty beam of the headlights. In uniform, hat still firmly on his head, he was waving a gun aimed drunkenly at them. The three shotguns fired at almost the same instant. Trujillo's body spun, arms flailing as it toppled. One of the assassins went forward and used his boot to roll the corpse onto its back. He administered the coup de grace by a final bullet to the head. They threw the bloodied body into the trunk of the sedan and drove off at speed.

By pure chance another army officer, loyal to the regime, was driving on the coastal highway and came upon the scene of carnage only minutes later. Recognising Trujillo's bullet-ridden car, he drove at once to his commanding officer – a certain General Roman – to report what he'd found and accompany Roman to the

Palace to take over control. Swept up by circumstance and with notable irony, Roman was escorted into power not by the rebels but instead by *loyal* army officers.

Thrown by this turn of events, the plotters called off their attack upon the Palace. The planned coup did not take place.

⁂

On landing at Ciudad Trujillo, Ramfis assumes control of the army with Rubi as his adviser and right-hand man. After a lifetime of waiting, Ramfis has been catapulted into the hot-seat of power and called upon to resolve a crisis. He's in poor shape to do so. Despite several 'cures', he's heavily dependent on drugs, and the event has sent him manic. His model in the use of power is his ruthless and deranged father, to whom vengeance was a creed.

At once the police are ordered to bring in the assassins. Within three days over 400 men and women have been arrested and are under interrogation and torture. A dozen others have been shot resisting capture. When General Roman's involvement is discovered he is ordered to report to the San Isidro army base, site of another notorious torture chamber, Kilometer Nine. There for days he is made to suffer, with eyelids stitched to his eyebrows. He is beaten with baseball bats, drenched with acid, exposed to swarms of angry ants, castrated and shocked for hours on end in the electric chair. Finally, while still twitching convulsively with life, his torturers discharge their weapons into his body, which disintegrates in the hail of fire.

In Miami, Flor receives word that Ramfis is '*Muy malo*, worse than Trujillo.' Low on funds and concerned about her inheritance, she flies to Ciudad Trujillo where one of Ramfis's generals fetches her to meet him. On the short drive to his fortified beach house the car is stopped ten times at roadblocks by armed soldiers demanding identification.

She finds her brother holed up with a German showgirl from the Paris Lido. He is drinking, on medication and in a high state of nerves. He tells her, 'Those Americans are impossible. I can do nothing, be nothing. Everyone is trying to impose ideas on me. Even my mother is driving me crazy.'

In the luxurious beachfront villa Ramfis is attended by Flor's ex-husband Rubi and his polo team, now become Ramfis's henchmen. All of them are wearing civilian clothes. His yacht *Angelita* is berthed at the nearby dock, engines fired-up, captain and crew on duty.

Flor is here to seek reassurance about her legacy. Can she have $25,000 in advance? Ramfis promises she will receive the money within days and she returns to Miami.

On 19 November Ramfis's nerve gives way. He cracks. Boarding the *Angelita*, already loaded with art-works and booty, he takes with him his father's body. Accompanied by his gang – though not Rubi, who is now back in Paris with Odile – he sails for Guadeloupe. From there the party catches a plane to Paris, instructing the *Angelita*'s captain to sail for Cannes. On landing in Paris, Ramfis flies on to Brussels where he is admitted as a patient to the clinic where he has stayed before. It is announced that he is receiving 'sleeping treatment'.

Not until he wakes up days later does Rubi learn that the *Angelita* has been intercepted by a Dominican gunship. The treasures it contained have been confiscated, but Trujillo's body was put on an Air France plane to Paris.

Rubi is incensed at the lily-livered way Ramfis has bottled out of power. He's invested years of his life in this jerk, taught him everything he knew. Odile and he (and all his earlier wives) have put the creep up, fixed him up with women, launched him on society, provided food and drink, endured his loutish company. For what? For this? For Rubi to lose the plantation Barbara Hutton bought him on the island, to lose his job as ambassador, to lose the car and driver, the first class travel, the perks, the diplomatic status… Seething with anger Rubi calls a press conference – well attended because the Dominican Republic is news. With Odile at his side he calls Ramfis a loser and junkie retard, 'the most cowardly man in the world'.

Meanwhile the Benefactor completes his final journey to land in France. During his lifetime he's been accustomed to honour and respect but his reception at Orly is sadly lacking in ceremony – indeed in any dignity. Not a soul is there to meet him and claim his coffin. He's put in a freezer to await collection.

CHAPTER 20

ODILE RODIN, PARIS, INDEPENDENCE DAY, 4 JULY 1965

This polo match is the last in the series. Other teams competing for the Coupe de France have been knocked out and this game between Baron Elie de Rothschild's team and Rubi's Cibao La Pampa will decide this year's champion. It's a bright sunny afternoon and the elegant wooden stand of the Bagatelle Club in the Bois de Boulogne is filled by men wearing light suits and women in colourful dresses and hats.

The competing sides, mounted on ponies that can accelerate from zero to thirty-five mph in seconds, are dressed in white breeches, team colours and white helmets. On the large field it is not always easy to distinguish the players from one another, but Rubi stands out. He wears a red helmet, as he always has.

Odile is seated in the clubhouse stand in a small group that includes Oleg Cassini, Igor's couturier brother. She and Rubi have continued to enjoy the good life since his involuntary retirement from Trujillo's service. They've divided their time between Paris, Deauville, Cap Ferrat, New York and Palm Beach. They've become members of a classy circle. Igor has been pals with the Kennedy family for years and Oleg is the designer chosen to dress the First Lady. The Rubirosas have sailed with them in the presidential yacht and been invited to the family compound of Hyannis Port. Lem Billings, a friend of Kennedy since Choate prep school, says,

> Only once did I see Jackie lose her composure because of another woman. It was over Odile Rodin, the young wife of Porfirio Rubirosa… Jack and Rubi had been introduced by Igor Cassini. They had one thing in common: a burning interest in women. They became friends; Jack and Odile became better friends. Rubi, never particularly prone to the vagaries of jealousy, didn't seem to mind; Jackie minded a great deal… Jack could be shameless in his sexuality, would simply pull girls' dresses up and so forth. He would corner them at White House dinner parties and ask them to step into the next room, where they could hold a "serious discussion"… it was typical of how he dealt with women.

It takes money for a couple to follow the international lifestyle chosen by the Rubirosas and to keep up with its competitive milieu. And it requires a fortune to maintain your own polo team, that's a hobby for the likes of the Aly Khan and Elie de Rothschild. Rubi still had cash but he was not *rich*. There is no money coming in now, no embassy to which he can charge his household expenses and the limo when required. He'd never *saved* money, his business was spending it.

The couple did not cut back on the extravagance of their way of life, but he did spend more nights at home sparing his liver and resting up. There were usually a handful of chums hanging around the house and Odile was free to go out with them if she wished. Oleg Cassini says, 'Odile exhausted him and made him jealous. In a weak moment he admitted, "All my life I've controlled women – every woman I've ever met, except this one. She is under my skin."'

As a couple what media attention they received was an occasional listing among guests who were there, but as actors in a marriage in trouble they rated a mention. The columnist Suzy ran a blind item about an ageing playboy sipping hot milk in front of the TV while his wife was on the town having an affair with one of his young friends. 'Odile ruined his life,' says Zsa Zsa Gabor.

❦

At the Bagatelle Club that afternoon, Cibao La Pampa are the victors in the hard-fought match with a score of 2½ to 2. They gain the Coupe de France and the triumph demands a special celebration, for which traditionally the leader of the losing team will pick up the tab.

Odile and Rubi drive home to shower and change. He tells her what to wear for the evening ahead. She says, 'He counselled me on my hair (he loves chignons). On which jewellery I should wear (he prefers simple), on my outfits (these are very important to him). I haven't bought a suit, an outfit, a coat in which he hasn't accompanied me to give me his judgement. He would put me under the shower if my hair was too lacquered.' But she found ways to defy his fogyism, such as going out without knickers beneath her couture dresses.

They leave the house taking two cars, Rubi the Ferrari, Odile the Austin. It is not a dinner party they're headed for but a rout at New Jimmy's, the in-club of the moment. They pitch up around 10 p.m. when the joint is already roiling. This is *the* party of the night, the A-list throng the bar and space around the tiny dance floor. There is loud music, good-looking couples dancing the Twist, a crowded room with people shouting to be heard above the din. This is Rubi's scene, the habitat where he's on show, on form, most alive and most himself.

At 4.30 a.m. the crowd has thinned but the revel is still kicking and when Odile says she's going home he's not ready to leave. Oleg Cassini is still there, 'Champagne was being poured into the championship cup; everyone was laughing, drinking. I remember looking at him. He was trying to smile but the fun had gone out of him. His eyes were dead. He said to me, "Oleg, let's go out. We've had enough of this. Let's go and have a drink or two."'

They go to Calvados, open all night. Rubi has sunk a lot by now yet Oleg says, 'He could hold his liquor better than anyone I knew.' But drink has turned sour in him, he's gone flat. 'I'm not happy,' he tells Oleg. 'It's always the same thing. I don't have any money. I don't know if I can sell my house. I don't know what's going to happen... Odile is impossible.'

Oleg tries to cheer him and Rubi rouses himself to say, 'Hey *mon vieux!* Come back and stay with me at the house. We can have another glass of champagne and talk.' But Cassini has a meeting early next morning and refuses. 'I remember thinking I should go with him.'

⚜

At 7 a.m. the Allée de la Reine Marguerite, which cuts through the Bois de Boulogne in a straight line, is almost empty of traffic. A Frenchman on his way to work gets into his parked car, either glances or fails to check his rear mirror, and pulls out. A Ferrari sports car travelling fast clips his bumper and rebounds. Its front wheels hit the kerb and it takes off to ram into a tree.

The Frenchman runs to the crash. The driver is slumped forward, his chest crushed into the steering column. He's struggling to extract the unconscious figure from the wreckage before it explodes when by pure chance an ambulance passes. He flags it down. The paramedics help free the driver and rush him to hospital. But it's already too late, Rubi's spine is broken and he is dead on arrival.

CHAPTER 21

AFTER RUBI

After such knowledge of Rubi, what forgiveness? In the instant of his sudden death five wives and Zsa Zsa became widows-in-law, bonded by their relationship to the once-loved one. How did they feel about him?

He had played a seminal role in all their pasts, been a lead character in their lives – though perhaps not *the* leading character. One cannot but be struck by the dominant father figure looming over most of their childhoods.

Flor Trujillo had been twenty-two when she divorced Rubi. In the following years she ran through eight further husbands. She'd been in Montreal when she learned of her father's assassination. 'I wept tears of love and bitterness. I felt that I myself was dying, for I had no existence, no personality apart from Trujillo.' When she got home the island was in chaos. Hysterical people swarmed the streets wailing, 'The father of all of us has been killed.' Ramfis was back with Rubi at his side. He'd seized power, and her ex-husband was about to tour the country with his own entourage to announce the 'New Program'. Flor was filled with scorn. 'Feckless playboy Rubi a politician? The very idea was comic... And it was high comedy to see Rubirosa riding his horse up George Washington Avenue, where once Trujillo had promenaded nightly, flanked by twenty or so henchmen.'

Flor's tone of contempt is clear, but it is the sole instance of it. Neither she nor any of his wives spoke badly of him afterwards. And neither did they repine or show bitterness at the financial cost and damage he'd done them, as many might in the circumstances. Partly this may be because these women all possessed wealth and an international circle of friends. They were not lonely in rejection, nor short of invitations. A variety of would-be lovers and would-be husbands stood available. Riches are a solace to the afflicted, you do not have to languish. As with other surgical operations, wealth can fix a broken heart.[†]

Despite the humiliation she suffered in her five-year marriage, Flor recovered her spirit when she broke free from Rubi. She'd married him to get away from her father, but it is inescapable to conclude that he was only a substitute for her monstrous parent, the Great Benefactor, and from *that* relationship it would seem she never escaped, even after his death.

⚜

For Danielle Darrieux, when aged twenty-four and married to a much older husband who had become a father figure, Rubi appeared on the scene at the right moment. She was ready to make a gesture to assert her independence and he was perfectly suited for the situation. The role was there for him, she invited him to

---

[†] Or at least assuage it. Philippe Woog, inventor of the electric toothbrush and mega-rich in consequence, incurably Belgian and one of the most miserable men on earth, when questioned on the disjunction between wealth and happiness agreed there was none but said he'd rather cry in his Rolls-Royce than on the subway.

step into it. For a while he filled it well, but then she fell in love with him...

The day she learned of Rubi's death she was filming *Les Demoiselles de Rochefort* with Gene Kelly and Catherine Deneuve. She had paid a high price for marrying him. Obtaining his freedom from imprisonment cost her her reputation and career. For over two years she lived in fear of reprisal and death. In 1948 she wed the writer Georges Mitsinkides, remaining happily married to him until his end in 1991. Following her pardon, she'd resumed work immediately. Between 1945 and 2008 she acted in seventy-eight movies, thirty-five stage plays, and twenty-eight TV productions. She was a trouper who played her part nobly to the end of her career.

⁂

After divorcing Rubi, Doris Duke picked up Joey Castro, a Mexican pianist at the Mocambo Club in LA, telling the barman to put him on her tab. She'd been thirty-five when she married Rubi, in personality as dominating as her father Buck, yet incapable of love or care. There was nothing naïve about Doris, she was a journalist and she'd researched him thoroughly. She knew he was a crook, a thief, had been involved in murder. She believed she could handle the relationship as she had with Buck, she was in charge and held the chequebook. But in Buenos Aires and later in Paris the frequent humiliation, gossip and ridicule wore her down to the point where she slashed her wrists.

Following separation from Rubi, Doris embraced the services of the first of a series of Indian yogis she hoped would restore her youth and cure a skin condition that increasingly troubled her. Joey Castro was said to be 'neurotic and volatile', he hit her over the head with a bottle and later broke her jaw. When she learned of Rubi's death she was with another lover, Edward Tirella, who records, 'She said Barbara Hutton had always been jealous of her. Rubi was the love of her life and Barbara stole him. "We could never get along but I still love the man."' Tirella himself Doris accidentally ran over and killed – he was planning to leave her.

A new lover, Moroccan Leon Amar, reported, 'She hated being what she was. She said the only family she had was her dogs.' Neither dermatologists nor Indian healers could cure Doris's skin problems. Her body was disfigured by white blotches, though it did not prevent her pursuing sex. The doorman to her New York block said, 'She brings these young studs in here and they're up there fifteen or twenty minutes. I don't know what she pays them.'

In 1971 she legally adopted Chandi Heffner, a follower of Hare Krishna whom she believed to be a reincarnation of her dead daughter. To please her, Doris bought a Boeing 737. Its pilot said, 'She went along with everything Chandi wanted ... I think it was fear.' In 1991 Chandi was dumped without notice. When Doris had a fall and broke her hip, her butler Bernard Lafferty began to make himself indispensable. Doris's housekeeper says, 'In March 1993 Lafferty told me she had suffered a stroke and was dying. I was asked to witness a codicil... Doyle [her lawyer] pushed her hand along the page, guiding the hand.' Doris's nurse says, 'Dr Kivowitz told me it was time for Miss Duke to go.' She was put on a morphine drip and given an injection. The cause of death was stated to be pulmonary oedema. She was eighty-one years old. Lafferty was left $5 million. He took to wearing her clothes and jewellery, cut and dyed his hair in her style and ordered her maid to make up his face in the same manner. He even started speaking in the same whispery voice as his dead mistress.

In the fall of 1957 Barbara Hutton called a press conference at the Paris
Ritz to announce her sixth marriage to Baron von Cramm. Three
weeks later she returned to the hotel one afternoon to find him on
his knees servicing a room-service waiter. She chose her last husband
in Raymond Doan, half Vietnamese, an amateur painter. An impoverished Laotian family was induced to adopt him, giving him their
ancestral title, and in 1964 Barbara became Princess de Champassak.

Then Rubi died in the Bois de Boulogne, only a few hundred
yards from her apartment, Jimmy Donahue committed suicide,
Reventlow expired during heart surgery, her son Lance died in a
plane crash. She sat in bed fully made-up, wearing all her jewels. Her
facelift had collapsed, her eyes were failing, she never got up. She
was sinking into a stupor but her prodigious will sparked for the last
time when her lawyer Mattison came to say goodbye. 'Graham,' she
said in her sweetest voice, 'I think you're the biggest con artist I've
ever met. Now get out of here and let me die in peace.' She did so
aged sixty-six in May 1979 and was buried at Woodlawn Memorial
Cemetery, NYC. No member of the press attended the ceremony.

What was the secret of Rubi's allure – apart from the obvious?

Part answer is that he was custom-made for the sort of
experienced women who invited him to their beds. He came unac-
companied by any emotional baggage or hang-ups, and you could
take him anywhere, he was a distinctive accessory to wear at any
gathering. He provided sex, fun, company and drama. He was also
the perfect girlfriend to take shopping. He knew which clothes
showed off a woman best and he adored spending.

There existed many elements in Rubi that were feminine. Vanity,
flirtatiousness, wilfulness, inordinate passion and a taste for drama

are predominately, though not exclusively, female characteristics. The downside was that he was entirely self-centred and didn't know the meaning of love. At the same time he was Peter Pan, the boy that never grew up, who liked nothing better than boxing, fencing, racing cars and playing with his toys.

⚜

Soon after Odile Rodin had met Rubi, he invited her mother to join them for dinner where she'd said, 'You will never be able to keep up with her, and you will be made most unhappy in the end.' It proved to be the case. Did he suffer? Probably. Did she? Perhaps not. Maybe it was as well it ended when it did, as the role of geriatric cuckold would not have become him. Afterwards, Odile sold their house for a substantial sum, remarried, chose the seclusion of a private life, gave no interviews and erased Rubi from her past.

⚜

So why do women marry shits? Or if that is too wide and stereotypical a question, why do some women choose to marry one while knowing full well what he is?

This book represents an attempt to elicit an answer to the query. A presumptuous venture not undertaken alone, but with the help of three female editors not unacquainted with life.

Tales of men who behave badly to women litter the pages of history since antiquity. It is rarer, much rarer, to learn the woman's side to the story. Very often they were in that relationship because they'd had no choice, they'd been obliged to marry a monster. But that is not so for the women in this book. They *chose* to marry Rubi, they embraced their fate.

Notes toward *why* may be gathered from these pages while read-ing of their childhood and upbringing; that is, the explanation lies within *them*. But this does not answer the question in regard to Rubi, their chosen one. Why was he irresistible?

He was dangerous, therefore exciting? He was volatile and passionate yet also *sooo* cool? He raised a woman's morale, made her feel special and desirable? Further, he made her more attrac-tive in others' eyes, providing a boost to self-worth prickled by a frisson of jealousy? But that jealousy was well-founded. Rubi was programmed to stray, a wife was destined to be betrayed. Knowing his past, did each think she would be the one to *change* him? They weren't innocents in the world, how could they have deluded themselves so?

Yet life was exhilarating in his company. To be with him was to live hard, with the accelerator floored and the needle flickering into the red zone. It raised the pulse rate. You were never bored, as so often with other men. He kept a woman on her toes, you had to stay sharp. He surprised you, made you laugh. No row could endure for long, it was solved by sex. And sex was wonderful with Rubi, he was the most attentive and sensitive of lovers. And most men aren't?

Zsa Zsa Gabor's affair with him had lasted on and off for a tempes-tuous four years. After not marrying him she went on to wed five more husbands. When she learned of Rubi's death, 'I cried for him, for his charm, for his passion, his verve, for our love, our romance … he mesmerised me.' Years after his death, while married to her fifth husband, she went to visit his grave in Père Lachaise cemetery. 'At first I couldn't find it … eventually I did and saw that no flowers marked the last resting place of the most famous playboy the world has ever known. Instead an old Christmas tree had been placed on the grave. It was July.'

It is appropriate that Zsa Zsa, who most resembled him and knew him best, should have the last word.

If I hadn't followed my heart and hadn't capitulated to my passion for Rubirosa, and had, at that moment, concentrated on my career, my life might have been completely different. As it is, I did follow my heart, I did let passion overrule judgement but I didn't care and, to this day, I still don't care. Out of all the many lives I've lived up till now – my life with Rubirosa was the most exciting.

ACKNOWLEDGEMENTS

A number of people have been of significant help while writing this book: Stephen Brough, Ernest Chapman, the Benjamin Fishers, Peter Mayle, Mark Ramage and Vivien Tyler.

Particular thanks to Gill Hoffs for research, Christine at Valiant Services, my agent Julian Friedmann. At The Robson Press to my editor Sam Carter, James Stephens, Katy Scholes, Nam Cho and Jennifer Hamilton.

A NOTE ON THE SOURCES

I am most indebted to Shawn Levy's fine biography of Rubirosa, *The Last Playboy*, Fourth Estate, 2005. I have also drawn upon the following sources:

Brown, Peter H., *Such Devoted Sisters: Those Fabulous Gabors*, St Martin's Press, 1985

Cassini, Igor, *I'd Do It All Over Again*, G P Putnam & Sons, 1977

Cassini, Oleg, *In My Own Fashion*, Simon & Schuster, 1987

Crassweller, Robert D., *The Life and Times of a Caribbean Dictator*, NY Macmillan, 1966

Delaunay, Pierre, *Just A Gigolo,* Paris, Olivier Orban, 1987

Diederich, Bernard, *The Death of the Goat,* The Bodley Head, 1978

Duke, Pony and Thomas, Jason, *Too Rich: The Family Secrets of Doris Duke,* Harper Collins, 1996

Frank, G., *Zsa Zsa Gabor: My Story*, Arthur Baker Ltd., 1961

Glass, Charlos, *Americans In Paris. Life and Death under Nazi Occupation*, Harper Press, 2007

Hersh, Seymour M., *The Dark Side of Camelot*, Little Brown, 1997

Heymann, David C., *Poor Little Rich Girl: The Life and Legend of Barbara Hutton*, Random House, 1983

Humbert, Agnes, *Resistance: Memoirs of Occupied France*, Bloomsbury, 2008

Jennings, Dean, *Barbara Hutton, A Candid Biography,* W.H. Allen, 1968

Kelley, Kitty, *His Way: The Unauthorised Biography of Frank Sinatra*, Bantam, 1986

Leigh, Wendy and Gabor, Zsa Zsa, *One Lifetime is Not Enough,* Headline, 1991

Mansfield, Stephanie, *The Richest Girl in the World*, Pinnacle Books, 1994

Maxwell, Elsa, *RSVP*, Little, Brown, 1954

Moats, Alice Leone, *The Million Dollar Studs,* Delacorte Press, 1997

Nemirovsky, Irene, *Suite Francaise*, Chatto & Windus, 2004

Rubirosa, Porfirio, *Mis Memorias*, Editorial Letra Grafica, 2000

Sanders, George, *Memoirs of a Professional Cad*, G P Putnam & Sons, 1960

Servat, Henry-Jean, *Les Trois Glorieuses,* Pygmalion, 2008

Spada, James, *The Man Who Kept The Secrets,* Bantam, 1991

Van Rensselaer, Phillip, *Million Dollar Baby: An Intimate Portrait of Barbara Hutton,* G P Putnam & Sons, 1979

Vanderbeets, Richard, *George Sanders: An Exhausted Life,* Robson Books, 1991

Vargas Llosa, Mario, *The Feast of the Goat,* Farrar, Straus and Giroux, 2001

Magazines

Look, interview with Flor Trujillo by Laura Bergquist, 15 June 1965

Night & Day, article by Phillip Knightly, 26 November 1994

Sunday Times, article by Shawn Levy, 4 September 2005

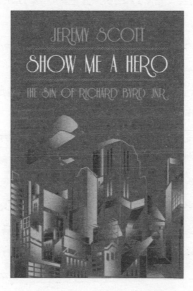

Also available from The Robson Press

HELL ABOVE EARTH

STEPHEN FRATER

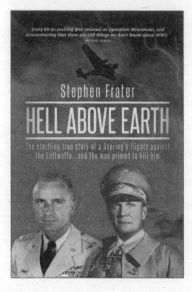

An unforgettable and thrilling tale of two WWII bomber pilots who forged an unexpected friendship in the flak-filled skies over Germany.

The air battle over Nazi Germany in WWII was hell above earth. For the British it lasted six years, for the Americans three, and the final death toll was 125,000 Allied aircrew, including 56,000 from the RAF and 26,000 Americans from the British-based Eighth Air Force. For bomber crews, every day they flew was like D-Day, exacting tremendous emotion and trauma. Death could come in many guises: an unlucky flak burst, Luftwaffe fighters that could appear anywhere at any time, or pilot error while flying less than twenty feet apart. Twenty-year-old US Captain Werner Goering accepted this, and even thrived on the adrenalin rush – he was an exceptional pilot. But Werner was also known to be the nephew of Herman Göring, Commander-in-Chief of the Luftwaffe – and because of it he became a marked man.

"Every bit as exciting and unusual as *Operation Mincemeat*, and demonstrating that there are still things we don't know about WWII."
MICHAEL KORDA

320pp hardback, £20
Available from all good bookshops or order from
www.therobsonpress.com

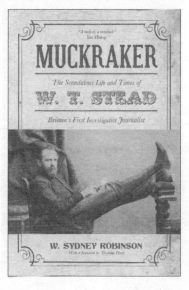